Widows and Patriarchy

WIDOWS AND PATRIARCHY

Ancient and Modern

Thomas A.J. McGinn

Duckworth

First published in 2008 by
Gerald Duckworth & Co. Ltd.
90-93 Cowcross Street, London EC1M 6BF
Tel: 020 7490 7300
Fax: 020 7490 0080
inquiries@duckworth-publishers.co.uk
www.ducknet.co.uk

© 2008 by Thomas A.J. McGinn

All rights reserved. No part of this publication
may be reproduced, stored in a retrieval system, or
transmitted, in any form or by any means, electronic,
mechanical, photocopying, recording or otherwise,
without the prior permission of the publisher.

A catalogue record for this book is available
from the British Library

ISBN 978 07156 3743 2

Typeset by Ray Davies
Printed and bound in Great Britain by
MPG Books Limited, Bodmin, Cornwall

Contents

Preface	vii
1. Introduction	1
2. Classical antiquity	18
3. Late medieval and early modern England and Germany	49
4. Modern England and the United States	105
5. Conclusion: Widows in history	156
Notes	165
References and further reading	205
Index	225

For Áine and Éile
Memoriam quoque ipsam cum voce perdidissemus,
si tam in nostra potestate esset
oblivisci quam tacere.

Preface

I first became interested in writing this book after the births of my daughters, Áine Maeve (7 April 1998) and Éile Rose (25 August 1999). Much of my earlier work had been devoted to various problems associated with the phenomenon of patriarchy in past time. Examining the status and role of women in ancient Roman society was a useful way for me to approach this subject. Prostitution, marriage (and especially the relationship between spouses), concubinage, and adultery, among other subjects, loomed large. With my daughters in the world, I felt something more was required. So I dedicate this book to them. I hope they find it useful.

I am very fortunate to have had the advice and assistance of a number of excellent readers, who have read some or all of the typescript. My profound thanks are due to Susanna Braund, Paul Cartledge, Lesley Dean-Jones, James Ely, Bruce Frier, Judith Evans Grubbs, Joel Harrington, Dennis Kehoe, Cynthia Patterson, Michele Salzman and Merry Wiesner-Hanks. I am most grateful to Vanderbilt University for a sabbatical semester and other key research support. I am once more indebted to Mr James Toplon and his excellent staff at Vanderbilt University's interlibrary loan office, in particular, Rachel Adams and Marilyn Pilley. I would also like to thank the staff at Duckworth, above all my editor, Deborah Blake, for invaluable assistance in getting this book to press.

As I indicate in the introductory chapter, the bibliographical references are weighted in favour of more recent scholarship and are not meant to be exhaustive. More references, and related material, appear on a website linked to my departmental homepage (www.vanderbilt.edu/classics/faculty). It is perhaps worth signaling that the nature and scope of this work have made it impossible to expand the bibliography after the summer of 2006, apart from rare exceptions.

1

Introduction

Design of the book

> Four times the nuptial bed she warmed,
> And every time so well performed,
> That when death spoiled each husband's billing
> He left the widow every shilling.

This rather arresting piece of misogyny was composed by Horace Walpole, forming part of a larger poem, and paying rank tribute to Bess of Hardwick, four times a widow in the course of the sixteenth century and the second wealthiest woman in England after Elizabeth I herself.[1] It eloquently if tritely rehearses the gist of the opprobrium commonly addressed to widows in that culture, as well as in a number of others. Such women were routinely assumed to be both sexually and financially avid. The theme has enjoyed an almost amazing popularity over time.

Why widows? The aim of this book is to explore the implications of what might be described as an analytical understanding of patriarchy. I take up the argument, advanced persuasively by Moses Finley, that ancient society was structured by a 'spectrum of statuses' and apply this insight to the status of women in different historical cultures. My purpose is to make the case that patriarchy has been far from monolithic in past time, precisely through an examination of certain aspects of the position of women, primarily that of widows, in three historical periods that are relatively well-attested and of considerable inherent interest: first, Greek and Roman antiquity, second, late medieval and early modern Europe, specifically England and Germany, and third, the nineteenth and early twentieth-century West, represented here by England and the United States.

My method is to harness Finley's point to a radical feminist perspective on citizenship that argues against over-privileging the public (or male) attributes of citizenship, above all the grant of suffrage, in analysing women's legal, economic and social condition in history. More important overall were distinctions in marital status, and it is on some of these that I focus. I hope to suggest, not merely that gender was at no time a unitary category either within or across past cultures, but more precisely what this means, without falling into the trap of constantly measuring women's situation from a standard set by and for males.[2] This perspective is in my view better suited to take the measure of both continuity and change for women's status and role in the more distant past as well as closer to the present day.

Widows and Patriarchy

Widows are potentially of great significance for this purpose, because they represent in all of these cultures a problematic category of adult women who are notionally independent of males. Their status and role become a focus for concern about gender relations, as though the widow were a sort of 'woman-plus'. The representation of widows can therefore say as much about the society that produces them as about widows themselves. Although this book concentrates on widows, it also comments where appropriate on other female categories in the three periods under study, chiefly wives and never-married women. For reasons that will be obvious, these types cannot be understood apart from each other. Asking questions about widows is to seek answers not only about them but also about women in general and the cultures in which they are found.

The starting point for this discussion is Greek and Roman antiquity. Throughout the book, I suggest what possibilities for investigation are tied to a differential perspective on gender role through a primary focus on the status of widows. Apart from their notional independence of men, widows are of interest because they are sexually experienced but, ideally in the cultures under study, sexually inactive, therefore a source of tension and suspicion, functioning as lightning rods for the praise and blame of women in general. This is not to deny that a woman's experience is defined by a number of other factors besides marital status, such as class, wealth, age, family size and citizenship. Intensive reflection on this type, combined with a series of summary observations on the other types already mentioned, wives and never-married women, in a series of different historical contexts, promises to shed light on those who typically sit atop the pyramid of a gender-based hierarchy: meaning males, especially upper-class males. Any true history or general theory of patriarchy would of necessity focus, as a point of departure, on all types of women and men, but that is not the aim of this more modest enterprise.

The idea that patriarchy constructs itself differently over time, shows significant variation from one society to the other, and rarely if ever exists as a monolithic entity in any given culture is a familiar one, as common perhaps as acknowledgment of the phenomenon as virtually universal.[3] There is much more to be done all the same. Scholars have offered many different definitions of patriarchy, a point to which we return below. The very pervasiveness of patriarchy makes it relatively impervious to analysis.[4] Some have attempted, vainly in my view, to discover its prehistoric origins.[5] Controversy is hardly foreign to the scholarship. There have been some interesting exchanges, for example, on the postulated evolution, if not the eclipse, of patriarchy in the transition from the early modern period to the modern. On this subject, one can trace a decades-long divergence of views, dating back to a work of Alice Clark originally published in 1919, specifically addressing the issue of whether capitalism and/or industrialism have helped or harmed women.[6] Feminist historians have vigorously debated not only the question of change, but also the

1. Introduction

nature and extent of women's subordination to men in past time.[7] In the Anglophone scholarship, one finds a particular emphasis on the model of a 'descent from paradise' to describe women's history in the modern period.[8] Among historians of ancient Greece and Rome, only occasionally is there registered a casual recognition of Greek or Roman society as a particular form of patriarchy, and not much more than that.[9] It is high time to start examining patriarchal societies as patriarchies.[10]

Contemporary feminists have in recent years been sounding the alarm that patriarchy is now morphing into a new, subtler, and possibly more pernicious form, a useful warning for any historian tempted by complacency.[11] For past cultures, we have increasingly sophisticated examinations of individual aspects of this complex subject, such as public policy on prostitution or the struggle for suffrage, for example. The logical next step is the development of criteria that allow a broad comparison of gender hierarchy in different historical contexts. This is the modest aim of this study. In order to proceed down this path, we must begin to risk generalization at some point. This book is not a history of patriarchy, nor does it attempt to present a unified field theory of gender hierarchy, but if it succeeds in providing some of the raw materials for such an enterprise, it will more than have achieved its purpose. Many intermediate steps seem possible, and even advisable, before attempting such a goal, however.

Examination of the historical record in broad terms puts us on guard against the tendency shown by some historians of reading the modern record on the status and role of women as a steady march of progress to the present day. Viewing women's history optimistically in terms of a linear evolutionary model that postulates increasing success not only distorts the past in a 'presentist' manner, it also misunderstands the present, where an overthrow of patriarchy is nowhere in sight.[12] Just as there is no 'Golden Age' for widows in prospect for the immediate future, so it is impossible to find one in the past.[13]

My approach reaps the benefits of cross-cultural study while seeking to avoid the trap of ahistoricism.[14] In a simpler sense, our information is often so spare and of such indifferent quality that examining a problem from a single vantage point, such as a unique culture or period of time, is unproductive.[15] There is some value in attempting to capture, even within limits, a sense of the enormous diversity of human experience.[16] The historical experience of widows, despite some appearances to the contrary, is extremely diverse, when such factors as period, region, legal culture, social status and economic level are taken into account.[17] This is important because in the sources deriving from a number of past cultures categorizations of women often obscure important differences among them, especially class differences.[18] What is more, these classifications are peculiar, as a rule, to a given society, so that terms like 'elite', 'aristocracy', 'upper class', as well as 'sub-elite' etc., are going to show differences in

3

meaning from culture to culture. Even in antiquity 'elite' in classical Rome meant something different from what it did in classical Athens.

The problem of historical periodization looms large in the historiography of women's studies. Feminist historians have been for some time alert to the challenge of the *longue durée* and on the whole sceptical of assumptions that events and processes otherwise of great consequence had much direct and immediate impact on the majority of women. So it might seem absurd to wonder if, among women, widows had a Principate, a Renaissance, a Reformation, or an Industrial Revolution.

There are some obvious cautions to raise, however. First, we should ask how many men experienced these watersheds in any meaningful sense. History is a different matter for the elites of either gender than it is for the masses, especially for those who leave little or nothing to record their experience. Writing women out of the historical record is no solution to this difficulty, which is not to deny that this has already been tried. The trap of periodization, in that it defines historiographical expertise, has foreclosed important avenues of investigation that reveal real change in women's experience.[19] The recent fashion in microhistory has yielded excellent results, no one would deny, but there are limits to the usefulness of this approach that seem at times barely recognized.[20] By the same token, adopting a long-term perspective has both advantages and disadvantages.

While political engagement has been a great strength of feminist scholarship it must in the end yield to careful scrutiny of the historical record.[21] One can at least begin to move from uncovering the causes of women's repression to addressing the myriad ways in which women have coped with it, at least to the extent the sources permit.[22] It is one of patriarchy's strengths that it can accommodate, and even exploit, women's agency. The fact that patriarchy affects different women at different times in different ways means it has a history.[23]

It is worth asking just what kind of patriarchy a given society represents, what degree of subordination it inflicts on women, about its relative harshness or mildness. This question plays out over a range of cultural practices, including family structure, religion and the division of labour by gender.[24] Patriarchy's mutability and flexibility at times seem to increase when it is placed under great stress, and these qualities might be viewed as keys to its success, or durability, at any rate.[25] There is a great deal of continuity and similarity all the same, as well as contestation over women's status and role within cultures.

So it is fitting, after all, to adopt a conventional periodization as a framework for presentation. For example, the traditional citation of 1500 as the dividing line between medieval and modern works about as well for my purposes as it does for anything else.[26] I both invoke it as a divider and structure my examination so as to straddle it. Of course such demarcations remain in large part arbitrary, and we will witness a great deal of

1. Introduction

continuity over this entire period. The same is true of any imaginable alternatives. I have chosen the periods and cultures named above because they struck me as inherently interesting and relatively well documented. Marriage is the ideal state for adult women in all of them, which means that widows are in some measure anomalous and therefore problematic.[27] That does not mean that other choices for scrutiny are not possible, or even desirable, and it certainly does not guarantee that generalization to other societies, especially non-Western societies, is going to be automatic or easy.

It is worth emphasizing that this study is not as massive or as ambitious as it may look. The analytical and broadly comparative approach adopted here means a great debt is owed to the work of others. Little space is accorded description and a series of case studies precludes continuous coverage. Even within those case studies I prefer the emblematic to the exhaustive. In my view, such compromises are of essential importance. The comparative approach is necessary to open up our understanding of widows' status and role in any one culture. What facilitates it is the fact that loss of a husband raises broadly similar problems that are addressed in different ways across cultures.[28] It does, however, look past the uncomfortable fact that expertise in several disciplines is necessary to pursue research on widows in an intensive fashion.[29] Not all comparisons are equally useful, of course, but this approach, which is consistent with a moderate social constructionism, alerts us both to similarity and difference, continuity and change. While comparative evidence proves nothing by itself, it can suggest solutions where the evidence is otherwise intractable.[30] Nothing else promises to open up quite so much the experience of women across broad stretches of time and varieties of cultural practice. With some exceptions, historians have tended to use information on widows (and orphans as well) to write about poverty and duress.[31] My argument is that widows are of far more interest to us than that approach by itself might imply. So, this book is intended as an experimental essay, not the final word on anything, and it will not be necessary, for example, to cite – let alone discuss – all of the relevant literature on any point. I try to avoid piling up citations beyond a reasonable minimum. Because the book is fundamentally an exercise in comparative method, with a few exceptions I try not to rely on widow-scholarship from outside the central areas of focus. Many of my secondary sources cite everyone and everything since the birth of historiography, so there is no point in reproducing their efforts. I aim to cite only material dating from the last quarter of a century or so, when possible. The reason for this is that the notes attempt to provide a foothold in the scholarship, not a history of it. Where material is fairly homogeneous within a paragraph or, in a few bold instances, at the end of a couple of paragraphs, I reserve citations for the end, in a note; otherwise not. Notes are kept to a minimum in terms of number and content. While I am thoroughly dependent on secondary sources, I allude

5

to disagreement among my predecessors only on points of fundamental importance. This book can only rarely explicate, let alone resolve, controversy among scholars, at least explicitly. Attentive readers should find their efforts repaid, in that economy of presentation is the order of the day.[32]

A primary focus on widows also makes for greater economy. Orphans, for all their importance, are noticed only when necessary. Data on never-married women are generally harder to come by, and that for wives almost too copious. Scholarship on widows in antiquity is relatively abundant, something especially true for Rome, thanks to the efforts of Jens-Uwe Krause. The attention devoted to widows in the late medieval and early modern periods is even greater. The modern era itself is more of a disappointment. Apart from a few signal exceptions like the excellent collection of essays edited by Arlene Scadron, the subject has suffered from historiographical neglect.[33] In a larger sense, the history of widowhood remains to be written. We seem far removed indeed from that achievement, which must I think be preceded by a series of precise studies on various historical periods and cultures.[34] Microhistory has its role to play here. It is my hope that this experiment helps spur such detailed examination.

While the design of this work does not allow for a detailed treatment of primary sources, a few points can be made about their value. Before the modern era, we have little written by widows and from antiquity virtually nothing. This has promoted their lack of visibility in the historical record.[35] The same is true of women in general, especially sub-elite women.[36] Didactic or more generally prescriptive works dominate the literary tradition, so that it is, in effect, usually easier to derive a sense of how men thought widows, and women in general, were supposed to behave, than what widows actually thought and did.[37] One important implication is that women's own thoughts on patriarchy in their own day are largely beyond recovery for a good stretch of time.[38]

It is crucial to our understanding to establish how literary genre shapes both the expectations of the audience and the contents of a text, as well as to recognize that important aspects of one genre can cross over to another; the boundaries can be porous.[39] Different types of sources, viewed in isolation, can lead to radically different conclusions about the status and role of widows in past time.[40] The misogyny of some literary genres can effortlessly, to all appearances, distort reality.[41]

While the historical context of a work is essential to our understanding of it, it should not be assumed that a text renders an account of reality, for example, that it communicates the lived experience of gender role or marital status as opposed to an ideal of this. Even in the modern period, where widows, at least some of the wealthier and better-educated among them, at last directly speak to us in some numbers through such means as diaries and letters, the representation of widowhood is much more accessible than the reality.[42] The latter is more elusive the further back in time

1. Introduction

we proceed and in most cases can be grasped fully, or as fully as possible, only through particularistic studies limited both geographically and temporally.[43] This is to recognize that patriarchy itself is contingent and variable.[44] Widowhood is not just a literary construct, of course, and even as a construct it is a highly contextualized one.[45] Demography and economics are not the only realities accessible to us. Representation can both reflect and reinforce social reality, through its complex relationship with widely held prejudice. Some popular literary genres seem very well suited for reinforcing a sense of social identity, for example. The fact that negative portraits vastly outweigh the positive is not without implications for widows' freedom of action.[46]

Definitions

There are many fine definitions of patriarchy available.[47] In part this is because this is one of the most contested areas of discussion among feminists. While admitting that different definitions are possible, this book defines patriarchy simply as a gender-based hierarchy in which males are privileged. This hierarchy is variously manifested in the structures, ideology and practices of a culture. One can expect to find its traces in such broad areas of experience as law, the economy and social life. The advantages to this approach are that it opens up a broad field for analysis, while resisting circular argument.[48] For the same reason, I generally avoid using different language to describe patriarchy at different stages of historical development. My premise is that the fact of patriarchy is less interesting than its internal design, which is properly the main focus of research.[49] To this end, I propose to construct an analytical framework that will facilitate cross-cultural comparisons and hope to avoid the vagueness that characterizes so much writing on the subject.

Moses Finley's idea of a spectrum of statuses seems well suited to this approach, at least as a point of departure.[50] The various categories of gender classification must be understood in relation to one another.[51] Not all men have benefited equally from patriarchy, just as not all women have been equally disadvantaged.[52] Patriarchy is typically not monolithic in character, and often generates compensatory pressures that favour women. It is paradoxical, in that it is both socially constructed and to all appearances universal.[53] A comparative approach seems best suited to assisting our comprehension of such a widespread, complex, multifaceted institution. It must be kept in mind, however, that patriarchy itself has little explanatory power. Rather, it is the thing that must be explained.

The application of Finley's scheme, devised with men in mind, to women does not, I think, suit perfectly all of the types indicated above all of the time, namely, never-married woman, wife and widow, even in classical antiquity, but it is generally consistent with the different ways in which ancient society defined status for both men, who were not typically classed according to marital status, and women, who were more likely to be so categorized. This is even truer for women in the late medieval and early modern period, where these three marital statuses assume an outsized importance and are more recognizable precisely as a spectrum.[54] In traditional societies women usually do not fall into group or corporate classifications in the same manner as men.[55] The real surprise, I believe, is how well Finley's scheme seems to work for one or more of these types in the nineteenth and early twentieth centuries, the period immediately before most women in Western societies were granted the public functions of citizens or, as a radical feminist would say, their status as citizens was assimilated to that of males, albeit not as perfectly as is sometimes assumed.[56]

It cannot be emphasized too much how important the understanding of the social status and role of married women is for the study of widows.[57] The experience of the marriage that precedes loss of a husband in large part shapes the nature of one's widowhood. This holds true above all in economic terms, but there are also important implications for legal status and what may be broadly described as freedom of movement. The chances for remarriage are also to an extent determined by the prior marriage.[58] We might usefully describe widows as living 'in the shadow of marriage' in all of these respects.[59] Perhaps as important, Western societies with an exalted ideal of marriage tend to privilege an institution that we can describe as typically monogamous and androcentric, defining a woman's identity through her relationship to a male. This spells almost automatic marginalization for widows.[60] Such isolation can operate on a number of levels, moral, psychological and spiritual. The undeniable importance of marriage in all of the cultures under study explains why this has attracted a greater share of attention among historians than widowhood.[61]

It is also important to offer definitions of such terms as 'widow' and 'orphan'. The latter primarily refers to a fatherless child, if only because this seems to be the most common usage in the cultures under study.[62] A widow is a woman who has lost her husband to death and who has not remarried. The matter is not as simple as it might seem because there are other types of women without men who are at times assimilated to widows, such as divorcées, deserted wives and even never-married women.[63] Different societies offer different definitions, which is to say that the widow is often best understood as a cultural construct.[64] The problem intensifies in the cases, for example, of Mormon plural wives, ex-slaves, soldiers' wives and common-law wives with decedent male partners.[65] Poverty is a key factor linking these types.[66] Marital separation can be especially common in cultures without ready access to divorce.[67] We encounter from time to time the 'constructive widow'. For example, in eighteenth-century England the courts accepted that the civil death of a husband through banishment or the like created a state of 'civil widowhood' for his wife.[68] Concubinage has played a prominent role at times, for example in parts of

1. Introduction

medieval Europe, which raises the question of whether insisting on marriage with a decedent partner has much sense for defining 'widow'.[69] In some societies, the loss of a husband has relatively insignificant consequences for the status of a wife, a point that affects perhaps not the category itself but its content and/or the social meaning attached to it.[70] Even where this does not hold true, however, the widow can still in a very real sense continue to count as a wife.[71] There is, in sum, no universal category of the widow.[72] A simple definition seems best suited to take the measure of this radical complexity.

For the sake of economy and clarity, then, the focus of this book is on widows as defined above.[73] Singling out women who have lost their husbands to death facilitates cross-cultural comparisons. Widowhood is (overwhelmingly) involuntary, while never-married women are often perceived or assumed to have chosen their status.[74] Many of the latter have been able to lead relatively independent lives, although circumstances set them apart from widows.[75] To describe them I prefer, apart from some culturally specific exceptions, the undeniably charmless term 'never-married' to 'unmarried', 'virgin', or even 'spinster' because of the advantage it presents in terms of clarity and precision.

It is particularly true of many traditional societies, at least in the West, that widows are relatively highly valued, for example, within kinship networks.[76] Or their status might receive a religious validation, such as the reference sometimes made to the widow in late medieval Germany as 'Bride of Christ'.[77] In fact, the existence of widowhood, as distinguished from marriage and virginity, as a spiritual and ultimately social category in the West has been argued by Bernhard Jussen to be a product of Christian theology originating in late antiquity, chiefly with the writings of St Jerome, and reaching its full flower in the Middle Ages.[78] That argument has considerable force, as we shall see later in this book. All the same, widowhood has signified, for most women in the cultures under study, a falling off in economic and social status and so on the whole has been regarded in negative terms.[79] By the same token, moral status as a widow might be easily undermined by perceptions of inappropriate behaviour. For example, the mid-fifteenth-century Carthusian monk Erhart Groß believed that sinful thoughts placed in jeopardy a woman's status as 'widow'.[80]

For this reason it is not surprising to find that any typology of widows we might reasonably develop contains little that is positive,[81] even though widow-types can differ notably from culture to culture. The commonest stereotypes over time are two in number, one happy and one sad.[82] These correspond overall to the coarse dichotomy of 'good' and 'bad' woman-types found generally in patriarchal societies, in which, not surprisingly, they serve as instruments of social control.[83] There is the 'sorrowing widow', dependent and vulnerable, often isolated, a living metaphor for weakness.[84] Next is the 'merry' or 'lusty widow', who raises fears of sexual betrayal through both promiscuous extramarital sex and marrying down, often to a younger husband held in her thrall. Thus aversion to female hypogamy has been grounded in fears of the inversion of gender hierarchy.[85] The two types reflect the central (male) concerns about widows we saw above registered, after a fashion, in Walpole's verses on Bess of Hardwick: economic and sexual vulnerability that can have a corrupting influence on a widow's character.[86] Lusty widows appear to be more common by far than the other main type, or in fact any other type in literature, at least before the modern age. Representation tends to focus on widows at both ends of the socio-economic spectrum, while actual widows were more broadly distributed.[87] This is a sign that caricatures of widows reveal more about male anxiety than about socio-economic reality.[88] It is important to note that, despite the strong continuity in the literary tradition from antiquity to the present on this subject, not all merry widows are presented as merry in precisely the same way. They can, in fact, be highly malleable as a type.[89] In the words of one scholar, '[t]he lusty widow, for all her apparent timelessness and universality, is culturally contingent'.[90]

Fears about sexual predation merged in some cultures with attributions of more generalized malice, as many widows came to be identified as witches. If not sexually avid, the merry widow was at least imagined as sexually available, or such availability might mark the transformation of a sorrowing widow into a merry one. In other words, chastity, or the reputation for same, was the hallmark of the good widow. Any breach of modesty was liable to be construed as a sign of inappropriate sexual behaviour.[91] Sub-elite women were particularly likely to be deemed at risk.[92] A widow had to be especially careful to avoid consignment to the disfavoured category, as it was necessary that she inhabit one or the other. For example, the story of the widow in the Gospel of Luke who beleaguers a judge until he grants her a favourable judgement simply in order to escape her harassment, might validate the aggressive pursuit of a claim before the authorities in early modern England, but only up to a point.[93]

A more precise description (or, if you like, 'ideal type') of the widow would combine both of these elements in a non-prejudicial manner, recognizing widowhood as a stage in a woman's life that has tended to render women both vulnerable and autonomous, if in different ways and to a widely varying extent.[94] In all of the cultures we study in this book, widowhood was as much a social experience as a personal or emotional one. This is true even, or especially, where widowhood is socially defined as a 'natural' state for women, the terminus of the life cycle of a marriage. Poverty and grief have been bound together for many widows in a manner that crucially determines their experience and perceptions of this by others.[95]

At the same time, widowhood has never been monolithic, not only in the obvious sense that factors such as socio-economic status play a decisive role in shaping the experience of individual widows, but that the experi-

1. Introduction

ence of each woman can vary considerably over the course of her widowhood. Widowhood, like marriage, has its own life cycle, no matter whether it ends in death or remarriage. This cycle is especially marked in societies where a significant number of widows are relatively young. The presence of dependent children can have a major impact.[96] Just as when for any society we write *women* we really mean only *some women*, so when we write *widows* we really refer only to *some widows*.[97] In other words, generalizations about 'widows' are often meaningless or certainly do not apply to all of them.[98]

Widowers are a surprisingly elusive category, even in a modern setting. Men are not usually defined in terms of marital status, insofar as their social identity and/or economic well-being is not as negatively affected, if it is affected at all, by the loss of a wife. Their legal status does not change, and they are not closely associated with any of the attributes tied to either of the main types of widow, merry and mourning.[99] Moreover, when they lose their wives to death they tend to remarry, in a manner best described as early and often. Even where they do not remarry they generally find it easier to replace a decedent wife's domestic services than a widow is able to find a new provider.[100] No society known to me insists on widowers' remarriage or, for that matter, their death, as we find with widows in some cultures.[101] It is no mere chance that in both Greek and Latin, as well as in modern European languages, the word for the man who has lost his wife to death, where it exists, tends, unusually, to derive from its female equivalent, like widower in English, and this at a relatively late date.[102] There is no real male equivalent for widow-status in the cultures under study. Widowers scarcely emerge from the historical record as a moral or sociological type, except perhaps in the abstract. They receive only a modest amount of attention in the sources and even this is relatively late.[103] Anyone doubting the importance of considerations of gender in the experience of widows over time would do well to contemplate the contrast with widowers.

Categories of analysis

This book examines rights at private law, especially those regarding property and succession, economic privilege and its absence, freedom of movement in general, including the question of bodily integrity and fear of physical interference, and, finally, entitlement to decide whether to remarry and to whom. I treat these rubrics with a high degree of flexibility and pragmatism, examining, for example, the legal rules for remarriage under that category. In fact, the questions they raise are all closely linked to each other.[104] Paradoxically, to look at the situation of women under these different headings, for example, those of law and economics, is sometimes to gain a radically different impression of their status and role.

Since antiquity, widows – along with orphans – have been a byword for the weak and oppressed. Do the facts as recovered sustain this image or not? What does the answer to this question tell us about where widows rank in relation to other women in any given society?

After a brief introduction, each chapter begins with a summary of the basic facts, as recoverable, of demography for each time period.[105] The purpose is simply to gain an idea, to the degree possible, of the *numbers of widows*. The main focus is on mortality and nuptiality. First, were mortality rates differentiated by gender in any appreciable way? Second, while some cultures have early marriage and others have late marriage, what is crucial is the typical gap between the ages of spouses at first marriage. This is decisive both for the average length of widowhood and the sheer numbers of widows.[106] Next, what was the overall proportion of the population ever marrying? How did divorce and remarriage practices affect the numbers of widows?

From antiquity down to the early modern period we are left to some fairly unreliable sources in attempting to measure human populations, a fact well recognized by scholars, who are sensitive to the difficulties in reading such facts from literature, for example. Demographers characterize the last century and a half as the 'statistical era' when developed countries such as England and the United States have sought to record precisely and preserve accurately such data as births, deaths and marriages, creating a lopsided abundance of 'necessary knowledge' for this period.[107]

For each culture under study I introduce four rubrics to facilitate comparison. The first is rights at *private law*. A central question in this connection concerns ownership of property. The details of marital property regimes in each society allow for an understanding of the resources on which widows might expect to rely. Often the rights of never-married women and widows contrast starkly with the disabilities imposed on married women. At times the contrast that really matters is not so much that between wives and widows as that between married women and all other adults.[108] Marriage and its legal regulation matter a great deal for widows. Moreover, what women were entitled to, through the law of succession, both under a will and upon intestacy, was often of crucial importance, and yet was very often not under their unfettered control. They might not own or, if ownership was not possible, be able to exploit, a share of property adequate for their support outright and/or find it necessary to engage in extensive litigation to recover their due. Many a widow was subject to a (male) guardian, although guardians were equipped with powers that differed considerably from culture to culture both in law and in practice. Some or all of these factors might influence a widow's ability to leave property under a will. Rights to the guardianship and custody of children also vary. It is worth keeping in mind that just as the regulation of marriage has influenced that of widowhood, the reverse has also held true at times, with the rights of widows helping to determine those enjoyed by wives.[109]

1. Introduction

Law on the books hardly delimits the scope of our interest, but this is not to discount its importance. Law's coercive power defines a 'realm of cognitive possibility'.[110] There is detectable at certain times a tendency to convert social and moral issues into legal ones. Statutes, cases and juristic commentaries are inadequate by themselves, however, to convey a sense of women's experience with law.[111] They are often more a statement of an ideal rather than a reflection of reality.[112] The relationship of law to society is at all times a complex and difficult issue. We do well to remain sensitive to the limits of the law, that is, the gap between theory and practice. A splendid illustration of this pitfall derives from the contrast between public policy on family planning, which firmly discouraged it, and popular usage in the late nineteenth and early twentieth-century United States, which increasingly resorted to it. Here is a sobering example of the failure of law to govern behaviour.[113]

The limits on widows' exercise of their rights are often extralegal in nature.[114] Sometimes these norms become law, through processes that can differ radically from culture to culture.[115] The designation 'private' should not be pressed too hard, in law as in all else. Historians emphasize that until relatively recently most men were excluded from what we define as public life. For them, as well as for women, the household was the focus of experience, and the household itself remained in an important sense a 'public' institution, just as marriage did, at least to an extent.[116] To be clear, the categories of 'public' and 'private', as well as any dividing line between them, are cultural constructions that can change over time and from place to place.[117] Marriage is a good example of an institution that can be used to trace such transformations. It is an important means by which the state lends shape to the hierarchy of gender, so that marriage law helps define 'the people', a policy issue with a pedigree as old as Periclean Athens.[118]

Next is *economic privilege*. The first task is to take up a theme implicit in the previous rubric by examining the sources of wealth available to widows. Widowhood often entails a reduction in available economic resources, although this is not inevitably true, and, where it is true, its implications can vary from culture to culture or among widows within a culture.[119] All the same, economic considerations have helped make remarriage an attractive option for some widows (below). If they did not remarry, how were their opportunities for administering property influenced by such extra-legal factors as personality, age and social class? Some widows were able to borrow money in order to make up for a shortfall in the bequests made to them by decedent family members or accruing under the rules of intestate succession, while others might augment their patrimony, for example, through lending, but it seems most widows were compelled either to seek work or charity where available. Their experience of work in all of the cultures under study was in no small measure determined by a gendered division of labour that overall reduced their chances of finding a job, advancing in a profession, or receiving a wage that was adequate by any objective measure. Despite great material difficulties, widows often valued their independence, for example, when acting as heads of households. Their practice of leaving property in wills (where this was possible) in many cases shows significant differences from that of men, above all their deceased husbands.

The sexual division of labour has been argued to be a universal feature of human society, certainly traditional cultures. Yet the precise mix of tasks assigned to men and women varies considerably over time and from place to place. Like patriarchy itself, the division of labour has been flexible, allowing some women to prosper.[120] Overall, however, the pattern is one of de-skilling of jobs once they are assigned to women, with the introduction of new technology either denying women new opportunities or opening some up for them, but leading to a further devaluation of their work. The result is a 'gendered work environment', that is, work cultures segregated by gender in which the jobs are rigorously sex-typed, to the emphatic disadvantage of women.[121]

Economic change, as impressive as it might otherwise seem, has only really profoundly affected most people in past time in the long term.[122] The sexual division of labour appears to be a characteristic of patriarchal social organization, so that it could not, for example, be 'caused' by capitalism or the industrial revolution.[123] All the same, the implications for women of the immense changes in the structure of the economy occurring in the early modern period tend to be discounted in the recent scholarship.[124]

The third rubric, *freedom of movement*, embraces a range of subjects relevant to mobility both physical and social. It is worth noting that until relatively recently severe constraints operated for all women.[125] Widowhood is nonetheless often particularly associated with isolation and a reduced social role.[126] For many women it amounts to a trade-off that is variously articulated on an individual basis: increased independence as against increased vulnerability.[127] Elite women have tended to fare better on this score. On the other hand, the exercise of authority by widows is not a phenomenon strictly limited to the upper classes.[128] Equally important are the opportunities for appearing in public, a question closely bound both to conceptions of widows' sexuality and to the threat of actual violence, above all sexual assault. Imputations of immorality, which loom large in the art and literature of various periods, can act as a check on behaviour.[129] Chastity is an ideal often really accessible only to women of the upper classes.[130] Feminist historians in recent years have been admirably sensitive to the problem of gender and social meaning, while recognizing that representations of women can never tell the whole story.[131] Patriarchy's curious ideological strength often manifests itself in literature.[132] Widows, especially young widows, are a favoured subject, because both sexually attractive (or at least eroticized) and experienced. Because their experience was acquired within marriage, that is, in a manner condoned by society, they are at once capable of being viewed as both respectable and vulnerable, and potentially more difficult to control than never-married women.[133] Education is closely tied not only to a widow's earning-power, but also to the amount of social isolation she experiences, her self-image and ultimately her personal autonomy. It can be discussed only very tangentially in this book, however.[134]

Widows, despite various admonitions and criticisms directed at them, have often been engaged in activities, even at times of an official nature, in the so-called public sphere, where they have been particularly likely to be involved with the practice of religion as well as (certainly true of the more prosperous among them) of litigation. In the latter arena their interests were often safeguarded by authorities who viewed the protection of the weak as essential to the moral order and their own claims of legitimacy.[135]

The fundamental criterion to examine under this rubric is personal autonomy, the ability to make one's own decisions.[136] Patriarchy tends to rob women of initiative, although in individual societies this is always a matter of degree. It cannot be simply assumed that they are passive victims.[137] Widows especially are often compelled to make decisions on their own. At the same time, loss of a spouse's companionship and support often bears a high emotional cost. Under the rubric of 'freedom of movement' we deal with various cultural processes, ideologies and manipulation of symbols, in other words the means by which gender shapes social structures and relations.[138] Movement also denotes mobility, or, simply as a rubric, can suggest the lack thereof. It is an interesting feature of several of the cultures under study that single women tend to migrate to cities, where they often live in close proximity to one another, savouring the relatively greater personal freedom (in large part deriving from a heightened anonymity) and economic opportunities that the urban context offers.[139] Widow-residence is a phenomenon of interest across cultures.[140] It has obvious implications not only for widows' autonomy but also for local economic structures, a subject that has just begun to be explored.[141]

Finally, *remarriage* is not only a possible solution to the economic challenges and social isolation, where present, of widowhood, but the only available exit from this state apart from death. All the same, this 'solution' is not an easy one for many patriarchal cultures.[142] Some societies have stipulated a period of mourning for a deceased spouse or at least a time of waiting before remarriage, but these have very often been ignored. Under this rubric it is useful to evaluate the degree of choice operating for widows, meaning choice of both partner and whether to remarry in the first place. Factors of age and wealth are relevant here, as well as attitudes to female hypogamy ('marrying down') in a given culture. Frequency of remarriage is as important as the motives for it. Comparison with the experience of widowers is especially enlightening on this score. Of course legal, economic and psychological factors are highly relevant. Lack of desire (or of a need) to remarry is often bound up paradoxically with the opportunity to do so.[143]

We do well here to guard against unfounded assumptions that widows were, in this or that culture, regarded for economic reasons as highly desirable marriage partners or not. Nor is a widow's own desire for remarriage something to be taken for granted.

While this study does not have much space to devote to descriptions or analysis of bereavement, this is not to underrate its importance.[144] It is undeniable, for example, that memorialization of a husband can play a key role in legitimizing a widow's status, something of particular significance in the case of ruling families.

Plan of the book

The book contains four chapters beyond this Introduction: one chapter on each historical period under study, plus a conclusion.

Chapter 2 examines Greek and Roman antiquity. For Greece, this means roughly the second half of the fifth and the whole of the fourth centuries BC and mostly Athens. For Rome, the period under examination extends from c. 200 BC to c. AD 250. The vast bulk of our literary and legal sources for each culture derives from these periods. Greece, here represented almost exclusively by Athens, again simply because of the extent of the available evidence, and Rome present a typology of women's status that, like most other features of social and cultural life, remained fairly stable and consistent over a long period of time, which does not mean of course that it was monolithic or free from controversy and criticism. A brief excursus on widows in ancient Judaism and Christianity points the way for future developments, by examining how widows came to be a privileged object of material assistance and how an ideal type was constructed for them, as part of a threefold series of marital statuses, that dominated the Christian West for over a thousand years to come. The transformation of the classical tradition on widows in late antiquity, chiefly at the hands of St Jerome, sets the stage for notable changes in the late medieval and early modern periods.

In Chapter 3 we turn to England and Germany, in the late medieval and early modern periods. More precisely, this is the late fourteenth through early seventeenth centuries, or approximately 1350 to 1650. In contrast to classical antiquity, this era presents a typology that turns out to be highly unstable. Women's status(es), including that of widows, underwent radical redefinition at this time, as patriarchy found itself under sustained challenge. In the end, the categories remained but the content and meaning attached to them changed a great deal. I have chosen England (here exclusive of Scotland and Wales, for the sake of simplicity) and Germany, chiefly because they are relatively well studied with respect to women and

1. Introduction

widows. Both England and Germany experienced the Reformation, an important point, as is the fact that they experienced it in different ways. For both areas, this period, in a reworking of the sexual order, generated all sorts of questions about and challenges to the status and role of widows. There is no doubt all the same that much is to be gained from similar study of a society that remained Catholic during this period, as did precisely significant parts of Germany.

The late nineteenth and early twentieth centuries, specifically the period from about 1850 to about 1925, are the focus of Chapter 4. Here we examine England (inclusive this time of some material from Scotland and Wales, when necessary or desirable) and the United States. This chapter outlines the story of how significant changes in the law, generated in some measure by developments in the economy and society, succeeded in breathing new life into the question of women's status and role. The lion's share of attention was devoted to married women, with important consequences for widows. This period immediately precedes the virtual disappearance of female marital status-categories in the wake of the unprecedented rise of the 'public' status of women overall. Although some of the disabilities imposed on wives remained in force for decades, the grant of full citizen rights to women marked an important watershed.

The concluding chapter, Chapter 5, offers a brief analytical summary of the main results of the study, along with suggestions for further research.

2

Classical antiquity

Greece and Rome

Ancient Greece was not one society, but a number of societies, spread out over the eastern Mediterranean for the most part, but extending to large stretches of its western shores (above all Sicily and southern Italy), the Black Sea and parts of the Near East. Their history begins in the eighth century BC, if not before, and stretches many centuries onwards to the empire of the Byzantines. The classical period is surveyed here, defined roughly as the century and a half from 450 to 300 BC, and we concentrate on Athens, which has preserved for us the best and most abundant evidence from this time.

The Romans too enjoyed a long and varied history, starting as a small community and emerging as a major superpower, a position they maintained for several centuries. The focus is on Rome's classical period, here defined as extending more or less from 200 BC to AD 250, which is when the vast bulk of the literary and legal sources of interest to us arises. This evidence is Rome-centred, although we will not hesitate to pursue the subject to the ends of the Empire when there is occasion to do so. Roman Egypt is a uniquely rich source of documentary evidence that reveals much about the lives of its sub-elite residents, most of whom were not Roman citizens, however, until the early third century.

Numbers of widows

We will never know how many widows Athens had in the fifth and fourth centuries BC, or for that matter how many Rome had in the four and a half centuries under examination. For Athens, we have fairly certain knowledge of as many as 48 of them, all evidently from the upper classes, given that our source of information is the corpus of private orations regarding lawsuits that must have concerned significant amounts of property.[1] What more can be said about the sheer numbers of women who lost their husbands to death or the chances an Athenian or Roman wife had of becoming a widow?

Most wives probably became widows at some point in their first marriages. This conclusion is buttressed by what information we have for the age gap between spouses among the elite, at least. The evidence for age at first marriage at Athens is spotty and anecdotal. It suggests that for upper-class women this was 14 to 15, for men 'around' 30, with the sources

2. Classical antiquity

indicating that men's age at first marriage varied more than women's.[2] For both men and women, it is likely that actual age at first marriage occurred within a range of years, rather than clustering close to an average age, even if we were able to reconstruct this. Unrecoverable though this range may be in precise terms, we can place it more generally in the mid-teens for women and in the late twenties to early thirties for men. Gender-differentiated life expectancy also had the potential to affect the numbers of widows. We are skating on very thin ice here, however. Based on comparisons with model life tables, which are extrapolated from modern demographic data and so controversial in their application to antiquity, life expectancy seems to have fallen between 20 and 30 years at birth, consistent with a very high rate of infant and child mortality, with men perhaps living a bit longer, about five years, than women.[3] Here the incidence, likely to be high, of death for women in childbirth has to be weighed against the effects of an almost continuous state of warfare that marks the Athenian experience of these years, and that reduced the numbers of male marriage partners. It seems safe to say that despite the apparent advantage in male life expectancy, the spousal age gap, large as it evidently was, mattered more than the effects of gender-differentiated mortality for our purposes, meaning more women would outlive their husbands than the reverse.[4]

As to sheer numbers of widows, it appears that almost all women who survived to adulthood did marry at least once, although this is largely a matter of inference.[5] Preferential female exposure affected the overall pool of marriageable women in the free population, although the degree to which this held true is impossible to calculate.[6] Divorce practice to some extent cut into the ranks of widows. The evidence does not suggest divorce was very common, but we simply do not know how frequent it was.[7] If we assume that the probability of divorce substantially increased for married women as they aged, then divorce operated for them in a way similar to male mortality. Remarriage reduced numbers in another way, and this does seem to have been frequent, at least among the upper classes (see below).

Over time, long experience of warfare might have had a self-regulating effect, in the sense that greater resort to exposure of females in the longer term came somewhat to balance a more or less consistently high rate of adult male mortality over time. Even so, there were times when the nature and extent of military activity meant that battle casualties were unusually high, and so created more widows than could easily remarry, certainly among the sub-elite.[8] A shortage of eligible males toward the end of the Peloponnesian War (431-404 BC) moved the Athenians to pass a law allowing a man to take, besides a wife, a woman for the purpose of bearing children.[9] The famous caution to widows urging them to avoid becoming a topic of conversation among men, attributed by Thucydides to Pericles in his Funeral Oration marking the end of the first year of the conflict,[10] makes even better sense from the perspective of the end of the war than from near its outset. By 404 a surfeit of unmarriageable widows was likely to have been perceived as a genuine social problem.[11]

The overall picture is very much the same for Rome, where the sources are more plentiful but in the end no less problematic. For life expectancy we are again left to the extrapolations found in Model Life Tables and explicit comparisons from more recent periods showing conditions thought to be similar to Rome, such as found in India and China. Supported by what little reliable evidence survives from antiquity, the Tables suggest that on the whole Roman life expectancy at birth ranged from 20 to 30 years. As with Greece, this assumes a very high rate of infant mortality.[12] The meagre evidence suggests a gendered differential in mortality, again with males living slightly longer than females.[13] Here too, losses of women from childbirth played a role in this outcome.

There is enough data for the Romans to reconstruct a class-related differentiation in age at first marriage, with a double tier in each case also showing a gender-based differentiation. What this means is that elite males tended to marry for the first time in their early twenties, elite females in their mid-teens, sub-elite males by around 30, sub-elite females by 20. As noted above, it is better to speak of a range of ages than of an average age at first marriage. For heuristic purposes, however, we can say that the average age gap between spouses on the sub-elite level was about ten years, while that for the elite was no more than seven, and in a number of cases evidently as low as four to five years.[14] This difference alone suggests, first, that most women lost a husband in a first marriage to death and second, that there were large numbers of widows, particularly among the lower classes.[15] In other words, the 'typical' marriage, when not interrupted by divorce, ended after less than 20 years through the death of one of the spouses, usually the husband.[16]

As with Athens, there is a strong probability that nearly all Roman women married.[17] Here too, the number of marriageable women was perhaps mitigated by a deficit in females, owing to preferential exposure, and impossible to measure, but especially perceptible among the elite.[18] Such a gender imbalance in favour of males at any social level is remarkable for a society that predates the modern demographic transition.[19] Rome was engaged in warfare for much of her history, however, so that there were times, for example, during the second Punic War (218-202) and its aftermath, as well as over the period of the civil wars of the first century BC, when widows and never-married women were relatively numerous.[20] The evidence for Rome on frequency of divorce does not support a high rate, although this problem must be approached with caution.[21] Remarriage, as we shall see, was more likely for higher-status widows. We can safely conclude that for Rome, like Greece, many more women than men were widowed, and that there were relatively large numbers of widows, at least on the lower social levels.

2. Classical antiquity

As for family structure, strong claims have been made for the predominance of the nuclear type both at Athens and Rome. Recent years, however, have seen a growing insistence on the centrality of the 'household' for both cultures. The household, a flexible and potentially more capacious institution, is easier to identify on all levels of society than family type. Meanwhile, the question of family structure has become more elusive, in that the available evidence does not speak decisively for any of the forms known from later periods.[22]

Greek widows and private law

Like all Athenian women, widows were jural minors, which meant they were denied a range of rights at private law that were accorded adult citizen males. Women were eternally subject to male guardians (who are generally thought to have possessed real authority), could not own land (a controversial point among scholars) and perhaps other property as well, including money, were not eligible for intestate succession from husband or father,[23] could not write a will, did not control their dowries, were barred from making financial transactions above the value of a very small amount of money, roughly three to six drachmas, without a guardian's approval, and required a male voice in a court to assert their thin residue of legal privilege.[24]

Widows enjoyed no special legal status as such. A widow, although freed from her husband's guardianship (*kyrieia*), would be subject to that of another male relative. If remarriage was not in prospect, a widow could, as a matter of law, choose to take her dowry and return to the household of her original guardian (*kyrios*) or stay in her husband's household under the *kyrieia* of her sons' guardians, or that of the sons themselves, if they were of age. Again, the guardian in each case would manage the dowry and the sons in the end would inherit it.[25] Any of these alternatives might lead to greater independence, vulnerability, or both. While a woman who had passed from the guardianship of her father to that of her husband is thought to have been able to appeal mistreatment by the latter to the former, it is unclear what assistance was available to women without fathers whose guardians failed them – or if the father himself was the source of difficulties. In one case, a widow, whose children had been defrauded by their guardian, who happened to be her own father and her decedent husband's brother (she had been married to her uncle, perfectly legally), took vigorous action to defend their interests. This episode suggests that sheer personality might count for a lot in the assertion of a widow's legal rights.[26]

Outside of Athens, worth noting is that the law code from the Cretan town of Gortyn, inscribed in the mid-fifth century but containing elements datable to an earlier period, has extensive protections for widows and orphans.[27] Some scholars believe that a number of rules favouring women from Gortyn (a Dorian settlement) also applied at Sparta.[28] At Sparta women could legally own land, and acquired it fairly easily through dowry and inheritance. Demographic realities further promoted the accumulation of property in female hands.[29] Thus Aristotle famously claims that in his day women owned two-fifths of the land at Sparta.[30]

Greek widows and economic privilege

A new school of critics has refused to take the Athenian widow's modest rights at law as the end of the story. They point to an active role played by widows in managing the family finances, mediating between members at variance with each other, and effecting their own wishes.[31] Widowed mothers managed their sons' estates until they came of age.[32] If necessary, their children, or at least their sons, were legally obligated to support them; in any case, they might enjoy a high economic status and an independent role in maintaining this.[33] A widow's status and role might depend on her relationship with her son(s), which was supposed to be close and affectionate.[34] Indeed, disharmony between mother and son tended to be blamed on the latter, and was taken as a sign of his personal and civic irresponsibility.[35]

A widow might even be described in male terms as a de facto *kyria* (= mistress/owner/guardian/manager) within the household.[36] It does seem that women were free to conduct financial transactions within the household and even perhaps among kin more generally without permission of a guardian.[37] Widows can be seen making small private loans to their sons-in-law.[38] Although not legally entitled to make wills, widows seem to have had their last wishes respected all the same.[39]

Although I agree that this new direction in the scholarship has unearthed important and previously neglected aspects of the widow's role in classical Athens, some caveats are in order. All of the widows mentioned in the orations are presumably upper class and so not representative of the entire population.[40] What is more, their role is described by males, invariably in a tendentious and self-justifying context that must, to depart from the very premise of a lawsuit, involve some measure of dysfunction. Their position, in fact, often appears precarious even as described, as though hard-won by sheer force of personality, determined in great measure by circumstance, chiefly the absence of a strong male figure to eclipse (and protect) them, and more than a little vulnerable on a number of fronts.[41] It is fair to say that ideally, at least, women passed from the protection of a father to that of a husband to that of a son.[42] The dowry may have represented a woman's share of her family's estate, and might be used (or the interest there from) for her maintenance as a widow, but it did not in any legal sense belong to her.[43] Widows were vulnerable to exploitation from their notional protectors.[44] In other words, legal protections, as impressive as they may be –

and at Athens they are, in some respects, impressive indeed[45] – are never the end of the story.

It is crucial all the same not to underestimate the importance of law. Whatever its actual success in influencing behaviour, something often beyond our ability to measure, law possesses some amount of ideological force through its very claim to guarantee a right.[46] Legal rules do not tell the whole story, but they relate an essential part of it.

On any estimate, widows, like other Athenian women, were completely deprived of economic privilege outside the circle of the household and close kin. No widow among those discussed here disposed of real estate, participated in commercial lending, or engaged in any other type of economic activity in the 'public sphere'.[47] Not one of the elite widows worked in the commercial sense of earning a wage for the benefit of family or household, as far as we know, although this must have been an inevitable aspect of existence for most poor widows, whose experience is documented, however inadequately, in other sources besides the forensic orations.[48] Prospects of employment were bleak at best for them. The gendered division of labour ideally allotted men outdoor and women indoor work,[49] a distinction that likely had harsh implications for many women who had lost their husbands. Work outside the home was associated with aliens and slaves, although lower-class citizen women must have been more active here than the sources allow.[50]

Even elite widows were vulnerable to exploitation and betrayal, not least from family members, as the experience of Cleobule, the orator Demosthenes' mother, with her husband's nephew Aphobus makes clear.[51] One piece of evidence suggests that grain was made available to widows and orphans at public expense, but the circumstances surrounding this distribution are far from certain.[52] Widows, like other women, could not rely on the social networks available to males.[53] Like other women they were absent from the courts, as litigants, witnesses, or even in supporting roles, excluded not by positive law but by custom.[54]

Greek widows and freedom of movement

Like all women, widows were isolated from a generous share of public activities in Athens.[55] Ideally at least, they remained invisible. It was a breach of decorum even to mention a respectable woman's name.[56] This usage was observed to the extent that of the 48 widows Virginia Hunter identifies in the private orations we know the names of only six.[57] Indeed, when Apollodorus questions the sexual propriety of his widowed and now deceased mother – the only instance of such a charge from a son in the extant evidence and perhaps the product of sheer desperation – he is still careful not to mention her name, Archippe.[58]

Pregnant widows were deemed especially vulnerable and so were among those entrusted to the protection of a public official, the *archôn basileus*.[59] For the most part, however, a widow's ideal protectors were her natal family.[60] As noted above, it was in theory the widow's choice to return to her household of birth or stay with her sons in that of her decedent husband. In fact, a son's direct role in her life, including co-residence, tended to increase with the passage of time.[61] Sons enjoyed some specific duties. They were supposed to defend their mothers against intruders in the household. They were also supposed to avoid offending her or damaging her reputation by installing a *hetaira* (here = 'mistress') therein.[62] Thanks to recent advances in scholarship, we are no longer beguiled by the ancient sources into thinking that Athenian women were kept under lock and key for their entire adult lives. The ideal was not one of seclusion, but one of separation, certainly from men outside the family, an ideal that was realized to an extent, at least by upper-class women.[63] A broad concern with a widow's sexual honour mirrors that which held for women in general but seems to have been especially acute for them.[64] Widows were exposed to slurs cast at them by opponents in lawsuits.[65] The quality and quantity of criticism directed against individual widows, however, may be taken to suggest that few of them effectively challenged the behavioural limits prescribed for them.

Widows past childbearing age or fortunate to have effective male protectors appear, to be sure, to have enjoyed a greater measure of freedom than others.[66] It has been argued that certain upper-class widows, especially after remarriage, enjoyed a prominent role in promoting the interests of their families.[67] Indeed, remarriage seems to have been the most practical means of escaping the constraints placed on their behaviour, a dilemma grounded in considerations of honour and shame.

Ancient Athens, like several of the other cultures under study in this book, had a vivid tradition of literary invective directed against older women. They were supposedly silly, superstitious and prone to drink. Various physical features were ascribed to them in a manner so as to suggest they occasioned reactions of disgust and fear. Moreover, they were socially marginalized, partially degendered, and at bottom dehumanized.[68] All the same, none of this ferocity seems to have been directed against widows in particular, which is to say that there is no good evidence beyond, perhaps, that of drama, that widows were regarded as a serious social problem,[69] apart from a few evidently brief episodes noted above, when unusually high losses in war depressed the number of potential marriage-partners and thus increased their numbers above the norm. A similar point holds for stepmothers, who were the object of widespread caricature and suspected of nursing hostility toward their stepchildren. Many must have been widows before remarriage, but their prior marital history as such is rarely if ever stressed. The stepmother was deemed wicked simply as a stepmother.[70]

Evidence of the anxieties generated by the effects of war is found in some of the later plays of Aristophanes (*Ecclesiazusae* and *Wealth*), where

2. Classical antiquity

the widow, whose aggressive sexual behaviour compromises her respectability, receives a notably higher share of attention than in his previous work.[71] Tragedy has even more to offer. Its widows may be broken down into two main types, the dangerous and the vulnerable. The first is guilty of betrayal, even if this is not intentional. Although utterly oblivious she can still prove disastrous, such as Jocasta in Sophocles' *Oedipus Tyrannus*. This example suggests that remarriage – the typical real-life Athenian solution to the problem of the widow – was not always assumed to be a panacea. The second category is composed of women whose loss of a male protector leads to the most abject suffering and exposure to outrage, including Tecmessa in Sophocles' *Ajax* (whose status as a concubine may heighten her vulnerability) and the heroines of various Euripidean plays, such as *Andromache, Hecuba, Suppliant Women* and *Trojan Women*, all four of which certainly or probably date from the period of the Peloponnesian War.[72] While the evidence of Aristophanes and Euripides falls in with other indications that widows were perceived as a social problem toward the end of the fifth century and the beginning of the fourth, Athenian drama, especially tragedy, is too broadly conceived to convey much specific information about this. It presents widowhood as a challenge in personal terms, a tragic aspect of the human experience that cuts most deeply on an individual level. It is difficult to reconstruct a sociology of the Athenian widow from such material.

As we have seen, widows did not enjoy a special status in law. The same also appears to have been true with regard to religion. Older women appear to have played a prominent role in cults such as that of Sabazios, but not, evidently, *qua* widows.[73] Widows in no sense seem to have formed a separate socially defined group. One important reason for this may have been that ideally and, at least among elite women, in actual fact, wives who lost their husbands appear to have routinely and quickly remarried.

Greek widows and remarriage

Remarriage among widows, at least the younger, upper-class widows known to us, appears to have been common and well-accepted, the latter to judge from the lack of evidence for popular criticism, such as the charivari (a community shaming sanction also sometimes called 'rough music') known to other cultures.[74] In fact, concerns with sexual reputation, undergirded by a belief that sex was recommended for reasons of a woman's health and allied with economic motivations, made a widow's remarriage highly desirable, despite the seemingly contrary example of (the non-Athenian, to be sure) Penelope in the *Odyssey*.[75] And so they evidently did remarry. Of 25 widows known to be of childbearing age, at least 18 were joined to new husbands.[76] Ease of remarriage was compromised at certain times by heightened levels of battlefield mortality for males, as noted above. Given the consequences for the mortality of husbands in comparison to that of wives, first, of the wide age gap for first marriage among the elite and, second, of losses on the battlefield in our period, remarriage behaviour of men may have had relatively little impact on the numbers of widows in Athenian society. Marriage of older widows, certainly those past menopause, was disparaged.[77] The two most important elements over the long term influencing a widow's remarriage chances were age and social class.

Younger widows tended to return – perhaps after a grace period of one year – to their natal families, often leaving their children behind, in order to await the possible arrangement by male relatives of a new match.[78] Where such family relations were unavailable, a husband might name a successor-spouse for his widow in his will, as happened with Cleobule the wife of Demosthenes the Elder and Archippe the wife of Pasio the banker.[79] Cleobule's remarriage did not in fact take place, although it is uncertain whether this decision was hers or that of her prospective husband, Aphobus, her husband's nephew.[80] The circumstances in her case appear to have been unusual in more than one sense and it appears that widows generally had little choice in whether to remarry and to whom.[81] One may compare Chrysilla, the widow of Ischomachus, who displaced her own daughter as the wife of Callias, although only after some difficulty.[82]

Some widows took up residence with their adult children, especially sons, or with their husband's family,[83] but remarriage is what rescued the Athenian widow, at least those of the elite, from social isolation and worse.[84] In re-entering what the Athenians deemed the only truly respectable state for an Athenian woman, the widow was removed from the situation of the vulnerable, independent and marginal. So Attic Old Comedy, which can be exceedingly cruel to the old woman as type, knew a respectable counter-type based on the idealized wife and mother.[85] The Athenian marriage ideal, although heavily infused with the values of a relatively extreme gender hierarchy, did allow women of the elite some opportunity to manage a household, to judge from Xenophon's *Oeconomicus*.[86] Lower-class widows presumably found remarriage more difficult, but certainty is elusive, since our sources are far less interested in them, as in the poor in general.[87] The same holds for widows who were not Athenian citizens. Social class and legal status seem to have counted for far more than status as a widow, though, as ever, younger widows probably remarried more than older ones among this group.

Roman widows and private law

Roman women, including widows, were in general much more privileged at private law than their Athenian counterparts. Demographic reconstruction suggests that most Roman women had lost their fathers by age 20,[88] which meant that few widows were in *patria potestas*, paternal power. Although there was a marital status (marriage with *manus*) that rendered

2. Classical antiquity

a wife strictly dependent on her husband in a legal sense, historians accept that this was rarely used for most of our period, while the guardians of adult women were not significant obstacles to the execution of their wishes, and could be dispensed with entirely in some cases.[89] All women not in *potestas* or *manus* were *sui iuris*, that is, of independent legal status, which meant they were eligible to own property, might inherit under will or through intestate succession, and could write a will, with a few restrictions that eased somewhat with the passage of time.[90]

Because few women married with *manus* in this period, then, most remained in their father's *potestas* as young wives and when widowed were already *sui iuris*. At the death of her father, a woman might expect a share of his patrimony, either through a will – her dowry represented only a part of her total claim, and the typical proportion is disputed – or on intestacy, on which all siblings were entitled to an equal share, regardless of sex. Daughters tended to benefit from inheritance under a father's will much more than wives under a husband's, although they often received a smaller share than their brothers.[91] On intestacy, spouses in a non-*manus* marriage could inherit nothing from each other under the civil law and were ranked only in the fourth class of heirs under the Praetor's Edict, the main source of procedural rules in Roman private law. This miserly regime probably encouraged many a husband to write a will and may have been designed in part to this end. One obstacle that arose for some women was the *lex Voconia* of 169 BC that prohibited testators in the highest census class from instituting females as heirs and leaving a legacy or gift in view of death worth more than what the heir received, which meant, for example, that a childless widow or sole daughter was entitled to no more than half the estate.[92] It was possible, however, to evade the statute through resort to trust (*fideicommissum*), while the rule on legacies was liberalized by the *lex Falcidia* of 40 BC and that regarding female heirs by the Augustan *lex Iulia et Papia*.[93]

Marriage, as opposed to the household itself, was not in essence an economic institution for the Romans, but a mechanism for creating legitimate offspring and transmitting property and status to them. For husbands and wives without *manus*, a separate property regime prevailed that prohibited spouses from making gifts of any value to each other by rendering them void. This rule was softened somewhat by an enactment of Septimius Severus in AD 206 that allowed gifts not revoked before death by the giver to stand, converting them essentially into gifts in view of death. Although the rule was gender-neutral, more widows than widowers would have benefited from it, since men tended to predecease their wives rather than vice-versa.[94] In principle, although a widow might profit considerably from her husband's largesse under a will, men aimed at minimum to preserve the same standard of living their wives enjoyed during the marriage.[95]

Whether or not a husband left a valid will, his widow was entitled to return of her dowry, which was in his ownership and control for the duration of the marriage. In practice the dowry served as a form of maintenance for the wife, although the husband was not, on the common view, strictly obligated at law to support her. Dowry was at any rate instrumental for a widow's sustenance and important to her prospects of remarriage.[96] Women were entitled to assert their own rights at private law, although they could not represent others.[97] So a widow (or her *pater familias*, if she had one) might sue for the return of the dowry. Although many husbands left this as a legacy in their wills (*legatum dotis*) or a more generous legacy in place of a dowry (*legatum pro dote*), under the Praetor's Edict a widow might choose between the bequest and a valuation of her dowry. It seems to have been customary to bequeath through legacy personal items used by the wife and to confirm gifts made during the marriage, practices that perhaps arose in the context of *manus*-marriage, in which the wife could own no property. Another commonly mentioned device (not to exhaust the possibilities) was bequest of the use and enjoyment, or usufruct, of property, such as a farm, to a widow, with ownership accruing to the heir, to whom the right of usufruct eventually reverted as well. Usufruct is thought to have been developed in the first place as a support for widows.

The Augustan marriage legislation (18 BC and AD 9) placed limits on the rights of spouses to succeed to each other under a will. Those without children in common might receive no more than a tenth of the other's estate with full rights of ownership and up to one-third in usufruct. Additional tenths were allowed for each child from a previous marriage and the *legatum dotis* was exempted from the calculation. One child from their marriage gave spouses complete rights of testamentary succession to each other, while three gave freeborn Romans the full slate of benefits under the law. It was possible to evade these rules through resort to trust until the passage of the Flavian *SC Pegasianum* and even afterwards through reliance on gifts in view of death until a later *SC* (a *senatusconsultum* or decree of the Senate) closed this loophole, a rule that held for the Severan loosening of the ban on spousal gifts mentioned above. Intestate succession to children's property was eased for widows with at least three children by a law passed under Hadrian, the *SC Tertullianum*.[98]

Widows were placed under only a few legal restrictions that specifically pertained to them. Marriage was not highly regulated at law, widowhood even less so. Most of the relevant rules deal with remarriage (below). A partial exception (partial because it also applied to divorcées) is a feature of the Praetor's Edict whose exact date is disputed. This built on earlier norms that involved supervision and surveillance of a widow's (or divorcée's) pregnancy and giving birth. These were set in motion on her request and designed to protect her child's claim to a share of her deceased husband's estate as well as the interests of his family in excluding a false claim.[99]

2. Classical antiquity

As with Greece, it is clear that 'widow' was not an independent legal category at Rome and it is disputable whether it even qualifies as a sociological type. Latin *vidua*, like Greek *chêra*, might refer to any type of unmarried woman, widow, divorcée, or never-married, or just generally to a 'woman without a husband', although there are texts where it not only can but must mean 'widow'. The most significant legal and social status for Roman women was that of the *mater familias/matrona* or respectable woman. Predating Augustus, and enshrined in his adultery law (c. 17 BC) as a vague standard of liability, these terms primarily referred to married women, but embraced widows, divorcées and never-married women as well.[100] Social status, age and authority mattered more than status as a widow.[101] The fact that upper-class Roman women typically married early and quickly remarried on widowhood helped the *mater familias/matrona* eclipse the other categories.

Roman widows and economic privilege

Widows, as suggested, were no exception to the general principle that permitted adult Roman women to dispose freely of whatever economic assets they possessed.[102] The lifelong male guardianship imposed on female adults presented no real barrier to enjoying this freedom, especially after the death of a husband.[103] Their assets might derive from a variety of sources, such as the dowry furnished by fathers, other relatives, and friends, material support from children, and testamentary bequests left above all by fathers and husbands.[104] There is some evidence that control of a decedent husband's property might help sustain a widow's authority over her children, although they were rarely bequeathed more than half his estate.[105] Widows brought up their children and attempted to safeguard their interests, above all their economic interests, either in cooperation or in conflict with the children's guardians.[106] The widowed mother was recognized as enjoying the central role in the raising of her children.[107] Tacitus, for example, means to present as exemplary the role taken by his father-in-law Agricola's mother Iulia Procilla in her son's upbringing.[108] Egyptian evidence shows widowed mothers active in arranging marriage and apprenticeship contracts for their children.[109] Women were barred in principle from acting as guardians, although by the early second century the emperors allowed, on petition, some widows to take up this responsibility regarding their own children.[110]

Children, if they had the means, were legally required to support their needy parents from the mid-second century AD.[111] The state did not provide a system of welfare for its elderly citizens in general, leaving plenty of scope for private initiatives, such as former masters remembering their ex-slaves in their wills.[112] Widows demonstrably relied – and expected to rely – on the support of their sons.[113]

Women's participation as patrons and clients in the business world is an important index of their social integration and they were every bit as interested in profit as the male members of the upper classes.[114] Their share of property relative to that owned by men is uncertain, and therefore open to dispute. It was almost certainly less, perhaps far less.[115] In any case, they did not escape criticism in their managing of resources. The wealth of widows, whatever its size and distribution, inspired a pronounced degree of male angst.[116] Wealth might attract a new spouse, promoting an inversion of gender roles, at least in the preoccupations of some male authors, a concern admittedly separate from, but in my view related to, the oft-expressed aversion to older women as sexual partners.[117] Widows might paradoxically be regarded both as victims and as predators.

The household in antiquity had more diversified functions and operated as more of an economic unit than in the present-day West, so that losing a (male) head might pose significant challenges for his survivors. Upper-class widows were typically competent managers of estates, to judge, for example, from Apuleius's admittedly self-interested praise of Aemilia Pudentilla's administration of her household.[118] There is no doubt that the economic implications of losing a husband to death were felt more acutely among the great masses of widows from the lower orders of society. They enjoyed little or no access to the sources of the economic assets described above. Opportunities for self-support were meagre for women in general, and even more limited for widows.[119] Women's job opportunities were highly circumscribed for reasons that were cultural as well as economic, while charity, public or private, was practically non-existent.[120] Widows' numbers were great and their poverty vast. It is clear why widows in antiquity were a by-word for vulnerability and misery.[121]

Roman widows and freedom of movement

While forbidden, like their Athenian counterparts, to participate in a range of public activities, Roman women were far from invisible, even ideally so. The ancients themselves noticed the distinction, with a famous text of Cornelius Nepos making a striking observation worth describing here. No Roman husband was ashamed to bring his wife to a dinner party: the 'lady of the household' (*mater familias*) reigned supreme at home and maintained a high profile in public. In the Greek world, on the other hand, respectable women attended dinner parties – even at home – only if they were strictly family occasions and were in principle discouraged from venturing outside the part of the house said to be allotted to them.[122]

Nepos may exaggerate both the degree of actual segregation for Greek women and, to some extent, the freedom of action available to elite Roman women, but the essential cultural difference he invokes seems valid. Seeing one's name published in a poem could be an honour for a Roman woman in Martial's day in a way unimaginable for a woman in Periclean Athens.[123] Roman widows might host dinner parties at their homes for

2. Classical antiquity

guests of both sexes, although it is less clear whether they could attend them elsewhere without reproach.[124] In other respects, they enjoyed a relatively broad freedom of movement. Widows were no strangers to litigation, to judge from a casual remark of Apuleius, from which we might speculate they were relatively visible in this area as well.[125]

Widows were unburdened from the responsibility of catering to a husband's sense of propriety and were typically under the control and supervision of no man, not even, in any significant sense, of their legal guardian, as we have seen. They enjoyed on the whole greater freedom, influence, and even, a bit surprisingly, respect than married women, both notionally and, as far as we can tell, in actual fact.[126] A mother's authority over her children was enhanced by widowhood, at least among the upper classes.[127] This does not mean that widows were beyond criticism, however.

Widows, as we shall see, were not as a rule branded by prejudice against them as a group or type. They constituted, as individuals, a kind of 'woman-plus', attracting at times a greater measure of praise or (especially) blame than others, perhaps, but not of an appreciably different kind. Older women in general, however, were doubly marginalized, by gender and by age, as we shall see.[128] Wealthy women were at least a partial exception to this principle. A friend warns Martial not to tangle with a widow who is both old and rich.[129] Even on the upper levels of society, however, there was no absolute guarantee against imposition, as demonstrates Pliny's story of how the villainous aristocrat Regulus tricked the widow Verania on her deathbed into leaving him a legacy in her will.[130]

Greater independence for widows meant that they were exposed to sometimes fierce criticism, mostly on an individual basis.[131] Ideally, upper-class women were retiring in their behaviour and reticent in their speech, a standard of conduct especially highly valued in the second century AD,[132] and one that is clearly at odds with a widow's notionally wide scope of action. This tension is frequently resolved in favour of anti-female invective. Widows were liable, for example, to be characterized as sexually aggressive.[133] Sassia's lust is an issue central to the criminal case as defined and defended by Cicero in the *Pro Cluentio*. The abuse he visits on Clodia Metelli in the *Pro Caelio* may suggest the limits some, perhaps many, men would place upon a widow's role, however indirect, in public life.[134] Clodia was impugned as an unmarried woman (and, further, implicated in her husband's death), but a widow did not necessarily escape criticism by remarrying, as Aemilia Pudentilla learned. Juvenal does not omit widows in his catalogue of female sexual excess, although he hardly devotes much space to them.[135] The elderly Ummidia Quadratilla was free to indulge her weakness for pantomime, a hobby Pliny the Younger disapproves, although she escapes serious censure by sheltering her grandson from it.[136]

This criticism, which reaches its full pitch in the patristic authors, should not be read as a mere reflection of actual freedom for widows, let

Widows and Patriarchy

alone adult women in general, although it is reasonably persuasive that the degree of freedom they enjoyed, or in some cases claimed for themselves, was an aggravating factor in provoking such reactions. Beyond this, such criticism suggests the truth of their exposed position in a patriarchal society.[137] Although they were not singled out, widows were clearly a concern of the controls on sexual behaviour imposed by the Augustan law on adultery.[138] Loss of a husband did not spell greater freedom in this area, as there loomed the penalty of the criminal law for sexually active widows. A widow's sexual misbehaviour – even when this was merely alleged – might reflect badly on her entire family.[139]

One important and enduring source of criticism of widows is the story of the Widow of Ephesus. There are two classical versions of this, one by Phaedrus, a freedman of Augustus who wrote fables in the early to mid-first century, and the other by Petronius, Nero's minister of parties and special events, as well as the author of a novel, the *Satyricon*, that survives in fragments.[140] Neither work is precisely datable, although most scholars view Phaedrus' verse rendition as earlier than Petronius' prose. The elements common to both are important. A beautiful young widow, overcome with grief, shuts herself up in her husband's tomb intent on starving herself to death, attended by a single slave-woman. A soldier assigned to guard the corpses of some crucified criminals comes across the widow and after a brief interval the two of them begin an affair in the tomb. While the soldier is thus distracted, one of the corpses goes missing. Struck by fear of serious punishment, the soldier explains the situation to the widow, who remedies matters by supplying her deceased husband's corpse to hang on the cross in place of the absent criminal.

The differences between the two accounts are also significant. One obvious point is that Petronius' version is considerably longer than Phaedrus' and so more detailed. For example, it sets the story in a certain place, the city of Ephesus. It is also framed within a wider narrative, in contrast to Phaedrus' stand-alone fable, a fact which assists, or at least complicates, its interpretation. The story is retailed by Eumolpus, a person of dubious merits, to an audience consisting largely of equally doubtful characters, in an atmosphere redolent of sexual (and other) intrigue.[141] Not surprisingly, its meaning is hotly disputed, but the most convincing explanation contrasts the import of Phaedrus, whose version is more or less plainly misogynist (although the weight of this falls on the very last line of the poem), with that of Petronius, which is at bottom satirical, lending itself to a variety of interpretations and enabling readers to extract diverse moral lessons from it. For example, some view the author as condemning the widow for her faithlessness, promiscuity, and self-absorption, rendered concrete in such acts as abuse of her husband's corpse, betraying him sexually with various attendant aggravating factors in play, and abandonment to excessive mourning in the first place,[142] while others see a humane sympathy for the widow's plight, coupled with an affirmation of

2. Classical antiquity

the value of choosing life over death. It is fair to say that the story contains plenty of raw material encouraging both misogynistic and/or widow-friendly readings, to give two extreme possibilities, while that of Phaedrus is both relatively monotone in nature, that is, more unambiguously anti-female, and also more consistent with mainstream Roman notions of desirable conduct on the part of widows.[143]

The impact of both versions on later literature was attenuated by the disappearance of Phaedrus' text from the ninth century until its rediscovery in 1596 (even manuscripts are lacking until about 1470) and of Petronius' version as well for much of the same period. Despite John of Salisbury's use of the latter in his 1159 classic of medieval political science, the *Policraticus*, it long remained relatively inaccessible. Phaedrus did, however, influence the version of the story found in the late antique collection of fables known as the *Romulus*. From this derived a flourishing medieval literary tradition of male anxiety.[144]

Many Roman widows were relatively young, but with increasing age came both privilege and vulnerability. Romans were decidedly ambivalent about old age, now praising and honouring it, now subjecting it to fierce criticism or even ridicule. Women tended to suffer from the negative side of this ambivalence.[145] Older women, as a somewhat paradoxical compensation for their marginality, enjoyed greater freedom than younger women, regardless of marital status. This made them well suited, at least in the male imagination, as go-betweens, e.g. procuresses.[146] They were liable to criticism for their allegedly repulsive physical appearance, putative drunkenness (qualities represented not only in literature but in art, where sculpture might portray them as wrinkled, toothless, drunkards), and supposed sexual voraciousness. They were, moreover, often identified with the practice of witchcraft.[147] Widows, perhaps because they were not automatically and absolutely associated with old age in antiquity, are relatively rarely singled out in this way.[148] Neither are they particularly identified with stepmothers, for whom the Romans developed a vicious stereotype, although many widows remarried men with children. This is true even for a stepmother like Agrippina the Younger, widowed twice, who advanced the interests of her son by a prior marriage to the detriment of her stepchildren.[149] She is vilified as a stepmother, not as a widow.

Social rank also mattered here, in the sense that the less advantaged were more vulnerable, for example, to the predatory and often violent practices of tax collectors, public officials and others, while enjoying far less autonomy overall.[150] Widows in their petitions to the authorities that survive from Roman Egypt stress their vulnerability, a style of self-presentation that appears to have been effective overall.[151] A degree of sympathy was felt for less fortunate widows, but it would be easy to exaggerate this.[152] Only upper-class widows were effectively integrated into extensive patronage networks of friends and clients.[153] These networks often included men, of course, as we can see from, for example, the poet Martial's deferential attitude toward his patron Marcella.[154] Surviving a husband enabled a widow with means to define what and who was important in the relationship, as the famous Pompeian funerary monument erected by Naevoleia Tyche for her deceased husband shows: it is more about her than about him.[155]

Children were a decisive factor in determining a widow's place of residence, tying her to her husband's family, and few seem to have returned to that of their birth. Widows living alone are often difficult to read out of the evidence, to be sure.[156] Although it has been argued that sons tended to remain with their widowed mothers after reaching adulthood and even marrying, the frequency of neo-local marriage (where the couple form a new household apart from both sets of parents) appears to increase along with social status. Nevertheless, this arrangement might change over time. The Romans felt a moral duty to care for elders that could extend to providing shelter for them. Widows often took up residence with an adult son, married or unmarried, a solution preferable to risking disrespectful treatment, or worse, from in-laws or outsiders.[157] Elite women often had a choice of two or more residences, both in town and in the countryside, as the example of Aemilia Pudentilla shows.[158] Lower-status widows may have kept their children with them even after remarriage.[159] Legally, the *pater familias*, if there was one, of a decedent husband had the right to decide where and by whom children were to be raised, but it is doubtful whether this claim was exercised very much on the lower levels of society.[160]

Roman widows and remarriage

Romans celebrated the virtue of the *univira*, the woman married only once, who remained loyal to the memory of her husband if he predeceased her.[161] A famous example is Cornelia, *Gracchorum mater*, who turned down a marriage proposal from no less a suitor than the King of Egypt.[162] All the same, it seems that most widows who could remarry did so, which suggests the existence of a counter-ideal that valued remarriage after loss of a spouse, a counter-ideal rooted in practical considerations.[163] The paradox of the *univira* is that Romans seem to have expected most or all respectable upper-class women to be married.[164] Loyalty to a first husband was not necessarily inconsistent in their eyes with marriage to a second.[165] The interest of a widow's children was valued far more than celibacy honouring a decedent spouse, an interest that might well be served by remarriage.[166] Restoration of dowry from a prior marriage, as seen above, could play an important role in securing a subsequent union.

Some of the very few legal rules specifically framed for widows concern remarriage. One example is the longstanding prohibition against remarriage for a period of ten months following the death of a husband, which was not extended either to widowers or divorcées, and which in the

2. Classical antiquity

classical period was explained in terms both of a concern with confusion of progeny, and so questions of legitimacy, and of a concern with the proper respect due a husband. Violation of this norm might be punished by the urban Praetor with procedural disabilities at law.[167] Widows were expected to mourn for their deceased husbands and were often praised for doing so.[168] Literary and epigraphical evidence demonstrates that grief over loss of a husband could be profound.[169] Widows' use of mourning clothes[170] and the limits placed on the expression of their grief as early as the middle of the fifth century BC [171] suggest the strength of the social imperative in favour of mourning a dead husband.[172] These restrictions included a prohibition against mutilating the face, which suggests *a fortiori* that widow suicide was unacceptable. In fact, women who killed themselves at the time of or just after the deaths of their husbands were widely admired, although the evidence also yields the sense that such behaviour might be regarded, at best, as above and beyond the call of duty, and so hardly a routine expectation. At worst it could be deemed excessive and unnecessary.[173]

Widows were required to remarry (like divorcées, who were given less time) by the Augustan marriage legislation, at first (18 BC) after a year, then (AD 9) after two years.[174] Upon the law's passage, widows younger than 20 or older than 50 were exempt, but the latter were rendered liable by later legislation that penalized on a permanent basis widows who had not remarried by the time they reached the upper age cut-off.[175] Before the law, anyone could leave a bequest on the condition that the recipient remain unmarried; afterwards, this was only allowed to the decedent spouse (although theoretically possible for both sexes, in practice husbands seem more often to have imposed the condition of widowhood on their wives), and even here, the widow might still remarry and receive the bequest, if she did so within a year (presumably after conclusion of the legally prescribed mourning period of ten months), and upon swearing an oath that her motive in doing so was procreation.[176]

Aside from the prospect of easier material support and social respectability, motives for marrying again included fears of vulnerability, loneliness (aggravated by a widow's need to hold herself somewhat aloof from society out of concern for her reputation), a concern with health (lack of sex was commonly thought to cause problems for women),[177] the desire for children (which was not always exhausted by producing them in a first marriage), and the demands of gender-specific roles within the household, which seemed to require the presence of a man.[178] A robust ideal of marriage flourished for both sexes,[179] as did a lively anti-marriage tradition, which was produced by and for men.[180]

Remarriage was common among upper-class women, but not so among lower-class women, especially after age 30.[181] For the former, examples of twice-widowed and remarried women, like Fulvia and Livia Iulia, can easily be found. For many of the latter, the ideal of the *univira* was more of a necessity than a virtue. Sub-elite Roman society had a large number of unmarried, and quite unmarriageable, widows, many of them young and burdened with minor-age children.[182] Women in the imperial household tended to marry especially quickly and often. Antonia Minor, widowed at the age of 27 by the death of her husband Drusus, is a rare example of a young widow in Augustus' family who did not remarry, remaining a widow until her death at the age of 72.[183]

Remarrying widows had much greater influence in the choice of a new husband and on what might be described as the dynamics of a new marriage than did first-time brides, who were ideally and often in fact the weaker partner.[184] This did not free every one of them from importunity, although wealthy women might assert themselves with greater success. Apuleius' Aemilia Pudentilla braved hostility from family members, but succeeded in marrying a second husband of her choice, despite the fact that he was perhaps ten years her junior and socio-economically her inferior as well.

Age and social rank were evidently the two most important factors in fostering or discouraging remarriage.[185] It seems that even widows with children, provided they were wealthy and prominent, had the opportunity to remarry no less than widowers.[186] They might balk, however, at the potential lessening of respect and authority occasioned by marriage to a new husband.[187] A common concern was with female hypogamy, that is, a wealthy widow marrying beneath her rank, a concern that extended to non-marital relationships, as the Widow of Ephesus story shows.[188] The evidence from Roman Egypt, on the other hand, offers a bleak sense of the remarriage chances of many lower-status widows, especially older ones, in contrast to the men, who as a group remarried more often and with increasingly younger wives as partners.[189] Roman males with children contemplating remarriage confronted a caution in the stereotype of the *saeva noverca*, the cruel stepmother, that was ever popular in literature, but it is far from certain that this was much of an impediment to them.[190]

Jewish and Christian influences

Widows posed a serious challenge for Christians. Their renunciation of remarriage, and so ideally of sex, validated a central Christian ideal. As celibates, they evidently seemed, at least to some, a greater prize for the Church than never-married women, *virgines*, because unlike the latter they had known sex and still were prepared to give it up.[191] On the other hand, making provision for their welfare was a daunting task. Christian ideology could answer to the economic and demographic exigencies of widowhood only up to a point. The responsibility of providing care was impossible to ignore, especially given the reception of a longstanding Jewish tradition and its refinement by a new faith in strong competition with its own antecedents. But the challenge of supporting massive num-

2. Classical antiquity

bers of widows and defining for them an acceptable role within the Church led to problems in the final analysis impossible to reconcile in the moral economy of the ancient Mediterranean world. This excursus focuses exclusively on those aspects of the Jewish and Christian traditions necessary for understanding the legacy of widowhood in antiquity for the late medieval and early modern periods. That means a focus on Latin authors in late antiquity and in particular on Jerome. At the same time, a number of other aspects of the law and life regarding widows are deliberately omitted.[192]

Various questions arise in connection with the long-term legacy of widowhood as just described. How did widows come to be viewed as privileged recipients of material assistance? What was the origin of the ideological construct of the celibate woman who had lost her husband to death, and how did this category come unambiguously to rank higher than married women, but lower than virgins?

The Jewish tradition itself appears to have taken its point of departure from a series of pronouncements concerning widows in the ancient Near East. These derive from Egyptian, Mesopotamian, Hittite and Northwest Semitic sources, above all, a couple of texts in the Ugaritic literature, that suggest protection of widows and other vulnerable persons was a particular duty, sometimes divinely sanctioned, of the ruler.[193] There are a number of references to widows scattered throughout the Hebrew Bible, among the earliest and most important of which is the injunction in Exodus not to mistreat them.[194] The duty of protection is crystallized in Deuteronomy, where it is articulated largely as a positive obligation to provide material support for widows, orphans and a third category of persons often called 'strangers' whose precise meaning remains a subject of controversy.[195] Every three years, the annual tithe had to be shared with widows, orphans, 'strangers' and Levites at a cult-site.[196]

Widows, orphans, Levites, and 'strangers' are also stipulated as beneficiaries of offerings at the Feast of Weeks[197] and the Feast of Booths.[198] Finally, during the harvest of grain, olives and grapes, the farmer is commanded to glean but once, leaving the residue for the widow, orphan, and 'stranger'.[199] The charity in all of these cases seems to be rather direct, although it may have been mediated to an extent by religious officials in all but the last case. Yet another text invokes just treatment at law for all three of these types, specifically ordaining that the widow not be deprived of clothing as a pledge.[200]

The concern with widows and the rest may have in part rested on a fear that some well-off persons might face a rapid and irreversible downward mobility as a consequence of a change of personal status.[201] Their fate seemed fortuitous, not moral, in nature, so that they might be regarded as deserving of assistance. In any case, these figures were all obviously highly vulnerable types. God was particularly disposed to hear their prayer.[202] Nevertheless, while God was their ultimate protector, this did not relieve others of an obligation to help them. Providing assistance to widows

Widows and Patriarchy

therefore helped legitimize the power of the elite. It laid down a bright shining line between legitimate authority and tyranny, which exploited the weak or at least turned a blind eye to their oppression. Widows emerge from Deuteronomy as a fully fledged moral category.[203]

When we turn to the status and role of widows in the early Christian Church, we can trace both continuity and change with regard to the Jewish tradition from a pair of nearly contemporary texts dating most likely to the period 80-100.[204] The first, from the *Acts of the Apostles*, recounts a bitter discord that arose, as the Church was growing rapidly, between two groups of Christians at Jerusalem, identified as the Hellenists and the Hebrews, a division marked by differences of language, culture and theology.[205] The former complained that their widows were disadvantaged in the daily food distributions, and the Apostles respond by appointing a Board of Seven to supervise these, leaving themselves free to pursue their mission of prayer and the ministry of the Word. The fact that at this early date (c. 36?) material support for widows is taken for granted (and seems more deeply rooted among the Hebrew speakers) suggests that the practice was taken over directly from the Jewish tradition.[206] No mention is made of remarriage – or not – of widows as a moral criterion.

Of significance is that the distributions of food acquired a new level of institutional sophistication at this time. The Church was already large enough, and contained enough needy widows, that these require special provision. They form not just an economic category but also a moral one – the moral status of those widows supported by the Church is clearly superior to that of those not so supported.[207] Also of interest is the hint of moral competition in evidence – the matter is presented and resolved in a way that suggests that economic criteria were not the sole means of determining who was worthy of assistance. But this aspect of the matter remains unclear, and, importantly, the precise meaning of 'widows' (*chêrai*) in this text remains undefined.

The second passage, from a pastoral epistle attributed insecurely to Paul, addresses these issues head on.[208] It begins with an injunction to honour – a term containing both moral and economic implications[209] – the 'real' or 'true' widows. Widows who have children and grandchildren should look to them for support. The 'real' widow is the one left alone who places her hope in God, devoting herself night and day to petitions and prayers. A widow awash in luxury leads a living death. Providing for widows in one's family, especially one's immediate family, is obligatory for a Christian. Failure to do so is to behave worse than an unbeliever. To be registered as a recipient of Church support, a widow must be no less than 60 years old, and have been married only once. Her eligibility is secured by her good deeds: raising children, providing hospitality to strangers, washing the feet of Christian guests, assisting those in need, performing every good work possible.

As the epistle continues, there follows an instruction to reject as recipi-

2. Classical antiquity

ents of aid the younger widows, on the ground that their passions will alienate them from Christ and make them want to remarry, for which they will incur censure by breaking their first pledge.[210] They become lazy, idle, gossips flitting (or 'gadding', to use the technical term) from house to house chattering about things they ought not. Better for the younger widows to marry, produce children, manage a household and offer no ground for blame by those who criticize us Christians. Already, some (according to the author) have turned to Satan. If a female Christian has widows, evidently meaning in her household,[211] she should provide for them and prevent them from becoming a burden to the Church, so that it can provide for 'real' widows.

This text stands as foundational for Christian treatment of widows in the centuries to come, in the sense that it is one of the scriptural texts most cited in the regulation of their moral and spiritual status. All the same, many details remain controversial as to their exact significance. It is worth noting that the complex classifications set forth by this text find no precedent in the tradition of the Hebrew Bible.[212] Moral and economic criteria are intertwined, inextricably so in my view, in defining the widow who qualifies for support from the Church, the 'real' widow.[213] The Church cannot support everyone in need, and there is a concern especially with the behaviour of some of the younger widows.[214] Recipients of aid must have no alternative means available, such as family or personal resources, and in the latter case at least scathing moral criticism is levied against the widow said to be living in luxury. Poverty is construed as a moral ideal. The 'real' widow must be at least 60 years old and only once-married.

We should understand these requirements not so much as demographic as moral in nature. Thus it is easier to explain the concession to younger widows, who, it is claimed, will want to remarry, an act that might seem to render them permanently ineligible for Christian charity, according to the logic of this text, which advances both the ideal of celibacy and that of marriage. Marriage, however, ranks lower, precisely because assumed and, in this text, implied to be motivated by a desire for sex.[215] At the same time, it is clear that remarriage is the preferred option for the majority of widows in the community, in light of the restrictive qualifications stipulated for 'real' widows.[216] Given the demographic and economic exigencies described above, the rule is likely to have been more prescriptive than descriptive for many. Taken by itself, it is consistent with the counsel offered to widows by Paul in his first letter to the Corinthians:[217] better to (re)marry than to burn.[218] Despite the fact that this means breaking their first pledge, remarriage and its virtuous obligations are deemed preferable to the lifestyle of the young widow as described here. A record of prayer and good works ideally supports a widow's eligibility for support.

The obligation of family members to support 'their' widows is repeatedly stressed, as a concern emerges that not even the minimal standards of pagans, who provide private, but not of course community, support for

Widows and Patriarchy

their widows, will be met.[219] Widows ideally live in a state of dependency on God, their families, or a second husband.[220] The text breathes a spirit of moral competition with non-believers, as evidenced in the concern that the behaviour of young widows will provoke criticism from outside.[221] The idea of a register suggests an explicit grant of 'official' status as a 'real' widow, just as the insistence that private support where available frees the Church to focus on 'real' widows signals that its resources are, after all, limited. But it seems entirely predictable that some wealthy widows, widows with family, young widows and even morally-challenged widows might aspire to inclusion in a category that brought not only economic benefits but an enhanced, highly visible moral status. This does not mean that they formed anything like a clerical 'order of widows' in the way a number of scholars have argued on the basis of this (and other) evidence.[222]

Despite the rules laid down in *1 Timothy*, or perhaps because of their inadequate clarity, much ambiguity and controversy reigned over the status and role of widows both in the Church and in society at large over the next four centuries and beyond.[223] Now and again a harder or softer line is pursued. The criteria for eligibility for assistance laid down in *1 Timothy* become the standard, although one finds some difficulties arising with the age cut-off of 60 and the requirement that the widow have no alternative means of support in children and/or grandchildren.[224] There is evidence that different standards were advanced in different Christian communities and by various authorities: the age cut-off might be lowered to 50 years, women with very young children might be allowed relief, as also women with disabilities, etc.

Of course the entire issue of widows' eligibility for material assistance is caught up with the general debate over sexual renunciation, a point that cannot receive adequate emphasis.[225] Regional differences are seen as well as variations over time, especially in late antiquity, with the East generally showing greater rigour than the West.[226] The absence of a unified Christian position on the issue of widows, and especially of widows' remarriage, would seem *a priori* to place limits on the impact it could have on social life. Worth mentioning is Tertullian, who took earlier counsels against the remarriage of widows to an extreme of condemnation, especially as he turned toward Montanism.[227]

Remarriage for widows in late antiquity remained the norm, at least for those in the upper orders of society. Christian recommendations in favour of celibate widowhood could have little impact on the economic facts that governed the behaviour of most inhabitants of the empire. So the demographic effects of this teaching were minimal, as we shall see below. The defensiveness of the Fathers on the subject of widows' remarriage shows they encountered real opposition.[228] It is of some importance that much of their advice on this subject occurs in essays (e.g. Augustine's *De Bono Viduitatis*) and letters (such as Jerome's) intended for aristocrats (among whom they might circulate widely) and not in sermons addressed to the

2. Classical antiquity

general population.[229] An exception perhaps proving the rule is Ambrose's essay on widows (*De Viduis*), which many scholars believe to be a lightly edited sermon. It is relatively accommodating on the subject of remarriage.

Jerome was by far the most important source for the ideological construct of celibate widowhood that lived on past late antiquity. In circumstances that seem nothing if not contingent, he reinvented Christian widowhood, as a part of his overall redesign of the categories of female status and role. Although in the context of late antiquity, when he does not seem to have enjoyed widespread influence, his was only one of several voices advocating ascetical models for women, for us it is his long-term impact that matters. His work was later to stand, with some elaboration over time, as the dominant paradigm shaping women's experience and perceptions of that experience for many centuries to come.

The classical ideal of (elite) womanhood was the *mater familias / matrona*, ideally although not necessarily married, even as most upper-class women were married for much of their adult lives (see above). Jerome transformed this monolith into three unequal parts, fusing elements of the pagan tradition, the *mos maiorum*, with Christian ideals to create something vaguely familiar in important respects yet also quite remarkably new. Among his most important tactics was the way in which he precisely, emphatically, and in abundant detail ranked the three new female forms into (1) *virgines* or virgins, never-married women sworn off sex, and in some ways Jerome's most original creation of the three; (2) *viduae* or widows (there being no room for divorcées in this scheme), a compromise category comprised of the sexually inactive yet experienced; and (3) *nuptae*, the least prestigious and, from Jerome's perspective, the least desirable, in that they lacked the glamour of those who had renounced sex.[230]

Sheer originality was not the point here. What mattered more was absolute clarity, a wealth of argumentation and examples, and an aggressive style that carried zeal past the line of vehemence. Jerome was far from subtle in his ordering of the relative worth of the three (a characteristic no doubt essential for his later influence): virgins, he wrote, might expect a hundredfold reward in heaven, widows sixtyfold, and wives thirtyfold.[231] Before Jerome, widows appear to have had some claim to ascendancy among celibate Christian women, although virgins generally ranked higher.[232] The precise definition and relationship of these categories to each other and to other groups, such as married women, widowers, monastics and clerics, appears to have been still somewhat unclear before Jerome.[233] His reducing widows to an unambiguous secondary status below that of virgins was an important aspect of his ideological redefinition of widowhood.[234]

What was this new widow-type supposed to be? The key, as far as Jerome was concerned, was to abandon as much as possible the lifestyle of the wealthy and worldly *matrona*.[235] Like married women, upper-class widows often had a household to administer, although some degree of withdrawal from the world was preferred, better, removal to a country estate, or even retirement to an ascetical community.[236] As did the Stoics, Jerome believed that women enjoyed the same potential for intellectual and moral training as men (it is no coincidence that his advisees were highly educated) but thought that their talents were better devoted to the study of Christian texts than traditional Latin and Greek literature.[237] He also recommended physical labour as an exercise in humility, on the ground that spiritual authority derived from this.[238] Fasting was important as an antidote to (the recollection of) desire.[239] Jerome conceived of widowhood in no small measure as a penance for marriage.[240] Acts of charity (facilitated by the possession of great wealth) directed at the poor (in many cases widows themselves) and the Church itself might help compensate for the less than intense engagement with the ascetical life enjoined on many widows by their worldly obligations; on the other hand, generous distribution of patrimony might alienate them from their families, not entirely a bad thing, to his mind.[241]

Jerome in fact advocated cutting family ties, when this furthered an ascetical purpose. He held to this even to the point of slighting the interests of a widow's children, who could turn out to be a huge disappointment after all – witness the sorrows of the widowed mother of the Gracchi.[242] A widow's refusal to remarry might alienate and offend her family, which typically had other plans for her. Jerome emphatically discouraged remarriage. Although his position on this subject might seem more moderate than that of Tertullian, since he professes himself prepared to tolerate it if necessary on the basis of certain passages from *1 Corinthians* and *1 Timothy*,[243] serial remarriage was for him prostitution, a view that is sometimes phrased so categorically, however, as to embrace even a second marriage.[244] The influence of Tertullian is palpable, on this point and others.[245] Widows were in Jerome's ideal conception not only socially isolated and sundered from their families but also de-gendered.[246] He counselled a strong emphasis on *meditatio mortis* and envisioned widowhood as at best a kind of social death.[247] It is not surprising that widows who followed his precepts were regarded by some with suspicion, thought to be a source of danger, and their asceticism deemed highly antisocial, or worse.[248]

The contingency, meaning the non-inevitability, of the success enjoyed by Jerome's views on widows is well-supported by the evidence. Jerome often underrated the power and determination of his opponents and it is a bit surprising that his many personal defeats did not prevent the eventual triumph of his ideals. Both pagans and non-ascetical Christians with justice viewed Jerome as mounting an assault on traditional family values, and consequently women's decisions to remain celibate, whether as virgins or as widows, sometimes generated fierce conflicts within families. Among the upper classes, marriage, an institution designed to

2. Classical antiquity

secure the transmission of property and status from one generation to the next, as well as a useful tool in cementing political alignments, was a routine expectation of women, in both senses, that it was expected of them and by them. Many aristocratic Christians as well as pagans shared an appreciation of the virtues of marriage and family life.[249]

Even orthodox Christians, whose views on asceticism and much else, including the general conception of the new status and role of widows, were consistent with his own, differed with him on key points, such as widow-remarriage. Ambrose, Augustine and even at times Jerome himself took some distance from Tertullian and his extreme views on this subject, but with important differences among themselves. Ambrose and Augustine favoured sexual renunciation for widows, of course, but were careful to stress their tolerance for remarriage, on the authority of Paul, in a manner rather more sympathetic than Jerome's. In identifying remarriage of widows with prostitution, Jerome discounts every other possible motive, such as the financial, leaving only the sexual. (Re)marriage may have been a lesser evil for him than promiscuity, but it really was an evil.[250] Jerome interpreted the message of *1 Timothy* to suit this darker view of remarriage, whereas Augustine viewed this text as justifying remarriage for those widows who were not called to celibacy.[251] What was at stake of course in such debates was not just the relative value attached to widows' remarriage but the more basic question of whether marriage itself was a good or a bad thing.

Jerome's engagement with both allies and adversaries, although at times leading to political defeat, somewhat paradoxically helps explain the eventual success his ideas enjoyed, even if this came largely after his death. These battles encouraged him to refine his position, to clarify and simplify his message, and to develop an edgy, combative style that no doubt thrilled (when it did not exasperate) his supporters as much as it irritated and provoked his enemies.

There are other reasons one can cite for Jerome's ultimate success in this matter. The first is that in his new configuration of widowhood Jerome converted a lower-class necessity into an upper-class virtue. Poor women were on the whole unlikely to find suitable second husbands and were often forced to look to the Church for support. Wealthy women were far less in need of a male protector in the sense of providing for their physical safety or a contributor in the sense of offering financial support. Ascetical activity and its inherent moral respectability opened up the public realm for them as nothing before. Sexual renunciation spelled for them, at least in the early phase of the movement, novel possibilities of independence, personal growth and the exercise of a leadership role. Their experience of and talent for running large households were easily transferable to administering an ascetical community. A number of wealthy ascetics held on to their property and/or made arrangements for its preservation and transmission within the family. Elite women's level of education and their interest in the life of the mind deeply influenced the direction taken by Jerome. Some aristocrats found asceticism a welcome arena in which to pursue a new variant on an age-old ethic of competition for status. The new configuration of widow formed a category in which moral and social classifications overlapped, to an extent. It created a lasting conflict between the idealized Christian widow and the social reality of sexuality and, especially for the elite, remarriage. Lower-class women, many of whom did have an economic motive for turning ascetic, were able to rely on the moral example of their social superiors, whose engagement lent the new paradigm a considerable amount of its prestige, helping to move asceticism from the margins to the centre of both Church and society. Their sufferings and labours would now, surely, help them reap an everlasting reward.[252]

A further explanation for Jerome's success is that his threefold scheme possessed a kind of intuitive plausibility as a reflection of a woman's ideal life cycle, although this is not at all what he intended. The basic facts of demography remained fundamentally unaltered from the classical period, as described above. Most women married men older than themselves and at some point became widows. Whether or not they remarried, they thus passed through each of the statuses or lifestyles outlined by Jerome, after a fashion. Starting out as virgins (here, having more the sense of 'young unmarried women'), they then became wives, and then widows, in the majority of cases. Jerome, of course, intended 'virgin' as a lifelong state of dedicated celibacy, but to the extent his scheme seemed to align with the experience of the vast majority of women, and this too over many centuries to come, it acquired a validity that was not the less substantial for being indirect and unintentional.

Another reason for Jerome's largely posthumous success in promoting his brand of asceticism lies in his appropriation of the pagan Roman tradition. Like his Christian colleagues, Jerome drew on widows from the Old and New Testaments as models, and, as did at least some (although not all) of them, he also took great pains to identify his principles with traditional Roman values, the *mos maiorum*. This concept he thoroughly repackaged, in large part through careful selection, such as ignoring, on the precedent of Tertullian, the Vergilian version of Dido in rehabilitating her as a *univira*, in part through a combination of casual confusion of the facts and a deliberate distortion of the words and/or the sense of his sources. Some have accused him of even greater creativity, and it is worth noting that the wholesale invention of tradition was itself a time-honoured aspect of the *mos maiorum*. Following Tertullian, he appropriated a good deal of the pagan anti-marriage and anti-woman satirical tradition. His method, like that of the emperor Augustus centuries before, was to innovate (or at least to make the ideas of others his own) while claiming to return to tradition. His achievement was at least as great: the appropriation and transformation of literary and moral tradition that was in

2. Classical antiquity

important ways utterly alien to a Christian ethic in order to define a new set of norms that was to last a thousand years before effective challenge.[253] Jerome claimed to seek more than just an ideological renewal but an actual realization of the old values, itself a traditional assertion. He helped reshape both Roman and Christian identity in the sense that now it was possible to be a good Roman by being a good Christian, at least in his own conception of what this meant.[254]

Finally, it might be said that Jerome was fortunate, in important respects, in his opponents. Jerome waged fierce battles with adversaries who were in some cases highly influential in elite Christian circles and/or widely popular, such as Helvidius, the followers of Origen, Pelagius and his disciples, and Jovinian. This raises once again the insistent question as to how his views came to prevail in the end. The last two cases are particularly instructive.

One sign that the ascendancy of Jerome's views on widows and celibate life in general was far from guaranteed is the contemporary popularity of the opinions of the British monk Pelagius and his followers, especially in the period after Jerome's (forced) departure from Rome in 385.[255] They had much in common with Jerome in the sense that they believed that widows were a special concern of God, that they should be a model for other Christians, and that sexual renunciation was superior to marriage. The widow was for them a kind of 'Christian-plus' in the sense that she adhered to more than just the basic tenets of the faith, a point that is consistent with Jerome's views.[256] They likewise relied on *1 Timothy* for their conception of the 'true' widow, opting, however, for a threefold distinction of the holy widow, the pragmatic (concerned more for the welfare of her children than for that of her soul), and the bad.[257] The Pelagians accepted Jerome's threefold classification of women into virgins, widows and wives in terms of a differential reward in heaven, an important point.[258]

The Pelagians differed from Jerome above all in that they valued marriage more, and sexual renunciation less, than he did, in their belief that there was no special path for women to salvation, and that all good Christians were capable of holiness. Thus their conception of the ideal widow might seem to be a more attainable model, better integrated into the fabric of Christian society, than Jerome's more radicalized, marginal figure, although it is difficult at the same time to reconcile Pelagian ideals of perfection with the growing reality of a universal (and so far from perfect) Church.[259] The condemnation of Pelagius for heresy undoubtedly reduced the force of his challenge to Jerome. At the same time, Jerome's denunciations of the Pelagians marked something of a retreat from his earlier optimism about the liberating effect of asceticism on women. We now find a hardening of his views of celibacy as something meant for the Christian elite. He is readier to assert women's inferiority, and to advocate less independence for them from male oversight and control.[260]

Widows and Patriarchy

The popularity of Jovinian, who had argued for the moral and spiritual equality of dedicated virgins and married women, cannot be denied, but his condemnation for heresy at Rome and Milan, probably in 393, neutralized this as a serious challenge to Jerome.[261] It also left those, not few in number, dissatisfied with Jerome's anti-matrimonial views little choice but to try to square a circle by criticizing certain views of both men, that is, by asserting the good of marriage, sex and procreation on the one hand, and the value of the ascetical hierarchy on the other. This meant an acceptance of the principle of differential reward, in one form or another, among such diverse authorities as the unknown author of the *Consultationes Zacchaei et Apollonii* and Pelagius. Jerome's version was to stand up against all challengers, even Augustine, whose nuanced attempt to subvert the ascetical hierarchy by placing, like some of his North African predecessors, martyrdom above celibacy might have seemed less relevant to an increasingly Christianized society.[262]

Jerome shared a widespread ambivalence over women and their place in the Church and in society. Widows, as sexually experienced women, were an especially delicate matter. Here sympathy as well as respect for women's religiosity mingled with concern. Asceticism was for him a spiritual leveller between the sexes, to the point that women might be an example to men. But over time his outlook darkened, in part as an outcome of his many personal, political and doctrinal struggles. It was always easy to characterize a bias toward women as a sign of moral corruption or even heresy, a game that he himself played with some success. Despite the open texture of many of his precepts (true in the sense of class as well as gender), Jerome in the end developed a spiritual discipline that amounted to a lifestyle for widows. This differed little from that which he prescribed for virgins but that was very different from the rules which held for male celibates. He moved in a sense away from an ideal of an ascetical lay elite in favour of an ascetical monastic and even clerical elite. Jerome increasingly advocated the withdrawal from public life, the enclosure, and the subjection to male scrutiny and control, of widows and virgins, out of a concern with their health and welfare, but above all with regard for the preservation of their chastity, which their nature as women was thought to render at all times vulnerable.[263]

As for the material support the Church provided widows (and orphans) as early as the days of *Acts* and *1 Timothy*, for the non-Christian Greek and Roman world, this was, as we have seen, something new.[264] All the same, one might well be sceptical of its nature, scope and effectiveness.[265] Eusebius reports a letter of Pope Cornelius from AD 251 that has the Church in Rome supporting more than 1,500 widows and 'needy persons'.[266] John Chrysostom has 3,000 widows and virgins being maintained by the Church in late fourth-century Antioch.[267] These numbers represent perhaps only a small share of the genuine need.[268] In late antiquity we find, in addition to orphanages, old-age homes for widows supported by the

2. Classical antiquity

Church.[269] First the bishops and then the Christian emperors beginning with Constantine inherited the ideal of the benevolent ruler, protector and supporter of the weak and vulnerable, that arose in the ancient Near East.[270] As a metaphor for the helpless, the widow came to stand for the entire Church in the eyes of Augustine.[271] The ideology of ruler-legitimization inherited from the ancient Near East encouraged the development of a generalized norm that morally validated the protection of the poor and vulnerable, routinely symbolized by the figure of the widow, for many centuries to come.[272]

Although some widows benefited from such measures, it seems doubtful that the various forms of Christian, state, or private assistance could have helped the vast majority of those in need. At the same time, it is important not to exaggerate the failure, just as some have surely overstated the success, of these measures. Christian social welfare programmes reached thousands of persons as early as the mid third century, if, as seems correct, the figures for Rome are representative of other major urban centres. A measure of their success may be read from the fact that the emperor Julian felt it advisable to imitate them, in order to place his pagan renewal on a more competitive footing with Christianity.[273] Imitation here must be understood as the sincerest form of flattery.

Widows were in greater measure objects of patristic polemic than married women or virgins.[274] 'Widow' was a status within the Church to which elite women might well aspire, but the upper classes were only a very small percentage of the population in Christian or pagan society. Large numbers of poor women had good reason to view the prospect of losing a husband to death with apprehension. Some of the middling sort, of modest means but respectable, may have feared plunging into destitution after enduring such a loss. It has well been observed, of what we should describe as the registered or 'real' widows in the early Christian communities, that '[m]ost of these were helpless creatures, destitute old ladies only too glad to receive food and clothing from the hands of the clergy'.[275] At minimum, one can say that the Christians were from an early period skilled at making a virtue from a necessity. If this seems a tad cynical, it does alert us to the importance of making distinctions of a socio-economic nature in attempting to understand the demographics of ancient widowhood. Nor must the evidence mislead. Post-classical sources for the first time in antiquity deal in detail with the problems of poor and sick widows. The greater numbers of widows attested in this period are thus not simply a product of Christian propaganda against remarriage. For the most part, only a small group of young and propertied widows who might have married again are affected by the change in values. They were in a position to contribute much, and to enjoy great influence.[276] Widowhood was a great opportunity for giving to the Church.[277] But in demographic terms, Jerome's showcase widows notwithstanding, they were of scant significance. Most – poor and older – had little or no option but to accept their unmarried status as permanent. The moral reasoning of *1 Timothy* is revealed as circular, and one might assert the same of its economic assumptions. But it did confer some pretence to dignity on the experience of those women whom life left few real choices.

3

Late medieval and early modern England and Germany

England and Germany

We look first at England, during the period roughly between 1350 and 1650. This enables us to trace the demographic and economic impact of the Black Death, which arrived for the first time in England in 1348, on the lives of widows, evaluate their status in the late Middle Ages, and see how this was transformed by the Reformation and other developments that played out well into the modern period. There is no bright line separating 'medieval' from 'early modern', but 1500 is as good an arbitrary division as any. We must be sensitive not only to change, but continuity as well, in the lived experience of these women, as far as the sources allow us to grasp this. Although politically unified for most of the three centuries under examination, England shows great diversity both of legal rules and of jurisdiction, especially toward the beginning of the period under study. After the Reformation there was also religious diversity, represented not only by lingering Catholic elements but also by the more extreme versions of Protestantism, some of which historians tend to lump together under the vague category of Puritanism.

In this period there were four overlapping systems of courts, all of which played a role in adjudicating disputes regarding women, particularly widows, and their rights.[1] Common law is perhaps best known because over the course of time it eclipsed all the rest, although during this period its main importance lay in the law of real property.[2] The courts of equity arose in the fifteenth century as a palliative for aspects of the common law regarded as unfair, recognizing, for example, the right of married women to own property, something strictly impossible at common law. Widows in particular were objects of sympathy. Customary (or manorial, in the countryside, and borough, in towns) law varied widely from region to region, manor to manor, and town to town, substituting, where it was valid, its own rules for those of the common law and regulating the shares of land in an estate due to heirs, including, of course, widows. Resort to custom diminished over the seventeenth and eighteenth centuries.

The ecclesiastical (or canon) system of law administered the rules of probate and its courts helped secure widows' inheritance of a share of their deceased husbands' personal property. Although the role of the ecclesiastical tribunals in litigation came into increasing conflict with the common law in the early modern period, they continued their administrative function, apart from a brief interlude at the time of the Civil War, until 1857. Ecclesiastical law also differed somewhat between the Northern Province (York) and the Southern (Canterbury). The relatively severe legal restrictions placed on English women at this time were both tempered and exacerbated by this diversity of legal systems.[3]

The focus in this chapter is also on the German-speaking areas of Europe, that is, most of the Holy Roman Empire, in the years from about 1350 to about 1650. This temporal emphasis facilitates comparison with conditions in England during the same period. At this time Germany faced largely similar demographic and economic challenges arising from the Black Death. Again the status and role of widows in the late medieval era are evaluated in order to witness how these metamorphosed in the early modern era under the influence of the Reformation and other developments that extend in their impact far into the modern age. And here too we opt for 1500 as a useful, if more or less arbitrary, dividing line between 'medieval' and 'early modern'. As with England, our interest lies in tracing not only change but also continuity in the experience of widows, to the extent the sources allow us to recover this.

Germany most certainly was not politically unified in the same sense as England during this period, but was composed of a wide variety of political entities, most enjoying their own legal systems. In the sixteenth century, the Holy Roman Empire, including the Swiss confederation, contained some 250 independent states consisting of an almost bewildering melange of electoral estates, secular and ecclesiastical principalities, and more than 80 imperial cities. The rules governing the basic elements of widows' status and rights in private law (as those of women in general) varied considerably from place to place. It was common to find competing jurisdictions within the individual political entities, a phenomenon exacerbated somewhat by the Reformation, although this generally had the effect of concentrating judicial authority in state hands.[4] Besides an abundance and diversity of local legal traditions, Roman law became increasingly influential in this period, although its impact differed widely from place to place. It also played an important role in the formation of imperial law, which asserted itself with increasing force at this time.[5]

Confessional differences are one more complicating factor, although not to be exaggerated as they relate to women and above all to widows. I attempt to call attention to differences between Protestant and Catholic, or among different types of Protestants, only where they are especially relevant.[6] More generally, among Protestant denominations the focus falls almost exclusively on Lutheranism for reasons of space. For all of the differences from place to place in religion, governmental structure, economic base and level of modernization, many of the forces at work on women's status and role were strikingly similar, as we shall see.[7]

The diversity of legal regimes and social and religious practices in the

3. Late medieval and early modern England and Germany

various states of the Holy Roman Empire makes generalization about the status of women and particularly that of widows difficult, and comparison with England even more so. What is more, the details are often a source of controversy among historians. Some geographical areas have, in part because more of their records have survived, been more thoroughly studied than others: this is especially true of imperial cities in southern Germany such as Augsburg, Nuremberg and Strasbourg. We will risk some generalizations, nonetheless.[8] We are also able to trace some similarities with England, as well as some important differences.

Our sources become richer in many respects in this period. Aside from the parish register documents that have been so important for demography, we have increasingly abundant legal records of various kinds, more evidence of a personal nature, such as letters and diaries, and an abundance of religious literature, such as sermons, treatises and advice books. Women appear more frequently as authors, especially toward the end of this period, although they remain a distinct minority as such.

Numbers of widows

The demographics of this core period, which extends roughly from 1350 to 1650, present a curiously bifurcated picture. For approximately the first 150 years, we are scarcely better informed than we are about classical antiquity. Beginning in the sixteenth century, however, the quantity and quality of evidence markedly improve, as historians are increasingly able to rely on parish registers (available much earlier for England than for Germany), which contain notice of births, deaths and/or marriages, to provide a more or less accurate picture of a local population, which can then be combined with similar archives to construct a set of aggregate results for regional or even national entities.[9] Access to such resources has, of course, hardly dispelled controversy.

Despite problems of evidence and disagreement among scholars, a number of factors conspire to suggest caution in simply assuming that the numbers of widows were huge, as is often done. There were some very serious crises of mortality, which include bouts of famine with attendant malnutrition, and many years of warfare. Among the most important of the latter must be counted two seventeenth-century conflicts, the Civil War in England and the Thirty Years' War in Germany. The most serious recurring crisis was the bubonic plague, also known as the Black Death, which ravaged European populations at different times between 1347 and 1667. This was just one of a series of factors promoting demographic decline, some occurring even before the mid-fourteenth century, a fact not always well recognized by historians. Following a period of growth, population declined in the early to mid-seventeenth century.[10] The increased demand for women's labour generated by the demographic shortfall inspired by the plague itself stimulated further decline, on one argument, as women put off marriage, never married, or – as widows – refused remarriage, at least in some well-studied locales such as York.[11] By the same token, demographic growth in the sixteenth century is argued to have had a negative impact on women in terms of employment prospects.[12]

Although on the whole epidemics and famines appear to have struck both sexes indifferently (a point sometimes contested), war had a graver impact on male mortality, thus reducing chances of widows' remarriage and increasing their numbers. The information we have for gender-differentiated mortality in England and Germany for this period points in different directions, some suggesting more females than males among seniors, some the reverse. Losses from childbirth certainly cut into the number of wives, and therefore of widows.[13]

Other factors affected a woman's chances of becoming a widow. According to the so-called 'European marriage pattern' discovered in 1965 by John Hajnal for Western Europe, in the period extending at least from the seventeenth century on, both men and women married late, the latter on average for the first time between 23 and 27 years of age, the former an average of some three years later. It is in general terms, however, better to imagine both men and women marrying within a range of years, rather than thinking strictly in terms of an average age at first marriage. Large numbers of both men and women, 10% or more of the population, and as high as 25% in some places, remained unmarried; in fact, information from the seventeenth century suggests that the incidence of celibacy increased in this period, as more than 20% of women of childbearing age never married; in early modern England perhaps only one-third of adult women were married at any one time.[14] The picture has been refined further, as the pattern discovered by Hajnal was seen to apply more narrowly to northwestern Europe than previously thought. Data from England show that age at first marriage fluctuated not only in the short term but over the long term as well, in response to economic and mortality phenomena of various magnitudes. Further, the age gap between first-time spouses was at times as low as a year or two.[15]

Members of the elite generally married earlier, evidently with a larger gap in ages, and proportionally in greater numbers in both the late medieval and early modern periods.[16] Naturally, this resulted in greater numbers of wives losing a husband than the reverse, a point that also holds for Germany, where a study of three noble families from 1200 to 1600 suggests that over three-fourths of marriages ended with a widow left behind.[17] Data concerning the nobility in southwestern Germany in the late medieval and early modern periods show sons marrying for the first time on average almost a decade later than daughters, although the gap closed somewhat in the sixteenth and seventeenth centuries. On the other hand, a far higher percentage of daughters married than that of sons, even as this gap also narrowed a bit over time, when percentages of both sons and daughters marrying rose.[18] Throughout this period, the families of

3. Late medieval and early modern England and Germany

counts and barons (the sub-princely high nobility) in this part of Germany therefore produced a relatively large number of widows, who remarried more often than the widowers in this group, an exception to the general trend. For broad sectors of the population in both England and Germany, but especially in the former, gender-differentiated trends with respect to remarriage (below) accentuated the imbalance, leaving a higher proportion of widows, who remained unmarried.

Peter Laslett has estimated from a sample of 100 communities that, in the period 1574-1821, 8.7% of English females were widows, while 3.5% of males were widowers. From these calculations Amy Froide has derived a figure for widows as 14.9% of the adult female population.[19] The gender differential here amounts to a significant difference, but it is worth noting that the data derive largely from a period when widow remarriage rates went into a notable decline (see below). Divorce was impossible before the Reformation, and for a long time afterwards remained negligible in overall demographic terms.

The question of whether a similar pattern, in age at first marriage and, ultimately, in the numbers of widows, held across the population in the years prior to the early to mid-sixteenth century is difficult to answer because of the absence of data from parish registers, a dearth that extends a century later in Germany. Much disagreement has reigned, with recent developments in the scholarship emphasizing a complex interplay at work between fertility and mortality. These scholars also point to regional and temporal variety in both the medieval and early modern periods, as well as to a greater overall continuity between them, even as the population began to rise in the early to mid-sixteenth century.[20]

It is possible that the impact of the Black Death and the other factors promoting population decline mentioned above had a set of consequences, some more obvious than others, that operated in the following ways. One of these was to reward women's entry into the work force, another was to encourage a late age at first marriage for sub-elite never-married women. At least for a time, the new demographic and economic situation allowed many not to marry at all (it did largely the same for widows regarding remarriage), while the age gap between spouses in a first marriage remained relatively narrow. In large part, then, it simply reinforced an already existing marriage practice. On this thesis the pre- and post-Plague medieval period saw overall demographic continuity with the early modern in terms of proportions of women never marrying and of the age at first marriage for those that did, apart from some variations, as economic opportunities for women increased, at least in some regions. It is important to recognize that various differences occurred across regions, between classes and over time.[21] The smaller the age gap between marriage partners, of course, the fewer the numbers of widows.

Economic opportunity for women is not, however, inevitably tied to a high or low age at first marriage and a high or low rate of remarriage for widows. Sometimes it encourages postponement or even abstention, sometimes the reverse.[22] In this period it might have done both, with varying impacts at different times and in different places during the late Middle Ages, at minimum. By the same token, it is plausible that a rise in real wages in the late sixteenth and early seventeenth centuries helped stimulate population growth, only to fall subsequently, leading to postponement and even renunciation of marriage.[23] So we may have before us a paradox in that the late fourteenth and fifteenth centuries witnessed a rosy economic scenario that discouraged nuptiality, while the early modern period saw an economic decline with a similar impact. This conclusion is, of course, far from certain.

The state of the sources and ongoing controversy among scholars make it difficult to gain great clarity over the numbers of widows in fourteenth and fifteenth-century Europe. Such uncertainty inspires caution. This is especially true because the evidence does not permit us to assume, for the mass of the population, either a large age gap between spouses or a differentiation in mortality by gender that significantly benefited women. Thus we cannot postulate relatively large numbers of widows either for this period, the last century and a half of the medieval period, or for the first 150 years of the modern, at least until the decline in the rate of widow remarriage begins to take effect, certainly, in England, by the early seventeenth century (see below). It is possible perhaps to declare such a scenario as, on the whole, unlikely.

It is probable that the pre-Reformation European population contained relatively large numbers of single persons, a group that includes widows, clergy, monastics, prostitutes and (other) never-married women.[24] In a typical scenario dating from before the modern demographic transition we would expect to find more women than men overall, especially among the unmarried.[25] It is difficult to be certain how large a percentage of these were widows, however. And here the word 'relatively' is of crucial importance. When historians of late medieval and early modern England and Germany claim, as they often do, that these cultures knew large numbers of widows, they often appear to draw an implicit comparison with the modern period, or rather with their perceptions of this, as opposed to, say, classical antiquity. In fact, widows form a higher proportion of the total population today than they did a couple of centuries ago, when they were more broadly distributed into different age groups.[26] As a result, they are perhaps less visible, at least to some observers. If indeed men tended to predecease their wives rather than vice versa, which seems likely, and widowers remarried sooner and more often than widows, while preferring younger women as partners, it is certainly safe to conclude that widows outnumbered widowers in the period under study.[27] On the other hand, a high proportion of never-married women, higher than that for widows (although balanced against a non-existent or very low level of divorce), and, less consistently, a high rate of remarriage for women, drove the

3. Late medieval and early modern England and Germany

numbers of widows down. In sum, great caution is required when writing of the 'large' numbers of widows in this period.

Another demographic factor of interest for the study of widows is that of family form. It was during this period, if not before, that, many scholars argue, the nuclear family emerged as the dominant type of family structure, so called because it consists in principle of the elementary triad of father, mother and children. This argument holds, with qualifications, for northwest Europe in general over the next four centuries and the United States in the period studied in the next chapter. As a social phenomenon the nuclear family is driven by the life cycle. Reflection on this fact has produced the 'nuclear-hardship' hypothesis, which has direct implications for widows. On this theory the nuclear form tends to impose peculiar difficulties for them (not that societies with other dominant forms, like the stem family, are a paradise for widows), because once adult children have departed the parental home to form their own nuclear families, no one is present who is capable of caring for an elderly mother (or more rarely a father). The result was, for many, a relentless threat of life cycle poverty.[28]

English widows and private law

By law, unmarried English girls were in the power of their fathers, while married women were 'covered' by their husbands, and thus endowed with the status of a *feme covert* in the context of the legal institution known as 'coverture'. This meant that under the common law neither wife nor daughter enjoyed an independent legal personality. Coverture was a legal fiction with real-life consequences. The fiction lay in the notion that the married couple were one person, the husband, who acted as the legal representative of the pair. He owned outright all personal property and controlled all real property. Wives could not make a will without the permission of their husbands under common law, although they could under canon law. Widows, on the other hand, who enjoyed an independent legal status, might own and inherit property, including land, sue and be sued in their own names, receive gifts and rents, borrow and lend money.[29] Unlike wives, they had great freedom to make wills. Not surprisingly, most women who made a will were widows, and this held true for them in relatively increasing numbers as wills made by married women declined, from perhaps as early as the fourteenth century, but more certainly after 1500.[30]

One can generalize by observing that in the period extending from the Middle Ages to the late nineteenth century the law of succession was relatively egalitarian between men and women but the law of marriage was decisively stacked in the husband's favour. Widowhood, as an exit from marriage that prompted certain benefits either under a valid will or on intestacy, represented a genuinely different, and overall improved, legal status for women. For men, however, losing a wife had no such serious implications.[31] Change in the legal rights of widows and wives did nevertheless occur during this time, and overall not for the better.

For much of the Middle Ages, widows were entitled to a relatively large share of the estates of their decedent husbands, whether the latter wrote a valid will, or not.[32] A part of these estates, of course, consisted of assets women themselves had brought to the union as a dowry or marriage portion, which could have had more than one source.[33] The widow's share was defined differently for real estate (if there was any), where a life interest in a part of the husband's property (which on her death was to revert to his heirs) was reserved for her under the common law in the form of dower, and for personal property (movables and leases of land), where she had a claim, under customary practice recognized by the canon law, to succeed under a husband's will to a fixed portion of either one-third, if there were children of the marriage, or one-half, if not. On intestacy, a widow with children still received one-third, while a childless widow received all her husband's personal property.[34] This generosity may in part be due to the recognition of widows under canon law as 'disadvantaged persons' (*miserabiles personae*) whom it was the duty of all clergy to protect and who were eligible for relief from a fund generated by one-quarter of parish revenues.[35]

In the case of dower, the percentage due to widows varied according to the type of common law tenure, amounting usually to one-third or one-half.[36] With customary tenure,[37] the widow's share was called free bench, and the size of this varied from manor to manor, sometimes amounting to the entire estate; unlike with dower, free bench was in many cases lost on remarriage, unless the widow or her new husband had paid – usually a substantial amount – to retain it. In some cases a widow would surrender part of the holding to the heir(s), adjusting the usage to the needs of her children.[38]

Even when dower amounted to only one-third of the land in the estate, the stakes were high, in effect, keeping a substantial amount of property from the heirs. Women did not hesitate in many cases to go to law to claim their share. Heirs, including sons, can be seen engaging in a variety of tactics aimed at thwarting widows' just claims, including resort to inaction, negotiation as a stalling device, collusive suits, allegations about the competence and integrity of their adversaries and even violence.[39] The level of litigation appears to have been a function of the size of the estate, not the gender of the plaintiff.[40] Widows did not need an attorney or male relative to sue for dower, although they show increasing recourse to the former in the late medieval period.[41] Where assistance was required, they favoured their own agents and representatives over male family members. Widows fairly dominated the ecclesiastical probate courts, and were well represented in other courts to the extent that they were the only group of women whose level of litigation approached their actual numbers in the population.[42]

3. Late medieval and early modern England and Germany

Widows were not always the passive victims of obstinate heirs and other antagonists at law. Sometimes they acted the part of aggressive and even unscrupulous litigants in a variety of matters.[43] Some knew how to advance the stereotype of the poor, vulnerable, good widow to advantage, even when the facts did not support this image. Studies of the available evidence suggest that widows generally enjoyed success in pursuing their claims, certainly in dower cases, although split results were not infrequent and a significant number of these appear to have been settled out of court.[44] Judges, at least in courts of equity, tended to sympathize with the impediments that coverture placed in the way of women while still married.[45] Widows were thought especially deserving of just treatment in part on the authority of the Bible, although poverty earned them sympathy at best, not real independence.[46] Well-connected widows did not hesitate to appeal to the king or his chief advisers.[47] Inheritance cases hardly exhausted the range of situations in which widows successfully pleaded their vulnerability.[48] More than in contemporary Germany, arguments about entitlement for community support and attempts to garner sympathy because of poverty appear to have carried some weight.[49]

Among widows, doweresses in particular could cause no small amount of difficulty. Simply by enjoying the life interest they held in their landed property, sometimes over the course of a long widowhood and multiple remarriages, they took valuable assets, even if they were destined eventually to return, out of the hands of a decedent husband's family, in particular, his heirs. Resentment tended to diminish if a widow had produced at least one male heir, but this was not always the case. Some doweresses took more than their share, while others damaged the property or otherwise lowered its value.[50]

Widows themselves were eligible for the guardianship of their minor children, and this was usually awarded to them (although a feudal lord could assert a right), with the result that they were able to administer for a time at least an even larger share of the real and personal property in their husband's estate.[51] In case of husband's intestacy, they were legally entitled to act as administrator of the estate and were likely to be named as such by the ecclesiastical courts. They also could be named as executor of a husband's will and it seems in most cases were so named, either as sole or co-executor (in the latter case often together with one of their children).[52]

In the late fourteenth and fifteenth centuries, developments in the law, especially that of succession, began to undermine the guarantees afforded to widows.[53] New means of conveyancing, namely the jointure, the trust for use and deathbed transfers (the first two were prenuptial agreements), allowed husbands to give a greater share of property to their widows, but also less if they wished. It remains uncertain, however, whether the majority did one or the other.[54] London in the period 1301-1433 witnessed a sharp decline in dower cases.[55] By the end of the fifteenth century, many widows' chances of receiving land outright from their husbands' estates were considerably reduced, a trend aggravated in the next century by a pair of laws, the Statute of Uses, from 1536,[56] and the Statute of Wills, from 1540.[57] A widow's right to a fixed portion of her husband's personal property under his will disappears from most of southern England in the late fourteenth and early fifteenth centuries. It survived in places such as London and the Northern Province until abolished by a series of statutes dating from 1692-1725.[58]

It is unclear whether the motive behind such changes was to enlarge the scope of (male) testamentary freedom, but this was undoubtedly one of the effects.[59] Now more than ever a widow had to depend on a husband's (and/or father's) largesse for her support. In cases of intestacy, the ecclesiastical courts had for years attempted to protect the interests of female and younger male heirs, where the common law rule of primogeniture dictated that the eldest son inherit all the land, by reducing in proportion or even eliminating the latter's share of personal property in order to achieve an overall equitable result. Widows therefore tended to receive more than their legally specified one-third. The 1670 Act for the Better Settling of Intestates' Estates rendered these practices illegal, although the courts, while paying lip service to the statute, often evaded its strictures, a practice less in evidence for the shares of widows, however, who were effectively penalized by this law, not least by its provision that reduced a childless widow's share of decedent husband's personal property upon intestacy to one-half, leaving the rest to his next of kin.[60] Both law and practice increasingly reinforced male control of property.[61] An ideology of patrilineal principle and primogeniture took root.[62]

The system of equity, in the years following the period under examination, saw some of its courts extinguished and the rest choked by a rising caseload, as many litigants, including many widows, chose this route over that of the common law, whose courts were decidedly less sympathetic to them.[63] At least one forum of equity, the Court of Requests, experienced no small difficulty in enforcing its findings.[64] Scholars have identified an overall trend in early modern Europe whereby it became increasingly common to deny women the ability to manage and transmit to others their own separate property.[65] This certainly seems to have been the case for England.

Not all women were rendered miserable or were utterly oppressed by the changes. Wealthy widows are an obvious case in point. Many husbands even of relatively modest means tried to provide for their surviving spouses as best they could, often through a lump sum of cash secured by a bond.[66] Remarrying widows continued in theory to surrender their property to their husbands on the doctrine of coverture outlined above. In practice, however, they were twice as likely as women marrying for the first time to preserve, through a prenuptial agreement, their property in their own name in an estate separate from that of their husbands.[67] Unlike the portion of personal property under the old rules, the settlement was deducted from the estate before payment of debts.[68]

The existence of such agreements, however, is not reflected in wills made by women. This period witnesses a decline both in the proportion of all women making wills and in their sheer numbers, as Parliament and the judiciary steadily stripped away widows' property rights. Although they continue to be the chief beneficiaries of their husbands' wills, widows began to enjoy less authority, as guaranteed by the law, over the disposition of property than before.[69]

English widows and economic privilege

A well-accepted principle in the scholarship on medieval widows holds that there was potentially a sharp disjunction between their legal status and their economic role.[70] The implications of this can easily be overstated, however. The traditional tripartition of women into never-married (virgins), wives and widows had an economic as well as a moral and social sense.[71] As ever, our focus is placed not least on persons with property, especially land, to pass on from one generation to the next. We do well to keep in mind, as a point of contrast between the rules of law given above and the economic reality described here, that in many cases much of value in an estate was probably handed over during the lifetime of the husband and so has left no trace in the historical record.[72]

That is not to deny that many women relied on the portions guaranteed them under the law, at minimum. 'Doweress' signified not just a legal entitlement but also a socio-economic status.[73] A widow's economic resources might extend beyond her dower and claims to personal property to include property she inherited, chiefly from her family or from her husband, who might leave her his business or rental properties, for example.[74] Amy Erickson has discovered that, at relatively modest social levels, fathers in many cases gave daughters, often at time of marriage, shares of an inheritance comparable in value to those they left sons. The latter were more likely to receive real property in their share, the former movables or simply cash. In fact, a major motive for making a will was to soften the impact of primogeniture at common law, which of course favoured the eldest son.[75] In a common scenario for a first marriage in London, the husband's contribution to the marriage was land and sometimes a business, that of the wife movables, including money.[76] Here is but one sign that women were generally less favoured as landowners than men, in terms of law, custom and sheer numbers.[77]

Widows, as we have seen, often inherited by will more from their husbands than the minimum stipulated by law. On the other hand, a widow whose husband predeceased her father-in-law might receive significantly less.[78] Some widows, especially among the elite, during the time of the Black Death did very well by virtue of the pattern of male mortality within their families, as assets accumulated in their hands. Lower-class widows, on the other hand, often found that the social ideology privileging the male-headed household had economic consequences for them, by limiting their ability to make a living.[79] Even among the more privileged, some had to reckon with a decedent husband's indebtedness.[80]

Guardianship of children, which as we have seen widows were routinely granted, at least in the medieval period, could mean a significant increase in capital at their disposal. Among the upper classes widows often negotiated marriage matches for their daughters, while at lower levels of society this responsibility tended to fall to the daughters themselves.[81] Widows in a sense enjoyed greater testamentary freedom than their decedent husbands, because unlike them they were not, at least in theory, bound to guarantee the economic viability of their children. Thus there was no need to be 'fair' in an objective sense. Widows were more likely to leave land to their daughters, to family members in general other than eldest sons, as well as to non-family members, including other women, than their husbands. They were also more likely to choose such persons, especially daughters, as executors of their will.[82] Although they could not bequeath dower property (in which they had only a life-interest), they were not under an obligation to provide a portion of their personal property to anyone, so that in this sense too widows enjoyed greater testamentary freedom than their husbands.[83]

Customary law, which made widows eligible for as much as one-half or all of a decedent husband's landed property, placed significant amounts of land in widows' hands in parts of the countryside. In pre-plague Brigstock, Northamptonshire, for example, women, most of them widows, held 10%-15% of the land.[84] In such situations, land was a widow's primary asset, even as levels of wealth among the peasantry might vary, and we see them taking full advantage in many cases, selling land to which they had title, profiting from the rise in real estate prices in the half-century before the Black Death, and even attempting to acquire title to free bench land through various devices, some of them devious, or to alienate such land with or without the heir's permission, which was technically necessary.[85] Even where widows did not enjoy such freedom in conveying land we find an overall similar pattern of exploitation of property.[86] In some places the widow's interest was for life, in others, until remarriage. Variation in customary rules was extreme, and change over time introduced even greater variation.[87] Differences in systems of land tenure might strongly influence women's economic status for better or for worse, as at times security for the many might stand in inverse relationship to opportunity for a few.[88]

A widow's standard of living was contingent on other factors besides the purely economic. Her relations with her husband's heirs might well determine how easily and how quickly she was able to claim her rights to property, or indeed whether she was to be successful at all in some cases.[89]

3. Late medieval and early modern England and Germany

Living in a solitary household did not always bode well for maintaining financial security.[90] Personality, and sometimes age, counted for a great deal in seizing or declining some of the opportunities afforded by widowhood, for example, if a decedent husband left a business to run.[91] The indomitable Bess of Hardwick, whose long life spanned most of the sixteenth as well as the early years of the seventeenth centuries, is a case in point. Each of her four marriages seems to have left her better off than the one preceding. She embarked on an ambitious programme of building that relied on iconography largely drawn from antiquity to advertise her virtues as a wife and widow, and rose to take her place as the second wealthiest, and arguably second most powerful, woman in England after Elizabeth I.[92] The mid-seventeenth century widow Lady Anne Clifford commissioned a painted triptych that in a manner granted her both male and female attributes and emphasized her role within her own birth family, eclipsing her two husbands, one dead, the other estranged.[93]

Widows possessing wealth and power were, not surprisingly, in a better position than others to make the most of their widowhood. Managing a well-to-do household, a large and complex business enterprise in its own right, might well have been part of their experience as wives, when their actual responsibilities often outran their legal right to act. For example, they might effectively conduct themselves as householders in case of a husband's protracted absence, and this at various social levels.[94] Widows tended to carry on the administration of a household after a husband's death more or less along the same lines as before, although with greater freedom of action.[95] Aristocratic widows in particular were often astute managers of property,[96] although there is also evidence of sound, careful management on lower levels of society.[97] In the upper reaches of society some widows could in a sense create their own role in society.

On the lower levels of society, as with the widows of peasant farmers, the challenges encountered were greater, the economic margins of safety and success appreciably smaller. Some widows of smallholders yielded their land in return for an annuity, essentially a maintenance contract, sometimes immediately on their husband's death, at other times after years of struggle. For some, remarriage was a solution to the economic challenges of widowhood.[98] For a widow of a master craftsman to achieve economic security, remarriage might be absolutely essential in order to keep the family business going.[99] The loss of the economic contribution of a husband weighed very heavily at this level of society.

Widows were the most numerous group of women heading households.[100] As such, they were far more likely to be found in urban areas than in rural, but within cities they often gravitated to the margins in search of cheap housing.[101] Throughout western Europe in this period cities contained higher proportions of widows than the countryside, although their numbers were somewhat reduced in England owing to the influence of the system of Poor Relief introduced in the wake of the Reformation. This financial support gave some widows the option of remaining in their home communities.[102]

Late medieval London widows had the freedom of the city, meaning the right to conduct trade in the town, and so might start a new business or continue that of a husband. Indeed, if a husband had a trade or a craft to pass on, they were more or less expected to do the latter, by training both male and female apprentices, remaining liable for their own debts, and even being entitled to retain guild membership, albeit without full enfranchisement.[103] Maintaining a decedent husband's household and business was socially valued. Often, as with tanners, this was an element in a man's bequest strategy providing for his wife.[104] Almost all known 'freewomen' of the city of London were widows, where women, whether single, married or widowed, worked at every kind of business.[105] Sixteenth-century records at all events suggest that relatively few widows did actually live up to these expectations of continuing a husband's trade or craft, despite existing charters and precedents. This was certainly the case by the century's end, a trend that continued in the near term.[106]

Even in the late Middle Ages women confronted a gender-based division of labour, justified in part by the theory of gender weakness, which meant that they were denied access to training, found themselves restricted to the lowest-paid sectors of the economy, and worked for lower wages than men while their work was rated as inferior, too unskilled in most cases to qualify for guild membership.[107] In towns widows found it difficult to enter occupations that required significant capital expenditure on tools or raw materials.[108] Male apprentices did not always tolerate working for a woman well.[109] Medieval peasant women were sometimes paid less for the same work men did.[110] Widows, as well as never-married women and a few wives, were something of an exception to the general trend, in that they enjoyed a few advantages not shared by other women, especially by most wives. Their work pattern was roughly similar to that of males, in fact, meaning that it was more full-time in nature and more stable.[111]

One interesting example of gendered economic activity is brewing ale, which seems to have held some respectability for women since it grew out of customary female responsibilities within the household. Often leaving a brewing business to a widow was part of a husband's bequest strategy. The participation of widows and other women in the brewing business declined over the fifteenth century, however, especially under the impact of the replacement of ale by beer, which allowed for a more sophisticated and complex system of production and distribution, effectively excluding females whether from reasons of economics, propriety, or both. This development was marked by sex-typing of work, segregation of the genders and association of a new technology with male expertise. Widows and never-married women were ill placed to compete even with married women but less so with men in an increasingly professionalized industry

3. Late medieval and early modern England and Germany

that demanded larger amounts of capital, more advanced marketing strategies and a sizeable labour force.[112]

There is general, although not total, agreement among historians that the effects of the bubonic plague known as the Black Death, which swept across England for the first time in 1348-51, causing the loss of at least one-third of the population (and which was followed at intervals by wave after wave of bubonic plague and other infectious diseases for many years to come), opened up unparallelled economic opportunities for women. Before this there had been a trend toward the feminization of poverty, especially in urban areas.[113] The boom of the late fourteenth century placed great stress on the labour market, and the heightened need for women workers softened, although it did not eliminate, the traditional gendered division of labour as well as the wage gap between men and women.[114] The post-plague economy generally seems to have made life easier for women living on their own, whether as widows or never-married, so that it encouraged postponement of marriage for the latter and allowed the former to forego remarriage, prolonging the demographic impact of the plague.[115] The benefits did not accrue to all women or even all widows, of course, and the same can be said of the fallout from the economic crisis of 1438-40, when a good supply of land, consequent to the continuing devastations of plague, made it easier for widows of varying ages to claim their rights to real property and younger widows to remarry if they wished, while older widows were in many cases economically hard pressed.[116]

As with the law, the long-term economic trends were not always favourable to widows, and there is reason to think that on balance they were negative for the majority of them.[117] Already by the mid-fifteenth century a demographic rebound encouraged diminishing dependence on female labour and fostered a new trend toward women's exclusion from various sectors of the economy. Late in the century recession occurred in many places outside the generally prosperous South West.[118] Conditions at that time are thought to have encouraged greater numbers of widows (and women in general) to enter marriage or prostitution, the latter phenomenon provoking concern among civic authorities, the former receiving increasing ideological justification.[119]

The sixteenth century saw a general economic decline, as an increase in population and inflation led to a decline in real wages that was not reversed until after 1650. The wage gap between the genders widened again.[120] Poverty emerged as more of a problem than in the preceding period of relative prosperity.[121] By 1620, women were, by and large, relegated to one of two categories of economic activity: assisting the operation of a family business/household (the two were not neatly separated) or seeking whatever employment they could find out of sheer desperation.[122] In the town of Battle in Sussex in the late fifteenth century widows were not as wealthy as the wealthiest ones had been a century earlier, and the evidence suggests a significant drop in the numbers of

63

independent widows.[123] The alienation of customary landholdings in Sussex denied many widows their rights to free bench.[124] The legal changes described in the previous section removed some of the guarantees of widows' material support, although of course many benefited from their late husbands' generosity, as in previous periods. Over the seventeenth century the ratio of marriage portion (what a woman brought to a marriage) to jointure (what she took away as a widow) for the aristocracy dropped by one-half, meaning a widow would have to live much longer to get the full value out of her dowry.[125] Daughters in the early modern period did not benefit from paternal bequests of land as much as they had in the Middle Ages, to the extent that heiresses were fewer than the facts of demography and the rules of the common law would predict.[126] The significance of this decline is more than economic, given the enormous symbolic value of land in that culture.[127] Overall, the picture is one of reduced economic opportunity and reward for women in the early modern period.[128]

Even well into this period, however, some widows continued to prosper. In some parts of England, they were paid better than married women.[129] Greater numbers of women, often widows, were employed in connection with Poor Relief.[130] Many widows of property who remarried found it possible to their retain financial well-being through adroit resort to prenuptial agreements.[131] Many husbands were generous with bequests, as noted above. Before the advent of the eighteenth century a number remained independent and in control of sizable estates.[132]

Not all widows were so well placed, of course. In this period poor widows, especially the elderly among them, were by definition dependent. They, together with their children, were prime candidates for the benefits of the new regime of Poor Relief that developed in the sixteenth and seventeenth centuries and that became a means of moral oversight of its beneficiaries. Widows were also assisted by private charity where available.[133] Many women could only work on a part-time basis, and found themselves relegated to the worst-paid occupations, such as spinning or knitting. Most widows worked on an informal basis. Poor widows often had to seek multiple means of earning money.[134] Reduced job opportunities meant women had increasingly to look to marriage as a means of survival.[135]

The 'nuclear hardship' hypothesis postulates that societies with the nuclear as the dominant family form, like England in this period and later, tend to leave a number of widows rendered economically vulnerable because in principle there are no children (meaning adult children) or extended kin in residence to care for them. Should we look to provision of vital assistance chiefly or exclusively by non-resident family members, by the community in the form of local Poor Relief, or through resources furnished by self-sufficiency? Scholars have developed a variety of responses, but the better view is that all three sources of support mattered for many widows in supplying the means not so much for a comfortable

3. Late medieval and early modern England and Germany

retirement as for sheer survival. The precise mix varied according to time and place. Coresidence with an adult child was but one solution.[136]

English widows and freedom of movement

To judge from the 1436 autobiography of Margery Kempe, which recounts in detail her entrepreneurial (mis)adventures, late medieval English women were no more hindered by coverture than were ancient Roman women by gender-based guardianship.[137] Some early modern observers liked to contrast the low legal status of English women with their relatively wide freedom of action in general.[138] This claim reflects a certain continuity with the medieval period, even that pre-plague. Although excluded from participation in a range of official activities that were reserved for males, medieval widows' zealous resort to the law courts suggests a penetration of the public sphere that, however limited, remains significant, and it is worth noting that women's access to litigation overall increased in the early modern period, even as some barriers to this remained. Whether they used attorneys or acted on their own, the development of minimal levels of expertise in legal matters and of a network of relationships beyond the household was necessary for them to achieve the success they manifestly enjoyed. Their freedom of action was vulnerable to constraint, however, both with regard to remarriage (below) and their ability to manage and profit from property. In general, their actions were grounded in a field of tension between the morally commendable and the merely permitted.[139] There were unwritten rules of conduct constraining women's behaviour that did not hold for men.[140]

As with their financial situation, a range of factors helped shape the personal choices available to widows, above all, wealth, rank, age and personality. An obvious point is worth repeating. Widowhood was experienced differently by different women.[141] Release from coverture brought both risk and opportunity.

Many younger widows lived at the head of a household populated by servants and relatives, including minor children, sometimes other widows, and not with their adult children. A choice to live with a grown son or, more typically, a daughter might be made later in life, however, and a decline in independent residency was seen in the fifteenth century.[142] Among the elderly in the early modern period, fewer women than men lived with a child, and more lived alone.[143] Indeed, the cultural preference of the English for the conjugal household in the late medieval and early modern periods was precisely what made it difficult to place widows under male control, with attendant opportunities and difficulties for the widows themselves.[144]

Widows might choose to devote themselves to religious and charitable works, which provided acceptable opportunities to socialize, both with other women and on occasion with males as well. Their intent might in part be to memorialize a decedent husband or to benefit other widows.[145] Some chose the life of the cloister, while others preferred lay vows that left them greater scope for independent action.[146] After the Reformation, widows were relatively free to pursue the faith of their choice, provided it were Christian, and to support financially others of like mind.[147] Many widows were active in the cause of Reform, just as others were prominent among Catholic recusants.[148]

Questions of reputation had an impact on women's freedom of movement. Simply writing for publication entailed a measure of risk, although some relied on the Gospel parable of the 'widow's mite' to justify making a contribution to literature.[149] The numbers and output of women authors rose dramatically during the period of the Civil War and Interregnum, as widows in particular assumed a more active role in a number of ways.[150]

Adultery, proven in court, was a bar to the recovery of dower, which encouraged some defendants being sued by widows to attempt to besmirch their character.[151] Slurs on chastity were widespread, and not without effect, generating, for example, some pressure to remarry.[152] A degree of uncertainty operated, as opinions over the precise definition of chaste behaviour might be complex, ambivalent and contradictory, so that the concept of 'proper widow' itself could be highly unstable.[153] There is no good evidence, however, that widows were as a group especially prone to violate the rules of sexual conduct that their culture prescribed for women, either in the late medieval or early modern periods. Widows might find it prudent to avoid patronizing taverns so as to not to encourage gossip. Moralizing criticism of alewives, which turned especially fierce in the early sixteenth century, cannot have made it easy for widows to pursue this line of work.[154]

Living alone made a widow particularly vulnerable to misogynistic slurs on her reputation, even on the level of the upper classes.[155] The greater freedom enjoyed by widows in general seems at times to have generated a tension that rendered them more vulnerable to this kind of attack.[156] The same point holds for various forms of harassment, criminal activity (such as burglary) and vulnerability to physical assault, including abduction-marriage as well as rape, to which widows remained particularly exposed.[157] Among women, they were far less likely to commit acts of violence, physical or verbal, than were wives.[158]

By way of moral criticism abortion was linked to widows, never-married women and wives of absent husbands.[159] In the late sixteenth century prosecutions increased for all types of disorderliness, including witchcraft, in which widows were often implicated, as they were in infanticide.[160] Widows were both accusers and accused in criminal cases, destroyers of reputations and among those whose reputations were destroyed.[161]

Women's public activity became subject to greater constraint between the sixteenth and eighteenth centuries, with important consequences for widows.[162] Where widows did appear in public, such as before the courts, severe limitations might be placed on their behaviour.[163] There was,

3. Late medieval and early modern England and Germany

however, a way to turn necessity to advantage. Because the impoverished and vulnerable aspects of widowhood were objects of sympathy, widows who were not particularly poor or vulnerable would claim such attributes in self-defence or self-justification, often with no small success.[164] Poverty, in the Christian ethic ultimately deriving from antiquity, was not simply an economic category but also a moral one.[165]

A curious echo of the ancient ruler-ideology resounds through the Middle Ages in the tale of the emperor Trajan, the widow and Pope Gregory, which despite its apparently classical pedigree is almost certainly a medieval confection. In essence, the story is that Trajan was leading his army to war when a grieving widow accosted him, demanding justice for the murder of her son. Trajan promised his help when he returned from battle, but the widow persisted, and the emperor granted an immediate hearing. Centuries later, according to the story, Pope Gregory was so moved by this model of just rule (so Christian in substance) that he expressed regret (by shedding tears or, in some versions, by praying) over the fact that Trajan's status as a pagan condemned him to eternity in hell. He then learnt that Trajan was rescued from his infernal agony through his, Gregory's, actions, but the Pope was cautioned not to repeat such an intercession and then punished. The story is elaborated in various traditions, the hagiographical, the humanistic (including John of Salisbury)[166] and the scholastic. Sometimes emphasis is laid on the link between legitimate rule and compassion for the weak, very much in the style of the ancient Hebrew ruler ethos, and at others the story is told in the manner of Jerome, contrasting pagan virtue with Christian moral failure. It passes from Dante to such authors as William Langland and John Wyclif (both from the late fourteenth century), who use it to critique the Church as an institution. Beside the written traditions, there was also a strong visual one.[167]

The literary tradition on widows in the Middle Ages and early modern period was a highly moralizing one. It derived some of its impetus from a medieval debate, the origins and causes of which remain controversial, over the moral nature of women known as the *Querelle des Dames*. This debate saw an important contribution from a French widow, Christine de Pizan, whose most famous work, the *City of Ladies* (1405), an attack on the illogic of misogyny, was translated into English in 1521. In the *Querelle*, however, criticisms of women were overall published more often and argued with greater force than were arguments in support of women.[168]

The tradition on widows presents in essence two stereotypes, first, a Christianizing ideal that configured the widow as a paradigm of virtue, enjoying the next-best status to perpetual virginity, or even one that was equal or superior to that of virgins/nuns, while an image equally rooted in Christian ideology and popular tradition portrayed the widow as a paragon of lust, a conniving, greedy, scheming and sexually rapacious creature.[169] This latter stereotype was bolstered by medical doctrine, inherited from antiquity, holding that women were more sexually avid than men.[170] In the first case, widows gained status and influence through sexual renunciation. By rejecting the very sexuality men used to classify them they escaped the ill effects of classification. Not that this gain was without limits or even cost in the sense that such empowerment could actually limit widows' freedom of action, since some form of confinement frequently accompanied chaste widowhood, in part out of concerns with their sexual vulnerability or availability.[171]

The negative stereotype of the widow finds ample representation in the tradition of medieval Romance. This genre presented a challenge to the idealization of a widow as chaste, since the engine of the plot typically demanded resolution by marriage to the hero, an easier outcome for never-married women than for the widow who thereby risked betraying her late husband's memory. The upshot was typically a great deal of misogynistic backsliding, as though the representation of the widow as sexually depraved was the inevitable default position.[172] All the same, the bankruptcy of such an outcome in an artistic sense if nothing else may have been at least implicitly apparent to some, so that one occasionally finds widows in literature who evade the extremes of both stereotypes. Chaucer might be thought at least partly successful in depicting Criseyde as a sexually active widow who is not irredeemably a whore in his epic amatory poem *Troilus and Criseyde*,[173] a portrait that must be balanced against his more famous representation of the negative type of widow (times five) in the person of the Wife of Bath, named Alison, from the *Canterbury Tales*. Many summaries of this story are possible, but to take just one, here the Widow of Ephesus (whose grief at the loss of her husband is cut short when she takes a lover in his tomb) tackles Jerome at his most misogamous. Alison, the Wife, revels in her multiple marriages (for example, meeting one prospective husband at the funeral of his predecessor) and delivers a blistering critique of the *Adversus Iovinianum*. So Chaucer plays the misogynist by denouncing misogyny, so effectively in fact that some have taken him, Alison, or both to be, after a fashion, proto-feminists.[174]

Between these two works, in 1386, Chaucer wrote (but never completed) *The Legend of Good Women*, a series of ostensibly sympathetic portraits of women from the pagan mythographic and historical tradition that is heavily indebted to Ovid's *Heroides*. Despite his protestations to the contrary, however, Chaucer's distortions, selective emphasis, sly concessions and self-contradictions undercut his noble aims as stated, which turn out to be no more reliable than the flashy self-deprecation of the Prologue. Here, for example, he has Cupid name Ovid and Jerome as authorities who praise women, an association that deconstructs itself. One of the tales concerning widows is a purported attempt to rehabilitate Vergil's Dido, but this is done in such an unconvincing way as to render her character

3. Late medieval and early modern England and Germany

even more dubious – if possible – than Ovid's portrayal of her in his collection of amatory epistles. Chaucer notably plays up the complications generated by the difference in status of the two lovers more than his classical predecessors.[175]

Beyond whatever debt owed by Chaucer, the tradition of the Widow of Ephesus enjoyed great popularity in the Middle Ages. John of Salisbury reproduced Petronius's version in his twelfth-century *Policraticus* fairly faithfully, although with a section title that prompts an anti-woman reading and suggests in turn how John understood Petronius ('On the bothers and burdens of marriages according to Jerome and other philosophers; and on the destructive quality of lust; on the sexual loyalty of the Woman of Ephesus and others like her'). John prefigures the early modern period in his reliance on the pagan tradition as an independent moral authority, although his aim of validating the standing of unmarried clergy through the denigration of women is consistent with medieval attitudes.[176] Phaedrus himself disappears from view from the ninth century until rediscovery in 1596, although his explicitly misogynistic version, widely transmitted through the late-antique *Romulus* and its medieval successors, shows a greater diffusion than Petronius in England and elsewhere, often being translated into modern European languages and adapted for school use and sermons, and finally surfacing, it appears, in a series of hugely popular late medieval collections of moralizing stories. One important trend to note is the Christianization of the tradition, as concepts like 'chastity', 'love', 'marriage', 'widowhood' take on new meaning in the moral and religious context that has altered considerably between classical antiquity and the Middle Ages. At the same time there is a double aspect to the tradition, the more popular one heavily moralizing and anti-widow, usually under Christian influence, the other more literary and ambiguous.[177] The Widow of Ephesus story therefore tends overwhelmingly to reinforce the negative stereotype of widow in this period.

Whatever the precise balance struck in the late Middle Ages between the two widow-types, the early modern period witnessed the victory of the negative.[178] This is part of a larger trend reflecting the rise of male anxiety over women's sexuality, independence (i.e. from men), and authority (i.e. over men) as evidenced especially in the popular literature of both England and Germany, beginning in the late Middle Ages.[179] The figure of the wealthy, assertive and sexually avid 'merry widow' was favoured by the dramatists of the period, although the image of the vulnerable victim does not entirely disappear.[180]

Comedy focused on the question of remarriage, beginning with *Ralph Roister-Doister*, a play dating from the 1550s, and extending through the works of Wycherley and Congreve in the Restoration. It has been estimated that one of every four comedies from (roughly) the first half of the seventeenth century deals with widowhood, and most of these were concerned with the issue of remarriage.[181] From these plays emerged the stereotype of the widow as desperate for a new husband.[182] One important aspect is the widow cast as evil stepmother.[183] The negative stereotype is so familiar and so highly developed that it receives sophisticated satiric treatment from Thomas Middleton in his comedies from the early seventeenth century, which treat 'the lusty widow' more or less as a projection of male fantasy and fear.[184] One comedy from this period, George Chapman's 1604 *The Widow's Tears*, adapts the story of the Widow of Ephesus with a sardonic twist, as a husband fakes his death, in order then, as a test of her virtue, to seduce his 'widow' over his putative corpse.[185]

Some Shakespearean widows, like Cressida, Gertrude and Tamora, are depicted as lustful and predatory, a threat to manhood and the social order itself.[186] Others, like Hostess Quickly in *Henry IV Parts One and Two* (c. 1597, 1598) and the Old Widow of Florence in *All's Well That Ends Well* (c. 1603), exemplify vulnerability and downward social mobility. Vulnerable can easily morph into vicious, however. Richard III successfully courts Lady Anne, whose husband he has killed, in the presence of her father-in-law's corpse (c. 1593).[187] Two contrasting images of Dido appear in *The Tempest* (1611), one positive, one negative, thus reflecting a dual tradition tracing back to antiquity. In fact, all but a very few of the 'good widows' in Shakespeare's plays are not wholly good or not securely widows.[188] It is the widow who proves to be the most untameable of the three wives in *The Taming of the Shrew* (c. 1594).[189]

An important influence, at least on the level of the upper classes, was the work of the Spanish humanist Juan Luis Vives, instructor to Mary Tudor and author of an important Latin treatise on the moral education of women, dedicated to the once-widowed Catherine of Aragon and published in 1523 (with a second edition in 1538), in three books, one each on virgins, wives and widows. This work, the *De Institutione Feminae Christianae* ('On the Education of the Christian Woman'), was later translated into English, German and other vernacular languages (in over 40 editions and translations in the sixteenth century alone), making Vives perhaps the single most important voice on widowhood in the early modern period.[190]

Vives, relying on a mix of ancient pagan and Christian authorities and examples,[191] rejects the moralizing viewpoint that simplistically held marriage to be good and widowhood to be bad. The loss of a husband was in his eyes not so much a matter of a loss of social status or an economic crisis, as a personal catastrophe for a woman. He combines a hard-line patriarchal perspective with a measure of sympathy, in that few of the (male) writers on widows in this period or beforehand reflect for very long on the emotional impact of widowhood. Vives emphasizes the widow's duty of 'soul care' to her departed husband, although he cautions that one can mourn too much. He concedes the possibility of remarriage when necessary (*1 Timothy* is an influence, although Vives is perhaps also simply attempting to be realistic, or at least diplo-

3. Late medieval and early modern England and Germany

matic)[192] provided certain conditions are met, such as respect for traditional gender hierarchy. All the same, he generally favours instead a withdrawal from the world by the widow as an exercise in self-marginalization, while recognizing her ability to make decisions and take responsibility for her actions, preferably, however, in a context of male control.[193] In a separate work on the duties of a husband he briefly discusses the status and role of men who have lost their wives, an innovative topic, and, rather remarkably, holds that the onset of menopause dissolves the rationale for gender hierarchy within marriage.[194]

The early seventeenth-century Protestant moralist William Page drew on the tradition of the pastoral letter known as *1 Timothy* attributed (insecurely) to St Paul in order to elaborate a threefold typology of widows, the bad, the miserable and the good. For Page, suffering redeemed the widow, although for him the matter of social rank was inextricably tied to the practice of virtue in that widows who achieved misery through their own effort and the grace of God were the 'real' widows, not those who were born miserable or who had misery thrust on them.[195] Page advised against remarriage, in that for him autonomy ideally allowed more scope for the life of desolation he saw as the path to true holiness.[196] Page's thesis in a sense is an elaboration of the traditional Christian view that saw virtue in the poverty and troubles of widows, but at the same time it represents a considerable ratcheting up of this ideal to insist on such suffering as a path to goodness.[197] One might say that he tried to make a necessity out of a virtue.

The link drawn by William Page between renunciation of remarriage and justification through suffering suggests just how the ideology of widowhood and the individual circumstances of many widows might offer the prospect of imposing certain controls on these refugees from patriarchy. The 'poverty' of widows was as much a moral as an economic status.[198] So Poor Relief available to widows in the early modern period had the goal to protect and to control, sometimes even to punish.[199] While safeguarding the employment rights of widows, authorities in some English towns forbade single women to live by themselves, clearly perceiving them as a threat to the patriarchal order.[200] Such relief then was more than just a question of providing Christian charity to the deserving, but there is reason to doubt that it succeeded even at this much, as the trend going into the nineteenth century had widows retreating from independence, at least on some levels of society, to live with relatives, just as households headed by women, many of them widows, tended to be poor and were becoming poorer all the time.[201]

The force of the negative stereotype of widow extended well beyond representation, of course. Accusations of material greed and sexual avidity, for example, were levelled at actual widows, to their detriment.[202] The tendency to regard widows' putatively unbridled sexuality as dangerous, to the point of configuring widows as witches, notably takes firm hold in

71

the sixteenth and seventeenth centuries.[203] Not all widows accused of witchcraft were old and poor, as the stereotype would have them, but it is all the more remarkable that the onset of menopause did not help shield them from such suspicions.[204] In fact, it is the idea of pursuing sex without the capacity to be a mother, the ideal status for women, that in part seems to have inspired anxiety about witches. The predatory and disorderly nature attributed to them signals that here we have to do with a form of the 'merry widow' type, so often found in the literature of the day, including its most popular forms, such as the broadsheet.[205]

Witch persecution is part of a tendency, parallelled in Germany, to attempt to subject women to male discipline and authority, ideally within the household.[206] Even the Puritans, who put a relatively high premium on the spiritual equality of women, insisted that a good wife was a submissive wife.[207] Like other women, widows found themselves caught between the strictures of moralists, who demanded passivity, and the requirements of social life, which rewarded active participation. Both forces shaped women's lives in paradoxical ways, and even some moralists, such as Juan Luis Vives, recognized that passivity could render women vulnerable.[208] Ideals of what a widow should do, and should be, possessed considerable force.[209] Widows could not be blamed for thinking that suffering was not all it was cracked up to be.

English widows and remarriage

A widow contemplating remarriage might have had a number of factors to weigh. If she remained single, the benefits of continued independence were conceivably balanced against possible economic vulnerability and threats to her reputation and even physical integrity.[210] Unfortunately, a general principle operated to the effect that the greater the economic need for remarriage, the more remote the opportunity, with some exceptions. There does seem to have been a strong connection between rates of remarriage, landholding by widows and the demand for land.[211] Women who could remain independent often chose to remain so, despite the oppressiveness of the 'merry widow' stereotype.[212] Upper-class widows enjoyed the widest discretion while the poor often simply not could find suitable partners, so that rates of remarriage were highest perhaps in the middle ranks.[213] As Poor Relief and almshouses became more available to widows in the late sixteenth and seventeenth centuries, there is evidence to suggest that this presented some poor widows with a viable alternative to remarriage.[214]

Recent scholarship has shown that the experience of patriarchy for men in early modern England varied considerably, with a larger share of the benefits accruing to middle-aged householders. It has perhaps ever been the case that some men have derived greater advantage from gender hierarchy than others. In fact, a shift can be detected precisely during this

3. Late medieval and early modern England and Germany

period, in which the status of patriarchal manhood came to depend less on age and marital status and more on class.[215] The question naturally arises as to whether the same point holds for women, particularly widows. For them, however, the class differences at work influencing freedom of movement (above) and remarriage seem to have formed part of a traditional bundle of benefits and disadvantages associated with social rank and did not, to all appearances, impinge materially on the question of marital status. This continued to operate as part of an overall classification for women throughout this period, even after it ceased to be important for men. The categories remained, even with a shift in their content and meaning. The effacement of marital status as a significant factor in the categorization of women in society had to await the outcome of developments in the late nineteenth and early twentieth centuries, as we shall see in Chapter Four.

Widowers, as compared with widows, enjoyed greater benefits (and/or had greater needs) and better chances in the matter of remarriage. They tended to remarry more often, more quickly, and with much younger partners, a pattern that seems to have held even for the poor among them.[216] The pattern, unlike that for widows, held across England.[217] As noted above, until the Reformation a third choice existed, more popular with widows than with widowers, that of withdrawing from the world into a religious order or of taking secular vows.

About a third of all marriages in this period were remarriages for at least one of the partners.[218] No rule in contemporary canon or common law prohibited new unions within a year of losing a spouse, and many remarried rather quickly, albeit in the face of some (rather mild, for most of our period) criticism.[219] Lengthening periods of mourning entailing delay of remarriage were in England (and Germany) a product of the Reformation that took hold slowly and unevenly.[220] Even pregnancy was no bar to pursuing remarriage, at least to judge from a case in late medieval London.[221] Husbands sometimes tried to discourage remarriage through framing penalties in their wills, but this practice does not seem to have been very common, as we shall see below. Some men were concerned to have a widow mourn them, such as the mid-seventeenth century William Cartwright, who, having lost two wives to death, commissioned a painting of the third dressed as a widow. She too predeceased him.[222]

Among the relatively well attested, because socially prominent, late medieval peeresses, about one-half remarried, some for a second or third time.[223] These women tended to marry second husbands of slightly inferior status, which was a delicate enterprise, given that the practice of women marrying down – hypogamy – was not highly favoured, while lesser aristocrats remarried slightly up, and a great deal of movement in the remarriage market can be described as horizontal.[224] Widows were thought to be inclined to marry men younger than themselves, something controversial, and perhaps exaggerated to some extent in criticism of the practice, although the phenomenon was far from invented.[225] Feudal lords from the king on down might attempt to compel remarriage through threat of confiscation of land in the period before the Magna Carta (1215). Afterward the permission of the king (or other feudal lord) to remarry, usually obtainable against payment, was still required where the widow had the benefit of land under military tenure from her husband's estate, since under settlements of dower and jointure the widow did not lose the property on remarriage. Enforcement of this rule in the late Middle Ages was driven by a concern with widows marrying beneath them.[226] But even this difficulty could be avoided through resort to trusts.[227] Upper-class widows, or at least a good number of them, seem to have enjoyed relative freedom in the choice of whether and whom to marry.[228]

Dower from a decedent husband made a woman an attractive marriage prospect, and moralists recognized, with regret, that wealthy widows were particularly likely to attract suitors and so to remarry.[229] This may have been particularly the case in districts where land was expensive and/or scarce.[230] Wealth is not inevitably an explanation in itself for remarriage, at least as far as the actual rates of this were concerned. This fact helps explain the contrasting experience in Elizabethan London of the widows of prosperous tradesmen and craftsmen, who remarried early and often, with that of the widows of aldermen, the majority of whom did not remarry, much like the widows of poor tradesmen and craftsmen.[231]

Marriage with the widow of a successful guild member was a sure path to upward social mobility.[232] At the same time, evidence from Stepney, East London, shows some early modern widows not at all prevented by their poverty from finding new partners.[233] In London we can detect a certain endogamy within crafts, as for example tanners tried to keep resources pooled within their ranks.[234] In some places marriage with the widow of a citizen conferred status as one.[235]

There is contradictory evidence on the rate of widow remarriage following the Black Death, but it seems that at least in some places this declined for a time.[236] Parish registers from the sixteenth century preserve much fuller information than is available for the medieval period, and show a rate of remarriage for widows of 25-30%, with almost half remarrying within a year of a husband's death.[237] Age, like wealth, was an important factor influencing remarriage throughout this period, as younger widows were always more likely to remarry than older ones, and women over the age of 50 relatively unlikely to remarry.[238] In Elizabethan London, young widows were more likely to marry younger bachelors than were older widows.[239]

Given that remarriage involved a move from independent legal status back to marital coverture, it is difficult for a modern feminist to understand why so many widows chose this path, in cases where they do appear to have had a real choice, especially because so few have left us clear evidence of their motivations. We have addressed above the most obvious

3. Late medieval and early modern England and Germany

factors, including concerns about finances and exposure to attacks on reputation and person.[240] All the same, these cannot always have been decisive, especially in light of an ideal that celebrated a widow's celibacy and devotion to her decedent spouse, so that the matter remains somewhat puzzling.

An answer to the question is suggested by a study of marriage litigation in late medieval York. In the fourteenth century, many more women than men initiated suits to prove the existence of a marriage, and tended to be more persistent in pursuit of their claims.[241] The evidence suggests that while male litigants were more explicitly interested in the financial benefits of a union, women tended to value marriage for its own sake.[242] The status of wife, with all that this entailed, including companionship and greater financial security, appears to have mattered a great deal to them, even when balanced against the independence enjoyed by widows and the never-married. Again, this is not to deny that they were also arguably more vulnerable than men as single persons, in terms of finances, reputation and physical integrity.

In the Middle Ages many regarded marriage as the natural state for women.[243] One consequence of Protestant Reform was, if anything, to raise its already high status even higher, while the moral value of widowhood came to be discounted. This did not end but only redefined the problem posed by a conflict between a social imperative expressed in a desire for male control of women's behaviour and the challenge of a moral or religious ideal of matrimony, a conflict that was especially sharp with respect to the issue of remarriage of widows. This subject remained a perennial focal point of male ambivalence, something that had long been a feature of the canon law, for example.[244]

Other factors might encourage marriage. Medical lore, as in antiquity, saw sex as a biological necessity for women.[245] Further, many English husbands were themselves perhaps not as harsh or controlling as the aspects of the law that 'covered' the legal personalities of their wives and tolerated wife beating. This is at least to judge from the frequently generous testamentary provisions they made for their widows, in which they relatively rarely attempted to interfere with remarriage.[246]

Many married women conducted themselves as though coverture did not exist. Finally, the experience of a prior marriage may have led many women to confront a new one with greater confidence. Widows tended to be more careful than other women in financial negotiations over marriage.[247] Even below the level of the aristocracy, they could, and often did, protect their independence and property through a prenuptial agreement.[248] Law could help fill a breach of confidence in a husband's good will, or in his ability to manage the finances.

Although women litigants continued to dominate the marriage court of York in the fifteenth century, there were fewer of them and they were less successful.[249] The reasons for this development are unclear, but it does suggest marriage, and perhaps remarriage, had become a less attractive prospect for women at this time. Certainly by the early modern period widows faced increasingly strident criticism of their decision to remarry, which, given the value placed on marriage over celibacy in the wake of the Reformation, is paradoxical. Some widows defied the trend, out of a persistent regard for marriage.[250] Although relatively few husbands made bequests to their wives conditional on continued widowhood, the percentage of those doing so rose in this period. Their motives are not always clear, but evidently concerns over the financial welfare of their children were paramount.[251] While medieval rebukes are on the whole rather mild, in the early modern period moralizing criticism of widows for insincere mourning and rapid remarriage appears to intensify significantly.[252] What was deemed undue haste in this matter might generate accusations of adultery and even murder, as a 1591 case demonstrates.[253]

Such uncertainties have prompted controversy among scholars, with many wishing to contrast an older Catholic hostility to remarriage with a newer Protestant tolerance of this, while some argue that the latter ran up against broad popular resistance.[254] For example John Webster's *The Duchess of Malfi* (1614) has been viewed as presenting a clash between rival theologies, with the Duchess and Antonio asserting a Protestant ethic supporting remarriage and her brothers representing the Catholic intolerance of this, if only in a distorted fashion. But neither Catholic nor Protestant views, certainly in England, were monolithic on this subject, nor were attitudes and practice so discontinuous over the course of the Reformation – if anything remarriage of widows declined as the society became more Protestant. It is difficult to imagine many a Protestant theologian approving the conduct of the Duchess, who marries (if she does 'marry') a man her social inferior in secret, without the consent or even knowledge of her male relatives, relying on her knowledge of canon law. At the same time, to interpret the criminal obsessions of her brothers, who in fact waver between prescribing celibacy for their sister and wanting to arrange a socially advantageous match for her, as somehow Catholic in nature, may not only distort doctrine – Vives is nowhere on record recommending the murder of widows who remarry – but misunderstand the aims of the author.

Webster appears more intent on exploring and adapting the implications of a Mediterraneanist honour/shame dichotomy for his Jacobean audience than in representing religious difference. Although their own conceptions of honour and shame were not necessarily the same ones held by contemporary Italians, concerns with the conduct of widows and its control by men were hardly foreign to the early modern English, whatever their faith. By the same token, religious doctrine, even change in religious doctrine, is but one element in a complex and controversial cultural mix where female opportunity and male anxiety (not to deny the existence of male opportunity and female anxiety) interacted with each other to yield variations in a pattern that reveals the presence of a double ideal, one

3. Late medieval and early modern England and Germany

favouring, the other disfavouring, the remarriage of widows, as we see play out in comedies and other popular literature of this period, where a widow's 'lust' can be read as a threat to men or as a sign of gender weakness. The author sets up a conflict of values that does not unambiguously cleave to the fault-line of doctrinal difference, a conflict at times difficult for a modern sensibility to construe, especially when impeded by a (commendable, in itself) sympathy for the Duchess.[255]

Whatever widows' motives for remarriage, they were often utterly discounted. One motive, especially for the elderly joined to a younger partner, was obviously to secure financial support. Contemporaries often found this difficult to accept at face value. For example, the authors of the conduct book literature of the time could only ascribe an unbridled lust to widows and greed for material gain to their partners as reasons to marry. The anti-remarriage ideology read from *1 Timothy* maintained its prominence, as we have seen above, although some Puritan authorities conceded marriage might be good for older widows.[256] Fear of gender inversion produced by female hypogamy, as widows married men their inferior in age, wealth and marital experience (and occasionally intelligence and/or moral worth) is especially prominent in this period. Moralists conflated desire for remarriage with desire for sex, driven by the prior experience of same. At all events, some men evidently found the prospective conjuncture of money, power and sex attractive, and there is tantalizing evidence that more women 'married down' than meets the eye. Even if they exaggerate, the moralists who decry the practice may well have had something to complain about.[257]

Remarriage rates for widows fell in the seventeenth century, a phenomenon that has been variously explained and remains controversial. The greater intensity of misogynist rhetoric, a growth in (male) individualism and decreasing mortality rates (less so in a large city like London) have all been cited as factors that helped foreclose remarriage both for men and for women, as the rate of remarriage plummeted in the seventeenth century and stayed low for centuries afterwards. Although younger widows continued to remarry at a higher rate than older ones, the overall proportion of widows remarrying seems to have fallen by as much as one half or more in some places. While demographic and economic constraints should not be ignored, and differences of age, wealth and location need to be taken into account, neither can the preferences of individual women be discounted. There is a strong possibility that the valuation which women, at least women married once before, placed on marriage changed over time.[258]

German widows and private law

In Germany as well as in England, marital status was the decisive aspect of a woman's legal status, in a way that it never was for a man's.[259] This was of course a reflection of the fact that gender difference was embedded in law, and reinforced by corresponding behavioural expectations and norms. Property law and the law of succession helped subordinate women to men. But even where a degree of formal equality, that is, equality in the formulation of law, existed, this might often contrast with real inequality in law, that is, inequality in its application.[260]

One important category of formal equality concerned citizen status. Women in the late medieval period were typically classed as citizens in German cities and villages, more or less on the same basis as men, which usually meant, for example, fulfilling a property qualification. Until the early modern period, citizen women in many places could grant this status to their non-citizen husbands simply by marrying them.[261] If adult and unmarried, women might be required to take the oath of citizenship. The idea that widowhood represented a distinct legal status for women crystallized in the requirement that the widow of a citizen take the oath where it was otherwise required only of male heads of households.[262] Overall, however, the legal rules regarding widows, like those for wives, differed greatly from place to place.[263]

Marital property regimes in late medieval and early modern Germany were extremely diverse, so that what follows is generalized, to a degree.[264] Wives could make their own wills without interference from their husbands, so that here, unlike England in this period, widowhood brought no great advantage.[265] There were two basic types of marriage with respect to spousal property rules. Under one, all property was owned in common, although during this period the husband came to be regarded as sole administrator. Married women, under the other major form of marital property regime, owned property apart from that which they held in common with their husbands, property they were free to buy, sell, lend or pledge without his permission or even knowledge.[266] All women, whatever their marital status, were excluded from alienating real property.[267] Never-married women and widows over 18 could own property, and so make contracts, borrow and lend without a male co-signer, in Nuremberg at any rate.[268]

In other respects the status of a married woman resembled the English institution of coverture. The husband was his wife's 'head' or guardian, represented her at law, answered for her offences, and had the right to discipline her, even corporally.[269] The male head of the household was empowered, increasingly over time, to exercise authority, even as his responsibility to the state grew as well.[270]

Married couples often enjoyed ownership of all of their property in common, a principle strong enough for many municipal codifications, as well as customary law in a number of locales, to resist the importation of Roman law rules stipulating separate property for husband and wife. The latter was thought too suggestive of absolute legal equality between spouses and so condemned as 'foreign'. In principle, Roman law, in the eyes of the Reformers, was too closely associated with canon law for their comfort.[271] In the other main form of German marital property regime,

3. Late medieval and early modern England and Germany

alluded to above, only a part of the property of both spouses was held in common, although all increase belonged solely to the husband, who had a usufruct over his wife's property as well.[272] The husband administered the joint marital property here too, a fact that could generate conflict if either spouse overstepped the bounds established by law. The wife enjoyed some transactional freedom to run the household and business but in principle the husband's permission was required to dispose of property held in common.[273]

The law of succession also shows great diversity from place to place, but allows a few generalizations to be drawn. Overall, there were not major differences in the treatment of men and women under inheritance law, although only rarely did a widow have an absolute right to a share of her decedent husband's estate, as in England.[274] Under the German rules a husband might receive two-thirds of the estate if his wife predeceased him, a widow one-third, if he died first, with the remainder split among their children.[275] The death of a spouse in many cities led to a separation of property to pay off the decedent's creditors and heirs. This device operated primarily as protection for widows, in that it allowed them to recover their dowry and personal property.[276] Usually a widow received as usufruct that part of her husband's estate that did not accrue to her as owner. The general rule was that she receive her dowry and the marriage gift. The first came from the wife's family, the second from the husband's, and together formed not only the basis for a widow's financial support, but the economic foundation of the marital union. The ratio between them differed according to region and over time, as did the size of dowries. The income from these funds constituted a widow's pension, a means of supporting widows that came into vogue during this period, replacing an earlier system of dower. As a rule, a wife could be excluded by her husband's will from receiving a share of his property or benefit from his largesse.[277]

A widow might be left a usufruct of husband's estate and/or be commended to the care of his family as a way of avoiding, in case of her remarriage, transfer of the property destined for their children to the control of a new husband.[278] Developments in inheritance law, in some instances derived from the Roman tradition, discouraged widows' remarriage, as we shall see below. One rule relevant to widows that was adopted in a number of jurisdictions was actually a feature of the law of Justinian, and so from a time long past the classical period. This was a forced share of one-fourth granted to 'poor' (originally meaning without a dowry) widows from a husband's estate.[279] The early modern period saw a greater emphasis on primogeniture, although it might be better to view this as one stage in a long-running state of tension between two vastly different ideals in the succession of property, one that stressed patrilineal descent and thus the claims of the oldest son, and a partible ideal that favoured the equal claims of siblings, especially brothers. There was at the same time a growing reluctance to allow unmarried women to manage their legal affairs, both developments to the disfavour of widows.[280]

Marriage contracts could set aside the customary rules on marital property and succession, and often the statutory ones as well, making generous provision for the aristocratic widow, for example. A study of a number of lineages from the sub-princely high aristocracy in southwest-central Germany of the late medieval period affords a wealth of detail on how such marriage contracts worked. There was on this social level a constant tension between the desire to continue the male line by having a sufficient number of children and the need to avoid dispersing the patrimony by having too many. In this period, we find an increasing tendency to render the bestowal of a woman's marriage portion, or dowry, contingent on her renunciation of a right to inherit from her parents, so that this practice became the norm by the fifteenth century, at least where there were sons as well as daughters with a claim on the inheritance.

In this setting, the contribution from the wife's family, i.e. the dowry (known as the *Heimsteuer* or *Zugeld*) set the level for the matching gift from the groom's side (*Widerlegung*), in that these were typically framed in a proportion of 1:1. Exceptions occurred in notable cases of female hypergamy (women marrying up), in which the dowry was greater, and female hypogamy (women marrying down), in which the matching gift was higher. In addition, the groom's family provided a castle or suitably fortified place as a widow's residence, plus a morning gift (*Morgengabe*), which typically provided the sole source of income for a wife during her marriage. The fear that a widow's subsequent husband might turn out to be a political and/or military rival of the decedent husband's family and yet come into possession of a strategically sensitive point in their territory led some to prefer alternative arrangements, by which a widow would have to abandon her residence on remarriage. In many cases, broader concerns were felt about the danger that a widow's portion might mean a loss for to a family's patrimony, or, at minimum, simply render inaccessible vital assets for a substantial period of time. Ultimately, much depended for a widow's welfare on the generosity, prudence and care shown by her father at the time of her marriage, when the contract was drawn up, although a husband's (or that of his father, if still alive at the time of marriage) disposition to her and the marriage was hardly irrelevant.[281]

In general, wives enjoyed significantly less control than husbands over the shared marital property under both of the spousal property regimes described above. Although in theory they had to be consulted when the latter engaged in any relevant transaction, the husband and the husband alone had the power to administer it. The ideology surrounding the law of shared marital property was a powerful one, but the reality saw much conflict between spouses. These were often difficult to moderate. The Augsburg City Council, for example, was reluctant to intervene even in

3. Late medieval and early modern England and Germany

cases where an unscrupulous husband was squandering a wife's property. Often wives were expressly prohibited from buying, selling, owning or making any legally binding contracts regarding such property under the theory of 'womanly freedom' (*weibliche Freiheit*), which was in actual fact a device designed to protect the interest of husbands rather than that of wives. This protection was curtailed, however, where wives acted fraudulently, made a profit or formally renounced its application. 'Womanly freedom' also did not operate for women whose jobs involved sale, purchase, lending and borrowing, a type known as the 'market woman' (*Marktfrau*).[282] It was entirely irrelevant for widows, who could act as they pleased, at least for much of this period.[283]

Wives in German states, then, did not have their legal personality eclipsed to the extent accomplished, at least in theory, by coverture in England. Their status is a mixture of the independent and the dependent. Their independence is reflected in their ability to own and inherit property, be paid wages, and their obligation to pay taxes, while the joint property regime for spouses that prevailed in many places suggests a fair degree of subordination. A wife's contribution to the material welfare of the household was reflected in legal and ultimately economic benefits that limned the prevailing hierarchy of gender. Their freedom of action is especially notable on the higher social levels, where elite women enjoyed considerable discretion in economic matters. The legal status of widows was, as a result, not the radical break with that of wives that we find in contemporary England, although widowhood did present a woman with a mix of new challenges and opportunities and, as we shall see, there was some change for the worse over time.[284] It is of course exaggerated to speak of the 'emancipation' of women, or even widows, in late medieval Germany, but their position in relative terms is far superior to that of the early modern period.[285] The conspicuous wealth and independence of some widows in the late Middle Ages may have helped provoke a reaction that operated to the disadvantage of those who came afterwards.[286]

Widows were in many cases not able to act as guardians, at least sole guardians, to their own children but saw a male appointed to this end.[287] This fact did not prevent some from continuing to exercise an important role in raising children nonetheless.[288] Widows were entitled to vindicate their interests before both Church and state courts. Like other women, they exploited the ambiguities of the law and the administrative confusion occasioned by the overlapping jurisdiction of different legal authorities to their advantage in obtaining or retaining hold of property. Gendered differentials in power often worked in their favour, as the courts were inclined to protect the interest of the weak. This tendency might generate some tension between the goal of asserting patriarchal authority and the effects of intervening in a given household.

By the late medieval period in many places the institution of women's guardian had practically withered away. Where this happened the guardian functioned only for procedural purposes or widows might even represent themselves in court. This changed over time, and later they were usually required to use a male guardian appointed by the court, who was typically a relative. A widow might, however, assert her rights by appearing on her own behalf and suing her guardian if she felt mistreated. Alone among women, widows enjoyed a degree of personal freedom to act in legal matters. The reintroduction of gender guardianship, in its newly enhanced form, has been argued to have had a greater impact on never-married women and wives. Even so, the sixteenth and seventeenth centuries, in part under the influence of Roman law in its early modern reception, witnessed both an increase in the power of guardians to the disadvantage of at least some widows and a decrease in the rights of the latter with respect to their children.[289] The aim of such reforms seems to have been to encourage remarriage and/or to tie the widow to her husband's family.[290]

In both Protestant and Catholic areas of the Holy Roman Empire in the sixteenth century, marriage law changed so as to limit the rights of wives. Even earlier, rules began to forbid women to purchase, sell, lend and borrow, as well as give money as a gift, without approval of a husband or guardian, although court records show women engaging in these activities on a routine basis. From the sixteenth century, many states began to require widows and never-married women to choose a guardian not only to represent them in court but to manage their property. The overall trend moved toward increasing suspicion of, and so attempts to control, unmarried women, including widows.[291] Exaltation of the married state generated sheer hostility toward the unmarried, including celibate clergy, monks, nuns and prostitutes.[292] Here we have to do with a kind of patriarchy-plus that sought the direct domination of all women, or at least as many as possible, by men.

A great concern lay with 'masterless' persons, that is, those not subject to male control at all or whose subordination was deemed insufficiently direct, effective or morally justified. Cities crusaded first against unofficial brothels, in the end moving to close their municipal establishments as well, and in 1577 an imperial law banned concubinage.[293] In Augsburg single women who were not citizens were forbidden to have their own households.[294] Laws now tended to prohibit unmarried women from migrating into cities, required widows to dwell with a son, and stipulated that never-married women reside with a male relative or employer.[295] These measures reveal the Reformers' agenda to be not so much an assertion of family values but of the interest of a male-dominated social order. Only households headed by males qualified for endorsement and protection.

The influence of Roman law, where present, tended to disadvantage widows and women in general. The German jurists took over the Roman terminology for dowry, *dos*, but without according the wife all of the protections she enjoyed under Roman law in antiquity. The idea of guardianship for women was imported from Roman law, but this was not

3. Late medieval and early modern England and Germany

accomplished in the form of the lax gender-based form employed by the Romans themselves. Instead it resembled the more robust type they had imposed on minor children of both sexes. Joint parental authority yielded to a form of Roman paternal power, *patria potestas*, which meant, for example, that widows lost custody of their children on remarriage or, where the strict Roman rule was received, even without remarriage.[296] Generally, family law proved more resistant to Roman influence than other areas of the law, but in matters involving the rights of women, it appears as if the German authorities cherry-picked, selecting only Roman rules unfavourable to women and rejecting those that were favourable.[297] In matters of gender, the logic of the law might be marked by circular reasoning, repetitive arguments or sheer self-contradiction.[298] Such phenomena are a good sign of the direct importation of social values and extralegal policy considerations into the rules. The inheritance of Greek and Roman antiquity, especially Roman law and early Christian thought, above all that of Paul in *1 Corinthians*, interpreted through the lens of male bias, operated to the consistent disadvantage of women, whose alleged inferiority was used to justify even the few privileges they were granted.[299]

Over the course of the sixteenth century women's legal position declined in both theory and practice. Husbands in this period were increasingly able to act unilaterally with regard to marital property, to the point where in 1564 the Nuremberg City Council allowed widows to pay only one-half of their decedent husbands' debts, partly in order to prevent them from requiring public assistance.[300] All widows, at least in Nuremberg, were required to have a (male) city official write their wills and inventory their property. Fewer wills over this period were written by women on their own and more were written by husbands and wives together, to the detriment of traditional female charities. As late as the early sixteenth century we find that most widows and never-married women selling property did so without any sign of intervention by a guardian, but that this changes dramatically over the course of that century, just as the absolute participation of women in sale and purchase of property sharply declines. The rules requiring intervention by guardians undergo a general tightening up throughout this period. The regulation of market activity was motivated by economic considerations in the medieval period, while in the early modern it was moralized, an element in the overall attempt of Reformers to promote spiritual renewal by moralizing all of society, or as much of it as possible.[301] The conjugal household stood as the smallest building block of the early modern political economy, but was no less important for that.[302] This development, and others associated in some way with religious Reform, did not promise well for the legal standing of widows.[303]

Not all women, nor even all widows, were adversely affected by the (re)valorization of married life reflected in the public policy of the early modern period. The intensified allegiance to the ideology of shared marital property, with its intimations of a common purpose, as well as the uniting of work and domestic space that signified a partnership in the household, was attractive to many women.[304] This made, almost by default, widowhood something more of an ordeal than in a society that privileged celibacy as a religious principle, but, as we shall see, some women were more than equal to this challenge.

German widows and economic privilege

Women's rights to inheritance, both from their families of origin and from their husbands, might leave them in a position of relative power and affluence as widows.[305] Among women, widows were the most active in commercial investment, despite certain limitations, and at times took a direct role in managing the family business.[306] Widows of master craftsmen could offer to younger journeymen, in terms of material marriage prospects, a good living in a trade with high barriers to entry, especially when, from the late fifteenth century, the guilds, much stronger than in England, began to restrict eligibility for admission to the husbands of masters' widows and daughters.[307]

Peasant couples, in some areas at some times, owned their farm jointly, and regardless of whether the farm estate passed undivided (*Anerbenrecht*) or not to the widow, these women were often regarded as desirable marriage partners, as though they were tickets to prosperity.[308] As in England, the vast majority of men and women worked in agriculture. Many if not most rural widows, however, were poor or even destitute.[309] For them the elaborate legal rules described above would be of little relevance. The same held true in the towns, where poverty was a common condition of women who had lost their husbands to death.[310] Most widows could not rely on inherited wealth, especially in the form of land, or on family support, but had to try to earn their keep, often as textile workers. Even those with some resources at the outset of widowhood might see these diminish over time. Some widows turned to crime.[311]

Where remarriage was not an option, economic circumstances, often determined in part by the presence of dependent children, shaped the experience of widows.[312] Some widows might, to judge from the situation in late medieval Freiburg, hand over property in connection with a contract for maintenance.[313] It is possible to generalize by pointing out that in Germany, like England, strictly non-economic factors often played a role in the degree of prosperity and material comfort widows enjoyed. As noted above, for many aristocratic widows, the diligence and generosity of a father and/or of a husband often mattered a great deal more for her financial status than any legal entitlement independent of the arrangements these men made. The age of her oldest son at the time of her husband's death might be a key factor in determining a widow's standard of living, at least in the near term. Despite the existence of legal rules

3. Late medieval and early modern England and Germany

designed to facilitate the transfer of property in an orderly fashion, hard-fought struggles between widows and their children or members of a decedent husband's family are frequently attested. In fighting these battles, widows were hardly guaranteed success. The gap between a widow's claims at law, and their realization in fact, might be a large one.[314]

Widows with material assets and high social status generally found the going easiest, of course. Wealthy widows displayed their generosity by founding religious charities and monasteries.[315] Those who had been married to merchants and retailers tended to be among the more independent and successful, since they had experience running the family business during their husbands' typically frequent and protracted absences. As widows they enjoyed something close to the freedom males possessed.[316] Noble widows, above all, in the middling to smaller states, often exercised rule even when married, during the illness or absence of a husband.[317] Widows and wives of members of the elite were often placed in charge of social welfare organizations sponsored by the state.[318]

As a rule, widows were less prosperous than they had been as married women, and when we move down the social scale, some very negative consequences attach to this principle. For example, households headed by widows tended to rank among the poorest in any given place.[319] Most widows, it seems, were left without adequate financial support.[320] Tax records, poor lists and other evidence show that widows ranked among the very poorest in society.[321] The groups of beggars often seen wandering from place to place in this period included many widows.[322] Restrictions on single women as household heads, discussed in the section above, had a dampening effect on their economic activity and prospects.[323] Unmarried women, including widows, constituted a large share of the ranks of day labourers. They were poorly paid as a rule, and were paid less than male workers aside from very exceptional cases.[324] Many widows were forced to turn to prostitution.[325] Older widows were even more conspicuous in their misery than younger ones. Poverty, old age and widowhood tended to converge to create a 'perfect storm' of sheer vulnerability.

Despite this bleak picture, there is no question that in Germany, as in England, many women benefited from the economic conditions that prevailed in the wake of the Black Death that first made its appearance in the mid-fourteenth century. In the late Middle Ages, a growing number of work opportunities for women arose that facilitated their ability to support themselves and thereby to live on their own.[326] With the advent of the early modern period, however, or even starting a little before, a tendency gained momentum that excluded women from a number of fields of economic activity, or at least restricted them to a limited range of them. Much of the exclusionary trend centred round the guilds, where widows lost some of the chief advantages they had enjoyed earlier.

In the medieval period urban widows' privileges allowed them to enter a trade or craft in place of their late husbands.[327] Early on, in the fourteenth and fifteenth centuries, guild records not uncommonly show both male and female masters, the latter sometimes engaged at a high level of participation even in heavy industries like iron making and roofing. A widow might run her husband's shop for as long as 15-20 years after his death.[328] In many guilds, however, a widow's right to operate a husband's shop was limited by the occasion of her remarriage, by a fixed period (ranging from three weeks to three years), or by the time required to train her son to succeed her. The rules differed by region and by craft and reflect the same ambivalence as that which held for widows' remarriage, with recognition of the need for support balanced against fears of independence and its implications for male supremacy. In most places, widows allowed to continue a husband's trade were forbidden to enlist apprentices if they did not marry another master, so they might earn a living but not become a source of competition for others. The paradox, sustained by a conflict in values, endured. Resolution in the early modern period tended in the direction of widows' exclusion. Support for widows was one thing, but actually allowing them to work could be problematic.[329] Over time, restrictions were imposed on widows' participation in crafts and trades in terms of time, assistance and object.[330]

Among women, widows tended to receive the most sympathetic treatment from male guilds. Other women, for example, were often compelled to migrate to places where guild control was weakest.[331] But even widows, as we have seen, faced severe restrictions, both of an economic and regulatory nature.[332] Throughout northern Europe in the fifteenth century, as the population began to grow significantly and along with it the numbers of workers, women's access to employment, increasingly hampered by the guilds, declined.[333] This helps explain why in 1475 Augsburg the number of widows in guilds was only 5% of the total, while by 1536 their participation appears to have dropped to less than 1%.[334]

From the time of the mid-fifteenth century, guilds began to make it more difficult for masters' widows to continue the operation of the family shop, compelling many of them to marry a younger journeyman or to abandon the business.[335] Women in general were gradually excluded from participation in the crafts and trades regulated by the guilds. Widows of master craftsmen were increasingly left to appeal to city councils for what had been a right, now transformed into a privilege.[336] Permission to carry on a husband's trade, at least temporarily, seems to have been but rarely granted in many places during the sixteenth century.[337] Some managed to overcome the disabilities imposed on them all the same, as the example of Appollonia Mair, a successful tanner in Augsburg, suggests.[338]

Women were hardly excluded from all occupations. Some jobs saw changes for both sexes, others no change at all.[339] Occasionally a widow or married woman would be placed in charge of an orphanage for girls.[340] Sometimes women found work as schoolteachers.[341] In general, however, they were relegated to the lowest paid and most unpleasant jobs, ones that

3. Late medieval and early modern England and Germany

required little training or initial outlay of capital, leading to a general decline in women's participation in the economy and its rewards.[342] So, for example, early modern Bavaria saw a decline in well-paying and respectable jobs available to women.[343] Only at the very bottom of the scale were men's and women's salaries even roughly equal.[344]

This decline is reflected in the decrease in the percentage of women buying and selling property from the sixteenth to the eighteenth century.[345] The ban on women's standing surety for third parties, including on a strict interpretation their husbands, a rule received from Roman law (the *SC Vellaeanum*), led to their exclusion from business networks, which became increasingly operated by males.[346]

Some scholars argue that, while in the Middle Ages tasks within the household had not been sharply differentiated by gender or status, at least in ideological terms, that now began to change, and the newly negative attitudes to women's work resonated both inside the household and beyond, signifying a structural change in the gendered division of labour.[347] Women now had to look exclusively to marriage, and not to work, for any possible rise in their status.[348] Women's work was redefined, ceasing even to be regarded as 'work' as it increasingly became separated from men's.[349]

The reality of women's low economic status validated the social prejudice that deemed them inferior, so that the actual gendered division of labour and its supporting ideology were mutually reinforcing.[350] Despite the tendency toward the segregation of the genders and the sex-typing of jobs (with the more specialized, prestigious and better-paid ones typically falling to men), the new norm did not precisely anticipate the Victorian ideology of 'separate spheres'. Women's participation in religion was hardly a private matter, as it would come to be regarded in the modern age. The early modern household was not a private realm set off from the public arena, in part because it ideally and often in actual fact served as a locus of production as well as reproduction.[351]

The impetus to the exclusion or restriction of widows and other women from the crafts and trades supervised by the guilds often came from journeymen, sometimes in conflict with city councils.[352] Their motives were in part to meet what they deemed an economic threat and in part to address what appeared to them as an ideological challenge to male authority.[353] So, for example, guilds denied women convicted of adultery their rights as widows.[354] This suggests the truth of an important point that has fairly broad implications. Exclusion of widows from guilds was not simply grounded in economic and political motives. Members were concerned with perceived threats to the honour of the guilds, a sense of honour jeopardized by working in close proximity to women and rendered more vulnerable by an increased emphasis on male bonding. The new ideal was the all-male workshop.[355]

Changes in the structure of the professions introduced a more subtle form of exclusion for women, including widows. The sixteenth century saw both the introduction of positions that were strictly new and the increased professionalization of existing ones. These included officeholders, doctors, lawyers, appraisers and Protestant pastors. Because of their public nature and/or the level of education they required, an education from which women were utterly excluded, widows had no chance of succeeding their husbands in these fields. Protestant ideology held marriage and motherhood to be the only true vocation for women, an end toward which their education should be directed.[356]

Marriage was ideally structured so as to provide an opportunity for material support and even a level of comfort. On this theory, the cooperative efforts of husband and wife pooled their resources to the advantage of both.[357] Despite the existence of rules of inheritance designed to benefit them, however, widows were often not so well placed in reality, as we have seen. Moreover, some of the societal mechanisms intended to favour them were sharply eroded in the early modern period. Denial of the right to continue operation of a husband's shop amounted to a denial of the right to sustain oneself. Devaluation of women's work was bad news for widows, who were severely punished, in economic terms, for a shift in ideology. There are, to be sure, examples of widows from the early modern period who prosper despite adverse circumstances, but these relatively fortunate women do not appear to have been representative in any true sense, because their circumstances were unusual. For example, a good number were born or married into successful and well-off merchant and commercial families. Several such women are found in the printing trade, such as Margarethe Egenolff of Frankfurt.[358]

Ideological shifts alone were not responsible for generating greater misery for widows, however. Toward the end of this period the devastation of the Thirty Years' War (1618-48) had a negative impact on the lives of many ordinary people, including widows.[359] Widows' poverty seems to deepen at this time. For example, in the years 1619 and 1657, widows comprised 51% of the poorest taxpayers in Munich.[360] There is, moreover, continuity as well as change on the level of ideology. While widows continued to serve as a symbol of poverty and vulnerability, the ruler ideology that derived validation from assisting them, a legacy from the ancient Near East, continued to be strongly felt, and was generalized for all orders of society. Thus piety could be a source of empowerment.[361]

German widows and freedom of movement

Some developments in this period met with resistance. Widows of master craftsmen objected, at times fiercely, to the new limitations placed on their rights to continue operation of their husbands' shops, which were among the very first of the new restrictions on women's participation in the trades and crafts to be laid down.[362] Despite the obstacles placed before them, women of all marital statuses were often involved in litigation, both as

3. Late medieval and early modern England and Germany

plaintiffs and defendants, in a wide range of cases that extended outward from strictly family and marriage matters.[363] Individual widows made appeals to all sorts of authorities, including ducal courts, city councils and guild officials, asking for release from the ever-growing restrictions placed on them and using a variety of arguments, including the assertion of widows' rights as a general principle.[364] Making a plea did not automatically spell success, however.[365] The influence of received opinion could be decisive even in the face of a woman's superb intelligence and social skills, and at times her elevated socio-economic status as well.[366]

Women were denied the vote in both city and guild elections and could not serve in an elective office, such as city councilman or mayor. These were, of course, traditional exclusions for which sixteenth-century male intellectuals found convenient justification in Roman law and Greek philosophy.[367] Otherwise, women, at least those with property, had rights as citizens, and enjoyed a status that many a property-less male, who were usually not citizens, might envy. Widows, as citizens, might be called on to contribute to the defence of their town.[368] Women might be, and often were, appointed as minor public officials. In many cases they were married to public officials and, like their husbands, made to take an oath of office, since they too carried out the responsibilities associated with his position (for example, running the town jail or a hospital), the range of which at times was rather broad. Like widows of masters running their shops, such women might continue in the office even after the death of their husbands, but only on application, and were granted this privilege out of a mix of considerations of charity and self-interest, the latter grounded in a desire to avoid burdening the welfare rolls.[369] Despite their lack of political rights, widowhood offered women the status closest to that enjoyed by men, and some of the more privileged among them, at that.[370]

Widows were in many cases inclined to participate in religious life, often in the context of quasi-lay organizations known as soul houses, which provided support in exchange for prayer for the souls of the founders.[371] In pre-Reformation Munich, the composition of such religious communities was decidedly mixed, including widows, aging female servants and women abandoned by their husbands and/or without a home.[372] Widows often took vows and entered convents, creating so much concern in late fifteenth-century Strasbourg that the city council intervened to place limits on how much property they could bring with them or leave at the time of death.[373] Before the Reformation, and in Catholic areas afterwards, different forms of religious experience were available to women, as ordinary laypersons, vowesses or nuns. Some abbesses were powerful and independent, answering only to the emperor himself.[374] Widows were also prominently engaged in the care of the poor and the sick, many of whom themselves were widows.[375]

Late medieval German cities had a fairly large percentage of their households headed by or composed of women, many of whom were widows.

In part, this was a reflection of the urban gender imbalance that prevailed at the time in many places and persisted into the early modern period.[376] As seen in the previous sections, such households were at all times economically vulnerable, and after 1500 were increasingly liable in some places to legal sanction, as the male-headed version increasingly received exclusive official and non-official endorsement and protection.

Reputation was a different matter for men and women. Young men could wander through the streets of the city by night without penalty, but such behaviour by women would encourage their identification as prostitutes.[377] Wives were expected to exercise care in exiting the house or admitting visitors in their husbands' absence.[378] Widows, even or especially as heads of households, were routinely subject to the stares and disapproving talk of authorities, neighbours and relatives.[379] Vulnerability to various forms of harassment as well as to rape was commonplace.[380] Widows found some scope for activity in the context of the market and the coffee klatsch.[381] In dress, they closely resembled nuns, at least ideally.[382] The Roman and German traditions were in conflict over the punishment of a widow for non-marital sex, which might be defined as adultery, on the theory that she had betrayed her late husband, but overall the more lenient German rules prevailed, and such acts, although illegal, effectively went unpunished, except that they might jeopardize chances at remarriage.[383]

The medieval debate over women's nature and role known as the *Querelle des Dames* was popular in Germany, as elsewhere in Europe.[384] This was important in spreading ideas and representations of widows, as well as of women in general. As in England, a kind of dual stereotype prevailed for widows. The figure of the poor, weak, and vulnerable widow was familiar, and provoked much genuine sympathy. The poverty of widows was a familiar aspect of the everyday experience of social reality, but also over-determined by the biblical tradition, which lent a timelessness to this quality. The poor widow was not only part of lived experience but also a social construct, and even something of a tautology at that.[385]

The impact of this stereotype on widows was not exclusively negative. 'Poor' widows were routinely deemed worthy of support.[386] In fact, requests to city councils by the widows of master craftsmen, stressing their poverty and need, and appealing in this way to their sense of Christian charity, stood a far better chance of success than those that argued the existence of a right.[387] The same held for widows applying to a council (or even to a regional authority such as a duke) for a variety of means of assistance, such as for a position as employment agent, for relief in a quarrel with members of a guild, for a license to run a tavern or market stand, or for an exemption from some of the restrictions imposed on them in operating a shop. In these appeals, they frequently enjoyed success even where we have reason to believe that their claims about weakness and vulnerability were not literally true.[388] The most pathetic pleas tended to be the most

3. Late medieval and early modern England and Germany

effective.[389] Even noble widows, in appealing to the powerful, were able to rely, with success in many cases, on the rhetorical association of weakness and vulnerability with widowhood when they were anything themselves but weak and vulnerable.[390] In life, as well as in literature, moral considerations tended to eclipse economic or legal ones, at least in the matter of rhetorical presentation.[391]

The other chief stereotype was the bad widow, uncontrolled in her sexuality and also predatory, on the prowl for a young man to marry and dominate. The widow cast in this role was considered repulsive, but the true source of repulsion appears to be female hypogamy, where a wealthier, older and/or more powerful woman dominated her lower-status husband.[392] Men's fear of submitting to women's lust was so palpable as to be reflected in the everyday language of sexuality and its popular visual representations, such as woodcuts showing men in cages being jeered by women who have ensnared them.[393] Older women were widely deemed to be in the grip of an insatiable lust, and capable at the same time of bringing young men to moral and financial ruin.[394] Men were told to avoid widows as marriage partners.[395] Widows and divorced women were often imagined as procuresses, while widows and midwives were configured as witches. Widows and their sexuality were particular objects of concern, so it is not surprising to find suspicion falling on them from various quarters, including family and neighbours, as well as church and state authorities.[396]

Male anxiety manifested itself in the belief that many a widow was all too happy at the death of her husband, if she did not in fact play an active role in bringing this about, and the Widow of Ephesus story, elaborated in many versions, beginning as early as 1412, enjoyed quite a vogue.[397] Its origins in Germany have been traced to the French medieval literary tradition, from where it carried over to collections of moralizing stories, such as *The Seven Sages*, and to new forms of popular literature, especially the genre of bawdy tales, known as the *Schwank*, that originated in the late medieval period. In such contexts this figure not only functions as a negative widow type but more broadly as a subtype of a negative female type, an exaggeratedly lustful, predatory widow who at best only pretends to mourn for her deceased husband and readily exploits the opportunities presented by her new-found freedom. This representation, bordering on caricature, is thought to have developed in part as a reaction, especially among the lower orders, to the positive portrayal of women and widows in earlier medieval German literature, especially epic, an eminently elite genre.[398]

Bernhard Jussen has rightly criticized the tendency of modern scholars to treat the story of the Widow of Ephesus as a supracultural, universal, archetypical set of male fantasies about female sexuality. The specific cultural context of each retelling of the tale is of crucial importance, and its misogyny, or at any rate the degree of its misogyny, is certainly not something fixed and foreordained. Moreover, the ideal of widowhood had significantly changed from the Roman conception – widowhood as a brief phase – to the medieval – widowhood as a career.[399] This view has considerable merit. In my view, however, the lack of explicit sexual content in some medieval versions may not be the end of the story. Often such content is strongly implied, sometimes through euphemism: 'consoling' the widow means more than drying her tears, for example. Remarriage, in a Christian cultural context, is often a simple stand-in for sex, in part because it is frequently assumed to be motivated by lust. The actual or potential fact of hypogamy typically aggravates matters, as in the original versions; sometimes the widow weds a complete stranger. The differences and variations are, at the same time, often not without significance. Suicide is more than an extravagant gesture but a grave sin as well, despite Jerome's extremism on the subject. To be sure, male anxieties about a wife's sexual betrayal after a man's death are remarkably durable, even after the Reformation. What lends the story of the Widow of Ephesus to almost endless cultural adaptation is that it presented a series of useful choices, not all of which were consistently available, however. One could (sometimes) choose a misogynist reading of Petronius's satirical text over a widow-friendly one, one could (sometimes) choose the more obviously misogynist Phaedrus over Petronius, or one could (almost always) take the misogynist tradition and make it more misogynist, either by heightening the element of sexual outrage or the degree of maltreatment accorded the husband's corpse, or both.

Moral teaching on widows in the medieval and early modern periods depended heavily on Jerome's articulation in the late fourth century of three moral statuses for women: virgins, wives and widows. By the late medieval period these had developed into legal and sociological categories as well, so that a woman's marital status defined her place in society regardless of her social rank or wealth.[400] Not surprisingly, Jerome's influence continued to loom large in the moralizing works of the age, even as efforts were made to soften the implications of his hostility to the remarriage of widows. This period saw, in a sense, a re-valorization, specifically for women, of Jerome's categories, which earlier in the Middle Ages had sometimes been applied to men as well as women, religious and lay, in other words, all of Christian society. Given Jerome's zeal for sexual continence, it is not surprising to find such slippage already present in his writing, as he urges lay Christians to observe the rules set for ascetics of both sexes.[401] Now we find a return to Jerome's idea of a strictly female classification, which, however, more clearly distinguishes between religious and lay, so that, for example, Juan Luis Vives can posit virgin, wife and widow as phases of the Christian (lay)woman's life cycle.

Two German-language medieval moralizing texts devoted to widows that have been intensely studied are a sermon on marriage attributed to the thirteenth-century Franciscan Berthold von Regensburg and a moral

3. Late medieval and early modern England and Germany

treatise on widowhood written by the Carthusian Erhart Groß in 1446 in the form of a dialogue between a monk and a widow. In the sermon, the loss of a husband is viewed as disastrous for a woman, prejudicing her status in society and exposing her to exploitation, yet, following Jerome, the author postulates a benefit in terms of a prospectively enhanced reward after death, sixtyfold, to be precise. Ideally, the marriage bond survives a husband's death, and the widow is the person chiefly responsible for the care of his soul. At the same time, the author shares the traditional concerns of Church authors with widows' libido and its implications for her ability to lead a chaste life, and so with a reference to *1 Corinthians* he concedes the possibility of remarriage. Otherwise, widows should enter the cloister. The alternatives anticipate the theme of *aut murus aut maritus* ('either cloister or husband') propagated by the Council of Trent, although they are not really reconciled in a logical sense.[402] The allowance for remarriage has the appearance of a concession to lay practice, at least upper-class practice, and the tension with the ideal of 'soul care' for the decedent husband emerges as an unresolved and for the author perhaps unresolvable dilemma between ideal and reality, or perhaps between two ideals, one favoured by clerics and monastics, the other by the laity.[403]

Erhart Groß lays out much the same dilemma, but in large part because he takes seriously the idea that a widow can live chastely in society, the contrast is softened somewhat. Groß, although sensitive to traditional concerns that widows' sexual experience made them even more vulnerable to desire than never-married women, is prepared to recognize the earthly advantages of the widowed state, such as independence of action, as well as freedom from fear of the dangers and uncertainty associated with a husband's moods, his death and her pregnancy. He discards Jerome's counsel to a widow to turn away from her family as too extreme and even discounts his differential of heavenly reward for virgins, wives and widows, so that they all receive the same benefits in the world to come, even as he retains the categories themselves. Groß is, of course, influenced by *1 Timothy*, and agrees with its advice to younger widows to remarry, although he in a sense rewrites this text to include a category of widows without children who merit particular attention. In defiance of the medical tradition inherited from antiquity, he insists that abstinence from sex is, or can be, healthy. Overall he is concerned to set forth for widows in the world a programme of prayer, fasting and self-denial, coupled with avoidance of inappropriate behaviour in dress and association with men, that allows them a lifestyle characterized by both dignity and independence. For Groß, the widow's ideal of poverty is not to be equated with misery, and he even allows her the consumption of wine within measure. Remarriage remains an option for those not suited for this regimen, but neither this nor the cloister is assumed to be the respectable choice of the religiously motivated laywoman, who is encouraged to take responsibility for

Widows and Patriarchy

her own comportment and not to be excessively concerned with what others might think.[404]

The briefer moralizing works on widows from the late medieval period, such as those written by Heinrich der Teichner, Michael Beheim, Albrecht von Eyb and the unknown author of the social satire *Des Teufels Netz* focus on similar themes, especially on the tension between the ideal of loyalty, above all sexual loyalty, owed to the decedent husband and fears of the sexual vulnerability of women living without male protectors. The first aspect manifests itself in the emphasis on the widow's duty of 'soul care', the second in a concession of the possibility of her remarriage. A highly selective reading of the tradition marks this literature, with its strong preference above all for *1 Timothy* and Jerome as authorities. Scripture famously does not sanction the eternal devotion of a widow to her dead husband; in fact, Jesus rather discourages this in denying the existence of marriage at the Last Judgment,[405] a passage routinely ignored in writing about widows in this period. Instead, authority for the importance of this devotion is sought in the world of nature, for example, the relentlessly monogamous behaviour attributed to the turtledove by Heinrich der Teichner. The exclusive and almost aggressive reliance on a male perspective in this literature is remarkable even in the context of a tradition that is the product entirely of men.[406]

The same tension between an ideal of loyalty to the dead and the needs of the living, reflected in moralizing literature of the later Middle Ages that is heavily indebted to Jerome,[407] also appears in late medieval folklore, a tradition if anything even more marked by male anxiety over the sexuality of widows. Here an important influence, resisted by the theologians, was the legacy of ancient medicine. Although Galen and the Hippocratics differed on the rationale, they agreed that sex was necessary for preserving the health of adult women, thus contributing to the assumption, fully accepted by this popular tradition, that widows were 'by nature' sexually insatiable and incapable of chastity. This reinforced the perspective that viewed women, especially widows, as inherently lascivious, and more so than men.[408]

Popular literature evinces an enhanced male anxiety about widows' potential for disorderliness after 1500.[409] A popular song from the sixteenth century deplores the insincere grief of widows. The contemporary writer Hans Sachs, by way of contrast, praises the loyalty of wives in antiquity who show their devotion in, among other things, choosing suicide after the deaths of their husbands, and concentrates on virtuous widows in his (self-described) comedies (one, for example, is devoted to Judith, another to the Widow of Sarepta).[410] Even Sachs, however, tends to portray widows in overwhelmingly negative terms as foolish and faithless in his satirical works.[411]

In the sixteenth century, Reformers began to undermine the clarity postulated by the threefold categorization of virgins, wives and widows in

3. Late medieval and early modern England and Germany

its application to laywomen. The focus of their attacks was of course clerical and religious celibacy. But they might be argued to embrace, if only by implication, even 'the priesthood of all believers'.[412] These polemics were bound to have an impact on widows and their place in society, an impact that was not limited to Protestant areas, as they had a decided influence on the thinking of Catholic exponents of Counter-Reform. Aegidius Albertinus, secretary to Maximilian I, ruler of Bavaria in the early seventeenth century, shared the suspicions entertained by Protestants over the sexual behaviour of nuns. Like Jerome, he did not hesitate to assert the virtue of pre-Christian pagan women in castigating contemporary vice. For him, however, the categories of social and sexual status broke down into female virginity, marriage and clerical celibacy.[413] In this scheme there was no room for widows, as in the traditional arrangement inherited from Jerome. Geminianus Monachensis, the seventeenth-century Counter-Reformation preacher from Munich, did manage to accommodate them in his definition of the sexual estates: ecclesiastical celibacy, virginity/widowhood, and, finally, marriage.[414] Even so, by lumping widows, still in the second rank, with never-married women he appears to diminish their importance. It is striking how the effacement of Jerome's longstanding influence had such negative consequences for women.

Attacks of Reformers on the canon law of marriage, clerical celibacy and prostitution aimed at (re)valorizing the marriage ideal.[415] Brothels and convents represented in different ways the power of women, something much feared and deplored.[416] The malign effects that this campaign had on widowhood were less intentional than, by and large, a matter of collateral damage, with widows the proverbial innocent bystanders. Widows, as sexually experienced women not subject to male authority, were, not surprisingly, considered a threat to the moral and social order. All sex outside of marriage was condemned (it is perhaps not too much to say it was demonized) as sinful. Before the Reformation the nunnery offered a sort of counter-marriage ideal for women that Luther, for example, assailed in his assertion of the status of wife and mother as the only desirable one for women.[417]

The Catholic response, crystallized in the Council of Trent's slogan '*aut murus aut maritus*' ('either cloister or husband') to prescribe the destiny of women, promised no better, although some were able to rally around the force of tradition and the figure of Mary to argue for female activism, at least in the religious life.[418] Within convents, now prone to physical as well as ideological demarcation, the model of the male-headed household came to prevail, depriving many religious women of their former autonomy.[419] Options for widows narrowed in important respects. For example, the convents that welcomed widows in pre-Reformation Munich were now accessible only to never-married women, in a curious reassertion of a principle of celibate hierarchy that hearkened back to Jerome.[420] Brothels were closed in Catholic, as well as Protestant areas, an extreme solution not followed in all areas of Counter-Reformation Europe.[421] It was not just economic necessity, but an altered religious sensibility, that put pressure on widows to find new partners, especially in Protestant areas.[422]

The Reformers tended to ignore widows, or simply to recommend they be married. Luther himself has relatively little to say about them. His letters to widows (eight out of the 64 we know he addressed to women) are certainly full of sympathy and support. He includes them, although he does not accord them any special status, in his ideal household. This was supposed to absorb and care for widows and other anomalous persons. On the authority of *1 Timothy* he prescribes remarriage for younger widows (after a year), and rejects this for older ones, who are assigned religious duties but not conceded the cachet that attached to celibacy before Reform. The Reformer Johannes Spangenberg amplifies this thinking in a sermon for a widow he composed in 1549.[423] Spangenberg relies on *1 Timothy* to urge remarriage for younger widows, but not as a concession to female sexual vulnerability, as the tradition had it. Now instead marriage is the state to be preferred for all, or all but the oldest widows. He expresses great sympathy for the state of misery and dependency shared by many widows.[424] In this he resembles the Spanish humanist Juan Luis Vives, whose work *De Institutione Feminae Christianae* was translated into German by Christoph Bruno in 1544, although of course Vives himself remains within the Catholic tradition on the question of celibacy and, more moderately, remarriage.[425]

The Reformers' assertion of male authority as the foundation of their programme of moral renewal had as its corollary an attack on all forms of female ascendancy, not just nuns administering their own convents. This was grounded in fears of women living apart (or 'under their own smoke', as the contemporary phrase had it), now no longer (simply) an economic but a moral concern.[426] In this way discrimination against single women extended from aliens to citizens.[427] In times of rapid change, the social and legal status of all women might be rendered precarious, and, indeed, women regardless of their marital status in Reformation Germany were suspected of being actually or potentially sexually promiscuous. Unmarried women were especially vulnerable to such fears, however, and they easily became the objects of suspicion, surveillance and gossip.[428] In 1613 a widow in Bacharach, for example, was imprisoned for frequenting back streets in doubtful company and for rejecting a suitor on the ground he was excessively religious.[429] Women's sex drive was thought to increase with age, raising the ante of suspicion and anxiety regarding widows.[430] The equitable emphasis on a single standard of sexual behaviour for men and women led to attempts at its implementation that were decidedly misogynistic.[431]

Although it had its antecedents, the witch craze was a phenomenon not so much of the medieval as of the early modern period.[432] Particularly after 1560, both Protestants and Catholics tended to view older women, espe-

3. Late medieval and early modern England and Germany

cially widows, as likely practitioners of dangerous magic and sorcery.[433] The witch played a perverted version of the ideal woman's role, a mother's evil twin, infertile yet sexually insatiable, present in the house, often as a servant, but divorced, especially as an older widow, from the structure of the household.[434] Laws against witchcraft were typically framed as gender-neutral, but their enforcement in actual fact, as well as the representation of the witch in non-legal literature, was a different matter altogether.[435]

The Reformers promised a spiritual equality for women that did not of course translate into political or social equality. This deficit was most apparent when women were criticized for engaging in forms of religious self-expression that were deemed public, and therefore properly the province of males. The Reformation did create new roles for women, among which were pastor's wife, domestic missionary and religious polemicist.[436] But even in the religious sphere as narrowly defined, notions of female inferiority tended to outweigh the ideal of equality. Protestant women writers of the sixteenth and seventeenth centuries were sometimes disinclined to praise marriage itself, and even resisted the insistent pro-matrimonial ideology of the new faith. They idealized as a role for themselves a kind of spiritual motherhood, consistent with the practice of celibacy, which helps explain the paradoxical interest in Lutheran convents characteristic of the age.[437] One now finds noble widows supporting the cause of Reform through their writings, including consolations composed for widows. It is striking in this context to find a widow invoking *1 Timothy* as part of an argument against remarriage, as the learned sixteenth-century aristocrat Elisabeth von Braunschweig-Lüneberg does in her book of consolation for widows.[438]

One important exception to the trend disfavouring widows in the early modern period is found among the nobility. There are many examples of widows in the middling to smaller German states who exercised ruling power and acted as guardians until their sons reached the age of majority. Others directed convents as abbesses. A widow whose family or who herself had made a proper widow provisioning by means of a marriage contract would find herself adequately supported as the legal and economic authority (within limits, that in part depended on the widow's rank) of a small territorial widow residence. In this way economic security was intimately linked with freedom of action. On this level of society, a widow's independence functioned as a class marker, a fact that explains why families provided for them as they did. Certainly the example of these women proves that not all widows formed part of a marginal group, a point that cannot receive sufficient emphasis.[439]

Many of these widows were formidable types, promoting the arts, supporting the Church or, later, furthering the cause of the Reformation. They were also, not surprisingly, adept at advancing the political and economic interests of their families.[440] The promotion of culture, especially in the context of memorializing a decedent husband, aimed, in an aristocratic milieu, not just at moral validation but also at securing political legitimacy.[441] Conflicts with family members, especially in-laws and sons, above all stepsons, and/or children's guardians, were not an uncommon experience for such women.[442] Contingencies such as an awkward personality, bad decisions, and ill luck could cause difficulties even for a highly privileged widow.[443] Sometimes several factors combined, such as psychological and physical problems, disagreements with family members, and financial pressures, to produce a decidedly adverse outcome. Such was the case for Barbara Gräfin von Württemberg-Mömpelgard (1536-97). She suffered from depression, migraine headaches and what today we would describe as anger management issues. Her reputation was not helped by her affair with a court official. It is fair to say that noble widows displayed a great range of personal styles, ranging from the highly active and engaged to the deeply passive and withdrawn.[444] More than most widows, they themselves enjoyed a freedom of action sufficient to have had a decisive impact on their overall success or failure as single women.

Reform, like Christianity itself, both helped and hurt women.[445] But after the initial revolutionary period women's voices are heard less and less in the sequel, a process that was repeated with the rise of new radical groups. Gender now began to trump social class, financial situation and personal qualities as women were identified first and foremost as women.[446] The public role of women in worship was all but eclipsed under Protestantism.[447] The newly gendered roles assigned spouses were a broader sign of this trend.[448] Even citizenship was increasingly conceived in gendered terms, as women begin to emerge more and more as decidedly second-class citizens.[449] Equality was all but impossible in the reconfiguration of the household, with the new emphasis placed on the temporal and spiritual authority of its male head.[450]

Religion, under the aegis of Reform, was something ideally managed and even imposed by men.[451] The hierarchical household was assumed to be necessary for the maintenance of discipline and order.[452] Women's authority was ideally derivative where it was acknowledged at all. Women were regarded as the problem, not as a part of the solution, to the challenges confronting society: an unceasing menace to economic, moral, social and political order.[453] In Catholic as well as Protestant areas the interest of the state was seen to align with that of male heads of households, as the former assisted the latter in promoting important changes in family, marriage and inheritance law.[454] A kind of competitive dynamic developed among the different forms of Christianity, largely to the detriment of women, and gender relations in general. The disorder introduced by the circumstances associated with the Thirty Years' War only exacerbated the tendency toward repression, while the Enlightenment was to reinforce the effects of absolutist regulation.[455]

The household and/or workshop, newly (re)valorized, was now a site of social control, and women, whether wives, widows or never-married, were

3. Late medieval and early modern England and Germany

its most obvious objects.[456] The city council in Augsburg, for example, was particularly concerned with what it considered the civic anomaly of the household headed by a female in the context of the lower orders and non-citizens.[457] Marriage was placed at the centre of the economic, social and political order, even as the household was over the course of time removed from the public sphere.[458] Both Catholic and Protestant regimes aimed at the domestication of married women. Once Reformers successfully characterized sexual desire as ineluctable, attempts at repression followed, which did not always respect religious lines. Women increasingly saw membership in a patriarchal household associated in a more exclusive way with respectability. The increased concern with the sexuality of single women, especially those of the lower classes, tended to identify their behaviour with prostitution. So alternatives to married life experienced a decline. An emphasis on the transformation of marriage in the age of Reform should not obscure the radical changes effected on prostitution, virginity (mostly, although not exclusively, in Catholic areas), and the single life in general.[459] The new rules on guardians, domicile and work hardly allowed widows to escape the implications of these trends.

This complex and ambitious ideal almost inevitably ran aground on the reef of harsh reality. Male fears about women's physical mobility represented a clash between the principle of enclosure and the economically grounded need for women to leave the house, especially among the middle and lower orders.[460] The authorities never enjoyed much success in reducing the numbers of female-headed households. Many men were simply unequal to the challenge posed by the authority granted to them. The archives abound in tales of husbandly drunkenness and domestic violence of an extreme sort.[461] Reformers ablaze with the ideal of the male head of household (in German, *Hausvater*) were compelled to confront a disappointing reality in the person of the violent, drunken, promiscuous, lazy, loutish, wasteful, absent, and, worst of all, irreligious adult male.[462] Many men found the demands of patriarchy challenging, so that male anxiety and vulnerability is paramount in this period.[463] The clash of ideal and reality encouraged a deep pessimism manifested, for example, on the part of the Augsburg City Council regarding the moral quality of married life. Close intervention to remedy the situation tended to produce results opposite to those intended.[464] The fragility of patriarchal honour was nowhere more apparent than in the context of its vigorous assertion. Widows were hardly poised to benefit from this fact.

German widows and remarriage

A mix of similar factors of economics, demography, ideology and the age of the prospective spouses played a role in the remarriage of widows in late medieval and early modern Germany as elsewhere.[465] Marriage remained an attractive option for many women because of its decisive role in shaping their status and social identity.[466] It also provided economic security and companionship. Other factors worked against a decision to remarry. As seen above, the loss of child custody attendant on remarriage was a strong disincentive. The widows of merchants, who were relatively well placed to carry on the family business without a husband, were less interested in seeking a new partner than others, although some yielded to the desire for children, especially if they were childless in their first marriage, or to a yearning for companionship.[467] Well-off widows in late medieval Freiburg, for example, seem to have been disinclined to seek new husbands.[468] The adverse consequences of warfare were not just economic in nature but felt in the reduced number of potential marriage partners, as with the Thirty Years' War (1618-48).[469] Criticism of widows' desire for remarriage as a manifestation of lust appears alongside other trends in late medieval and early modern popular literature.[470]

Matters stood differently for widows in the sub-princely high nobility of this period, to judge from the results of study devoted to southwest-central Germany in the late Middle Ages. Here we find important pressures, above all, a sense of insecurity deriving from contestation of their entitlements as widows, that prompted many widows to remarry, at times beneath their status. They seem to have enjoyed great freedom to do so, in contrast to their experience with first marriages, which were largely arranged by their fathers and families. Their freedom in choosing a new husband is reflected in concerns, sometimes realized in actual fact, on the part of a decedent husband's family that a political and/or military rival would be able to take possession of a widow residence, in the form of a strategically placed fortification, along with significant assets of an economic nature belonging to the family, as a consequence of marrying a noble widow. This prompted some efforts to discourage widow remarriage among this group or at least to attenuate its impact. A widow's birth family might pressure a widow to remarry or not to do so, depending on its perception of its interests. The wealth deriving from her widow's pension and other assets made her an attractive marriage prospect for many. Rates of remarriage for this group were correspondingly high.[471]

The only significant change among this same sector of the nobility during this period occurred with women's freedom of choice in first marriages, which seems to have increased in the early modern age. Widows from this group in southwestern Germany could not in any case be compelled to accept a father's, or a family's, candidate for a new husband and continued to enjoy the freedom to pursue their own preferences instead.[472]

The ideal of celibate widowhood was powerful enough to sustain itself even in the teeth of Protestant pro-matrimonial ideology, so that some widows remained unmarried, despite the fact that financial hardship by itself provided them with a motive to marry again. All the same, it is difficult to believe that the new faith had no effect in this area.[473] Marriage

3. Late medieval and early modern England and Germany

now more than ever was considered the only appropriate calling for women. Women's continuing interest in marriage, as well as their vulnerability in the matter, is suggested by their overwhelming predominance as plaintiffs in suits over promises of marriage, to judge from a sample from Munich extending over the late sixteenth and early seventeenth centuries. Widows as well as never-married women numbered among the complainants.[474]

The remarriage of widows nevertheless remained a delicate subject in the sixteenth century.[475] Even some Protestants had doubts about its advisability. Male sexual jealousy, suspicion of women and Christian hostility to sex combined to discourage the practice in some quarters.[476] The ambivalence over remarriage of widows balanced concerns with disloyalty to a deceased husband against fears of women's independence.[477]

Age may have been the most important factor in promoting or discouraging remarriage of German widows overall, although it was closely linked to class, or at least wealth, in a manner that often does not allow us neatly to separate the two.[478] Widows over 50 (and even 40) years of age tended not to remarry, whether because their economic status allowed them to get by on their own or they simply could not find a new partner.[479] Younger, propertied widows at times found it difficult to remain single.[480] Remarriage seems to have been relatively more common among the younger widows of Protestant pastors. On the other hand, financial provision eventually had to be made for older ones.[481] Princes, both secular and ecclesiastical, might reward supporters with an arranged marriage either to an heiress or to a rich widow.[482] Among peasants younger widows with property were much sought after.[483] Remarriage does not seem to have been uncommon, at least for younger widows and for men of various ages.[484]

Older women did not in all places and at all times outnumber older men, although widows do seem to have been more numerous than widowers.[485] This was partly because widowers tended to remarry more often and more quickly than widows, and at times in overwhelmingly greater percentages.[486] As elsewhere, widowers preferred younger women, especially never-married women, as new wives.[487] They married so quickly that they often ignored the regulations imposing a delay from the date of spouse's death – for both sexes – on remarriage, a delay that varied from place to place (nine months or a year was common, at least in Protestant areas; in 1563, Nuremberg required only three months), although often cohabitation might for a time substitute for marriage. Widows also ignored such rules, which do not seem to have been zealously enforced at law.[488] As in England, the rules imposing a mourning period before remarriage were of recent vintage. In fact, in the late medieval period some guilds had demanded the remarriage of a master's widow within a set time.[489] In sum, the relative numbers of older men and women did not determine the number of widows who remarried as much as did the (re)marrying behaviour of men.[490]

Widows and Patriarchy

A nice counter-example to the general trend, drawn from the sub-princely high nobility of southwest-central Germany in the late medieval period, supports this point. Men, typically much older than their wives at time of first marriage, tended to predecease them. Surviving husbands, however, tended to remarry only if their marriage had produced no sons, or in some cases no more than one son. Widows from this group show a relatively high rate of remarriage, provided they were still of childbearing age, meaning here younger than 40.[491] Such gender-differentiated behaviour regarding remarriage had an impact on the numbers of widows within this social group, although it can hardly have been significant for society at large.

As seen in the previous section there was a great concern with female hypogamy, much of which centred around widows. Limits were placed on the ability of widows to marry non-citizens or 'foreigners' in Speyer, Strasbourg and elsewhere.[492] So we find the Augsburg City Council in 1562 pleading with the widows and daughters of master craftsmen to observe a kind of civic endogamy.[493] There were important exceptions, however. Marriage among the daughters of the southwest German nobility in the early modern period was characterized by hypogamy both ideally and in actual fact. One consequence was that the size of dowries remained relatively small; another was that wealthy but lower-status widows found it difficult to attract marriage partners from this stratum.[494] Marriage with the widow of a master craftsman represented an important opportunity for social and economic upward mobility for journeymen. This was encouraged by the guilds, although their campaign to curtail the rights of such widows worked at cross-purposes to this end.[495] Despite its manifest importance, marriage motivated by financial motives was denigrated by idealists as immoral.[496] Cases in which a widow deceived a new marriage prospect with the false pretence of wealth were not unknown.[497]

Although there was no equivalent to English coverture, a widow's goods would pass into her new husband's control, or even, where common property regimes existed for spouses, his ownership.[498] To meet this concern, a late Roman legal rule was adopted by some authorities that transformed, on remarriage, ownership of property from a first marriage into a usufruct for the surviving spouse, with ownership passing to the children from that union. Although it technically applied both to widows and widowers, widows tended to be disadvantaged more in practice, and they alone lost access to their children's property on remarriage.[499]

Reforming widows

What, by way of summary and conclusion, can we say about the impact of the changes that occurred during the early modern period on the status and role of widows in England and Germany?

There was a time when historians thought the Reformation was good

3. Late medieval and early modern England and Germany

for women.[500] Over the past 20 years or so this idea has been the object of withering criticism by feminist scholars. Some have provocatively described the late medieval period as a 'Golden Age' for women, while others characterize the sixteenth century as a period of repression and even despair.[501] Almost inevitably a reaction has set in determined to emphasize the benefits of Reform for women, if at times somewhat in the spirit of describing the silver lining to a very dark cloud.[502]

The question of the impact of the Reformation on women is complex, even if we try to limit its focus to widows. Important questions remain. Was the situation of women all that privileged in the late Middle Ages? Were all or even most women really affected by the changes of the early modern period? Was this transition marked as much or more by continuity as by change in its impact on men and women of varying statuses? Were the changes that did occur caused largely by developments strictly outside the sphere of religion? Were there important differences in outcome between England and Germany?

No definitive answers can be posed to these questions here. It is sufficiently clear that widows were more vulnerable to the impact of change than most women. We have seen good reason for caution in assuming a huge number of widows in this period. There was never a true Golden Age for widows (or for anyone else). The late Middle Ages, in both England and Germany, do seem, however, to have offered such women an unusually high degree of both economic opportunity and personal freedom. Protections for widows spelled out in the letter of the law were not always respected in actual fact, something true in all of the periods under study.

The legal safeguards themselves were eroded considerably during the early modern period. This had important consequences for the content of widowhood as a category of marital status. In Germany marriage did not eclipse the legal identity of the wife to the extent it did in England, which meant that the status of widow was less privileged by contrast. Their state was, all the same, a mixture of independence and dependency. With the passage of time, the latter attribute received increasing emphasis in both places.

Economic opportunities for widows in both countries contracted during the early modern period. This spelled another kind of change in the content of widowhood as a category of marital status. Most widows were poorer than they had been as wives, and for many, if not the majority, this fact spelled real hardship.

The twin stereotypes of sorrowing and merry widow flourished throughout the late Middle Ages, and into the early modern period, when the popularity of the latter was especially prominent. The social meaning attached to widowhood changed for the worse. Remarriage rates for widows were driven more by the marrying behaviour of males than by the absolute numbers of men and women at various age levels. These rates were not automatically and inevitably tied to economic prosperity or the lack of it, which does not render such a link irrelevant, however. The Reformation had by and large an adverse impact on widows and women in general in both countries, regardless of creed. Marriage was revalorized at the expense of the single life, as was the ideal of the household headed by a male. Not all of the influences at work were fully or primarily religious in nature, as can be seen from the deterioration in the economic privileges accorded widows. For complex reasons, meaning more than just religious ones, widow remarriage seems to have remained over the long term at a higher rate in Germany than in England, where from the early seventeenth century it went into a steep decline. Despite the challenges they faced, many widows prospered, in defiance of stereotypes and ideological imposition.

4
Modern England and the United States

England and the United States

Our focus starts, again, on England (largely although this time not totally to the exclusion of Scotland and Wales), now in the period ranging approximately from 1850 to 1925. There are few really significant changes in the law affecting widows and more generally women in the two centuries between the end of the period examined in the previous chapter, that is, 1650, and 1850. Although the various systems of law described in the previous chapter still existed, the customary and ecclesiastical had yielded much ground to the nation-wide systems (or system) of common law and equity in the seventeenth and eighteenth centuries. Social and economic change is a different matter, as the growth of capitalism, industrialization and urbanization was matched by fundamental transformations in the size, composition and lifestyle of the middle and working classes. Many of the most important changes in these areas occurred precisely during this 75-year window, however. The authoritarian model of state and family promoted by the Reformation that privileged men was still very much in evidence in the mid-nineteenth century.

By the mid-1920s, on the other hand, this picture had changed profoundly. Discussion of this 75-year period allows us to trace some of the major steps in the gradual but decisive legal emancipation of English women and to learn of its impact on widows. Of course, the story does not end in 1925, but by then wives could sue for divorce from their husbands on equal terms, mothers enjoyed by statute rights identical to those of fathers regarding the custody of children, and women (or at least many of them) had the vote.[1] Common law courts had eclipsed those of the other three systems. Marital status still mattered for women's rights, but it ceased to be foundational, as it certainly had been before 1850 and remained for most if not all of this period. In the end, the fundamental legal categories of never-married, wife and widow virtually collapsed into one that more or less held for all women.

Much the same can be said for the United States at this time. Here too the period extending roughly from 1850 to 1925 witnessed basic changes in the legal status of women, beginning, in fact, as early as the late 1840s. The United States had famously derived much of its legal system, including the principle of wifely coverture, from the English, although with the important distinction that common law was supreme among the various types of law from the start. Not every colony established courts of equity, and where these survived their jurisdiction was eventually subsumed under that of the common law. Ecclesiastical and manorial courts did not find a home in the new world, apart from a very few brief experiments in the latter case. Other differences were not slow to emerge, sometimes at first partly inspired by a desire to mark a cultural difference with the quondam colonizer, but more often in response to a divergent set of political, social and economic conditions.

Private law in the United States has always been largely a matter of state law, and has historically shown great variation, not least in legal rules affecting women and widows in particular. America's territory was huge, its jurisdictions many, and until relatively recently few centralizing norms existed in this field, although the need for a national law of marriage was discussed for over 150 years before the actual appearance of anything remotely describable as such. There were 31 states in 1850, including California, which became a state that year, plus the District of Columbia and several territories, and 48 states in 1925, each with its own set of laws and independent jurisdiction, which displayed great variations in structure. The United States Constitution placed fewer restrictions on the growth of legal variety than one might expect. In the early twentieth century some states began to institute family courts, which played an important role in the experience at law of many women. This is one sign that legal change in different jurisdictions could take very different directions. New York, with its large population, central role in business and communications, and complex and numerous courts, produced more law than any other state for much of the period in question. By the end of the period, women had been granted many rights for the first time in private and public law, including, on the national level, the right to vote, in 1920.

The sheer bulk of sources increases exponentially in comparison with the early modern period, including such familiar types of evidence as letters, diaries, wills and court papers. Women were, in growing numbers, authors of these documents and came to make an increasingly significant contribution to literature, including the new genre of the novel. A flourishing tradition of women's fiction sprang up addressing such concerns as marriage and education, although this hardy exhausts the range of subject matter taken up by women authors, as the examples of Harriet Beecher Stowe and Edith Wharton will suggest. A new industry of women's magazines arose, and more and more women wrote works of non-fiction.

Numbers of widows

The period under study in this chapter, roughly 1850-1925, witnessed dramatic and relatively rapid changes above all in the areas of mortality and fertility. In brief, England and the United States, like other Western societies, passed from a regime characterized by high mortality and high

4. Modern England and the United States

fertility to one where low mortality and low fertility prevailed. This process, which historians have termed the demographic transition, has also emerged, since the second half of the twentieth century, in non-Western societies such as Japan and China. Although the timing, process, and causes of the transition have differed notably in various cultures and so have sparked lively scholarly debate, the results have been remarkably uniform. The entire phenomenon had a profound effect on the numbers and age distribution of widows in England and the United States during this period.

Since census data allow for more precision in estimating proportions of widows in various age groups, it is possible simply to summarize the relevant information instead of engaging in the more speculative reconstructions characteristic of previous chapters. There are some differences in the nineteenth century between Britain and the United States, but by 1900 mortality rates and life expectancy began to show a convergence. Simply put, in England the latter increased by about 10 years (from 41 to 51) in the last half of the nineteenth century.[2] The United States started its increase in life expectancy later, in the 1870s, but with similar results by the end of the century.[3] The Civil War (for the United States) and the First World War (especially for England) as well as the flu pandemic of 1918, caused huge spikes in mortality (in the case of war, this was true above all for males) that did not, however, derail long-term demographic trends.[4] The gendered differential in mortality was not large by today's standards.[5] For example, American women in 1920 could expect to outlive men by an average of 1.9 years.[6] English women in 1911-12 had an advantage of three years on average.[7] What all this means is that over the course of this period marriages increasingly lasted longer. But there was still a high incidence of widowed persons overall.

In England the mean age at first marriage for women kept roughly in the range of 25-26 in the last half of the nineteenth century, with a slight rise over time and regional as well as occupational variation. The age interval between spouses was generally just over a year.[8] The United States data show a somewhat lower mean age of 23-24 and a wider gap, of some three to four years, for the European-American population.[9] 'Mean age' here suggests a range of ages from the early to late twenties for both sexes, with women starting a bit earlier, in both countries. These estimates should not be taken to suggest that no difference existed between the elite and sub-elite. In fact, the latter typically married later.

There were in England, and to a lesser extent in the United States, large numbers of never-married women ('spinsters'), above all among the middle and upper classes, whose numbers swelled as the nineteenth century progressed, while fewer men chose to remain single.[10] In important ways, the profile of spinsters as a social problem fairly eclipsed that of widows.[11] Certainly, their existence reduced the sheer numbers of widows as a proportion of the overall population. In the late nineteenth and early part

107

of the twentieth century, divorce rates remained low in both countries, effectively blocking another exit from marriage and so having an indirect impact on the numbers of widows.[12]

Widows, as in other periods, seem to have been concentrated in urban areas, to judge from the data from nineteenth-century London, which show a high proportion of them.[13] It is perhaps worth pointing out, however, that there were groups and places in the United States where unmarried men prevailed in terms of sheer numbers. The mass immigration experienced by the United States for most of this period was characterized by a surplus of males.[14] A shortage of women plagued the far West for many years, helping to generate a distinct demographic regime.[15] This hardly means, however, that all women married young or indeed married at all.[16]

Remarriage of widows had been in a state of decline since the seventeenth century in England, a decline that continues over the course of this period. The 'greying' of the widowed population over time meant that relatively fewer and fewer of them remarried, a point that also holds for the United States. The effects of a drop in fertility, greater life expectancy and an increasing mortality gap between male and female seniors combined to generate more widows who were relatively advanced in age, both in absolute and relative terms. In part this is simply a function of the fact that in post-transition populations not only does life expectancy rise but also so does the proportion of the elderly overall, a phenomenon already very much in evidence for the period under study. This trend intensified over the course of the twentieth century, as widowhood became increasingly associated with age and less likely to befall women with dependent children.[17] The marrying behaviour of men also played a role in determining the numbers of widows, especially elderly widows, as we shall see below. Local studies from the late nineteenth-century United States show that up to one-third of women aged 55-64 were widows, a percentage that dramatically increases for older women, in contrast to the much lower proportions of widowers at all ages.[18] In 1910 nearly one-third of ever-married women aged 55-59 in the United States were widows.[19]

Census data, unavailable for earlier periods, allow us to be more precise about the numbers of widows in each society. In the second half of the nineteenth century the figures for British widows were, by age group, 3% of women aged 25-34 (against 2% of men who were widowers in this age group), 8% at 35-44 (against 4% of men), 16% at 45-54 (against 7% of men), and 30% at 55-64 (against 14% of men). These numbers fell slowly over the nineteenth century and more quickly in the twentieth.[20] Comparable data from the United States in 1900 show widows as 2.9% of women aged 25-29 (against 1.2% of men who were widowers in this age group), 4.6% at 30-34 (against 2.0% of men), 8.6% at 35-44 (against 3.6% of men), 17.6% at 45-54 (against 6.8% of men) and 32.3 % at 55-64 (against 11.9% of men).[21]

4. Modern England and the United States

Modern English widows and private law

Beginning in the middle years of the nineteenth century, male privilege at law began to erode significantly for the first time. Before this, the legal rules governing the coverture of wives had changed little since the mid-seventeenth century. Much of Barbara Leigh Smith's famous *Summary* of the laws pertaining to women, which appeared in 1854, could have been written in 1650, or even centuries before. All movables belonging to a wife passed irrevocably to her husband at time of marriage. The husband obtained possession and usufruct of the wife's real property and was obligated at law to support a co-resident wife, but there was no way to enforce this obligation, at least without resort to the dreaded Poor Law. Widows continued to outnumber wives by a long shot as writers of wills. Although the eighteenth century had witnessed some challenge to the absolute unity of husband and wife in coverture, in principle, her legal personality was still subsumed under his.[22] Queen Victoria was in an important sense an anomaly as the only wife in England not subject to the power of her husband.

An important exception to this lack of legal change was the development of the strict settlement. Commonly employed among the elite by the early eighteenth century as a type of jointure (known as 'equitable jointure'), this was established in a prenuptial agreement at the time of an eldest son's marriage, determining his income as a husband, his wife's allowance (or 'pin money'), her pension as a widow (not strictly guaranteed) and her children's inheritance portions. The husband became in effect a life tenant in the estate, which was entailed on the eldest son born of the union. This and other devices were employed to bar dower, in decline as a matter of social usage in the eighteenth and early nineteenth centuries.[23]

Increasing resort was also had to trusts, which were more flexible in that they might be established at any time. These effectively allowed a married woman to control her own property. Chancery (an equity forum) by 1725 approved the constructive trust, which did not have a trustee. By the early nineteenth century, however, trustees were held to be necessary for the establishment of a wife's separate maintenance contract. A married woman with a trust had full power to dispose of her personal and (after 1865) real property. It is difficult, all the same, to conclude that the position of either married women or widows had thereby improved. More than ever, widows depended on the generosity of a now decedent husband rather than on their inalienable rights at law.[24] The evidence as it stands, although far from clear, suggests that this development was not overall a good thing for them.[25]

An important motive for these devices, which in different ways placed a significant element of a male-oriented system of property under female control, was to avoid the consequences of the greed and incompetence of many husbands, especially as it became widely recognized that daughters might offer a better chance than sons of preserving a family name, in other words, of ensuring the transfer of wealth and status from one generation – of males – to the next. As women's perceived usefulness in transmitting titles and property increased, daughters were preferred to distant male kin and even sometimes to younger sons as vehicles to a family's rise in, or maintenance of, status. Propertied widows in particular might comprise a key element in a family's strategy in passing assets between males in the group. There was also a broad anxiety that women (and children) might become public charges if proper provision were not made for them.

Despite these concerns, wives remained vulnerable to being persuaded or menaced (in the traditional phrase, 'kissed or kicked') into parting with their property, at least until the doctrine of 'restraint on anticipation' established by 1839 some protection for the property accessible to them as widows. With regard to bequests left to daughters, an important development began to take hold in the early nineteenth century in that the practice of favouring the eldest sons now yielded to a more equal division of the parental estate, even as sons and daughters tended to receive different types of property.[26] The need for a high level of legal expertise to devise a strict settlement and the rule laid down by the Courts of Equity limiting eligibility for a trust to wives with property worth over £200 meant that these benefits at law accrued only to the relatively prosperous, although the nineteenth century saw a broader distribution of them through society over time. The disabilities of coverture weighed mostly on women of the middle classes, since those from the working classes and the poor, some three-quarters of the population, had few assets to protect, just as their husbands lacked the means with which to contest them at law. So it was only as a widow that many a middle-class woman might achieve a measure of equality with men.[27]

The Dower Act of 1833 essentially ended dower by allowing husbands absolute power to bar it. A prospective wife might negotiate a prenuptial agreement removing her husband's right to deny dower or providing for her own jointure, but otherwise she had from this date forward no guaranteed right as a widow to any portion of his real or personal property. The law thus eliminated a key entitlement of widows, although one that had already been eroded by changes in the law and social practice since 1650. The Dower Act also represents the beginning of an important shift in the regulation of women's status from private law rules to statute.[28] Virtually complete testamentary freedom operated in England from this date for well over a century, without substantial curtailment until 1975.[29]

It is important to recognize that a primary if contested goal of nineteenth-century feminists was the abolition of legal distinctions in marital status.[30] They have often been criticized for their almost exclusive focus on legal reform as opposed to pursuing social, political and economic equality between men and women, or at least between husbands and wives. Indeed, many of them embraced the gendered division of labour within the household even while rejecting it without, thus inadvertently contributing to the formation of women's 'second shift', wherein women worked a full day outside the home only to encounter a full range of responsibility for housework and childcare on their return. The inequalities they criticized were, all the same, egregious.[31] Their focus on marital status was further justified in that it always seemed easier to justify discrimination on this basis rather than on that of gender.[32]

Reformer Harriet Martineau described the Custody of Infants Act of 1839 as the first statute to check the oppression of wives at law. This law represented at best a partial victory for them, however, because it allowed a mother, under some limited circumstances, to retain custody of children only under the age of seven. Otherwise, husbands could assert their custody rights through writs of *habeas corpus*.[33] They could remove children from the family home during marriage and name persons other than their widows as guardians after their death. Victorian society began with the Aristotelian premise that the father alone of the two parents created life, an idea that continued to exercise an influence on policy regarding custody and guardianship for a long period. The courts, in implementing a judicial patriarchy that was, certainly at first, more traditional and less flexible than that promoted by their counterparts in the United States, upheld the principle that a father's rights over his children might be terminated only in extreme circumstances and even created new paternal rights. An attempt at reform in 1873 granted some rights to separated mothers, which were limited out of a concern that granting more might encourage wives to desert their husbands. The Custody Act of 1886 eliminated the status of the father as 'sole parent', which meant he could no longer utterly exclude his children's mother as guardian, a principle that was made retroactive for already widowed women. Nevertheless, it was not until 1925 that the law granted full equality to both parents in custody matters, and even then the courts tended to privilege fathers, for example, in disputes over the vaccination of children. The rights of mothers over their children within marriage remained circumscribed throughout this period, an important factor in the preservation of distinctions of marital status.[34]

Even aristocratic women laboured under the male bias of custody law, found access to divorce difficult (the first petition by a woman occurred in 1801), and were legally not entitled to their own earnings while wed. Their advantages of settlement and trust, resort to which was by now common among broad sectors of the middle classes, were jeopardized by the Courts of Equity themselves, which had become slow and difficult to use by the mid-nineteenth century, offering little effective protection for property relationships in general, not to speak of women's rights to property. The connection between the two became clearer, with the result was that even many elite women and men began to see a need for legal change. The complex rules of equity and common law were seen as producing a set of difficulties and constraints that interfered with the smooth operation of a growing consumer economy and the high value placed on providing financial security for women of well-off families.[35]

Critics had cited American innovations in divorce law as a model for reform in England, but the first major movement, overwhelmingly middle-class in substance, to change the legal rules affecting women crystallized in an 1856 petition seeking protection for the earnings of wives. Here too United States precedent was a key influence, in the form of a series of Married Women's Property Acts (MWPA) carried in a number of states by this time. But this reform was thwarted, and instead the Divorce and Matrimonial Causes Act was passed in 1857, which eased the rules providing for both divorce and judicial separation. Divorced and separated women were now granted the same property and contractual rights as an unmarried woman, and cast in a sense as constructive widows. The Act also established a new court in London, replacing the old ecclesiastical jurisdiction. A husband could divorce solely on the basis of wife's adultery, while a wife had to prove adultery plus another offence, as stipulated by the law. The Act contributed to the levelling of status among different types of unmarried women, while it reasserted the legal inequality of spouses and so a traditional view of proper marital hierarchy.[36]

The first limited protection of a wife's property not safeguarded by settlement or trust came with the MWPA of 1870. This was amended by later legislation, above all the Act of 1882, which effectively ended coverture, as far as property rights were concerned, although some details had to wait for resolution until 1935 and even 1964. Wives now had a right to their own real and personal property, as well as their earnings. This meant they could make wills as they wished and could also sue in their own names.

Not that this was an unqualified victory for feminists, however. Logic, flexibility and clarity in the law of property were more important motives in the passage of the nineteenth-century MWPA than the cause of women's rights. The MWPA turned out in fact to be a boon for husbands, who were thus able to insulate spousal property from the claims of their creditors, whereas wives had previously been able to use the law as a shield, relying on common law rules allowing them to make 'necessary' purchases on credit.[37] Reformers nevertheless promoted the 1870 Act and similar legislation with arguments that it would protect wives from irresponsible husbands, justify the ideal of companionate marriage and support the role of mothers in educating their children.[38] This series of laws well suited the now dominant ideology proclaiming separate spheres for men and women.[39] It gave married women with property the same financial responsibility for children as widows possessed, but was otherwise far from making their status equal. Nor did it make for the legal equality of husbands and wives, as its feminist supporters had hoped, but simply extended to all wives the protection previously enjoyed only by those with

4. Modern England and the United States

separate property. The 1882 MWPA, for example, offered married women protection, not equality.[40] The benefits of this series of laws for women are controversial, although recent research has shown that women on certain levels of society, who married after the passage of the 1870 Act, owned a substantially larger share of household wealth than their predecessors.[41] This has obvious implications for their economic status as widows.

Also numerous were the Matrimonial Causes Acts carried in the years between the 1857 Act and 1923, the year when men and women were finally given the same rights to divorce. The general tendency of this series was to confer increasing benefits on wives in separation and maintenance cases, reflecting a partial but growing acceptance of feminist arguments for spousal equality. Meanwhile, the Divorce Court established by the 1857 Act, through its mere handling of cases, opened up the behaviour of many husbands to criticism. This led to a curious, if circumscribed, disjuncture between cause and effect. The judges were concerned to uphold the patriarchal interest. By hearing the complaints of wives and censuring the 'unreasonable' conduct of husbands the court acted as a paradoxical agent for change. It defended patriarchy by yielding in some measure to changing ideals of marital behaviour, in a manner generally consistent, however, with the notion of separate spheres for the sexes and considerations of social status. The court recognized that the assertion of the male interest overall meant repressing the excesses of some males who were thought to abuse their authority. It defined both the rights and the limits to such rights, specifically regarding male coercion and female submission, more generally pertaining to gender hierarchy within marriage.

In the Divorce Court England saw the establishment of a judicial patriarchy that in important respects came increasingly to resemble the contemporary American version. The number of divorces remained below 1,000 each year until 1918, while legal separation cases stayed at about 10,000.[42] Before and after the 1857 Act, divorce was simply too expensive for many couples. Until the period after the First World War it remained relatively infrequent. Ninety per cent of matrimonial cases were handled through summary treatment in police courts, which were empowered to approve separation and maintenance orders, and often promoted reconciliation. Between 1897 and 1906, 87,000 such orders were granted. Many couples separated informally.[43] The overall trend was to reduce the numbers of widows, and at the same time to erode legal (and other) distinctions between them and married women, as well as among different types of unmarried women.

Another legal change of some significance to widows occurred in 1846, when Parliament altered the common law of torts by enacting a wrongful death statute known as Lord Campbell's Act. This law reversed the rule that held actions in tort to expire with the death of the plaintiff, providing the possibility of relief in such cases where death was caused either intentionally or through negligence. Eligible for damages were the wife, husband, parent and child of the victim.[44]

In 1869 a law was passed allowing women to vote in local elections, such as those for school boards, something deemed entirely consistent with their domestic responsibilities. Three years later a court decided that the doctrine of coverture prevented married women from exercising this right. This meant effectively that only widows and never-married women (or 'spinsters') could do so. In 1874 a women's suffrage bill was brought forward that would, if passed, have allowed all women to vote in Parliamentary elections, until it was amended, through what was termed a 'widows and spinsters' clause, specifically to exclude married women.[45]

The supporters of this 'widows and spinsters' clause clearly wished to preserve the system of multiple, fragmented civic statuses for women chiefly, as ever, to the detriment of married ones. By now, however, these multiple legal statuses had for a number of purposes collapsed into just two, married and unmarried, in anticipation of the eventual near total disappearance of these distinctions at law. Nineteenth-century feminists have often been criticized for placing too much faith in legal reform. This campaign admittedly had limited impact, as noted above, given women's disabilities in the political, economic and social realms.[46] The effects in each instance were never as great as supporters hoped and opponents feared. What is more, these feminists never achieved their goal of full legal equality between husband and wife. Some aspects of coverture had to wait for the late twentieth century for their removal and a trace of the institution remains even today. That said, there is no denying the scope of their accomplishment, the dismantling of the fundamental legal differences regarding women's marital status.[47] This was to have profound consequences for all women, not only widows.

Modern English widows and economic privilege

Aristocratic widows in general continued to enjoy most of the economic advantages shared by their predecessors in the early modern period, at least in theory – we cannot be certain if agreed-on jointure payments were in every case actually made. As in earlier times, they held an important administrative role in the 'big houses', although middle-class and even working-class women also managed their households, even in the teeth of prejudice that doubted their business sense.[48] In financial terms, elite widows were in the vast number of cases more than secure.

For middle-class widows, or at least some of them, life could be more precarious. Most male wage earners had low average incomes that discouraged the accumulation of savings and so investments that might generate income after their deaths.[49] Widowhood made clear the extent of women's economic vulnerability among both the middle and lower classes. Marriage was an economic necessity for most such women, which meant

4. Modern England and the United States

widowhood in turn presented potential difficulties, even calamity,[50] though recent research has somewhat qualified this dark assessment. Those who were well provided for, in terms of having been set up in a business or with investment income, were able to live comfortably, as is suggested by a study of their wills. These women appear to have enjoyed considerable freedom to dispose of their property as they wished, with the beneficiaries often being single women, including other widows, and a minority were able to find work in a range of respectable occupations. Thus not all widows were in financial terms vulnerable and powerless.[51] It remains an open question to what extent their economic activities validated, defied or redefined conventional gender roles.[52]

Throughout the nineteenth century much of the population remained engaged in agriculture, even as the percentage declined, from about one-third in 1801, to about one-fifth in 1851, to about one-eighth in 1901.[53] The experience of women's work in this sector of the economy changed but little.[54] Mechanization at first rendered the less-expensive labour of women attractive to employers. In the longer term it also helped narrow the range of acceptable tasks for female workers, pushing them into lower-paid, lower-status jobs, even as a changing ideal of the feminine discouraged their employment, leading in turn to their eventual withdrawal from agriculture. Conditions were so discouraging that even widows on Poor Relief were said to decline farmwork.[55] A situation of dire poverty reigned in the countryside, where the largest group of those receiving assistance or entering the workhouse consisted of widows with children. The rural poor were scattered and isolated. Even marriage was a gamble, but the single life was less secure. The lives of women married to agricultural workers were harder than those of wives among the urban poor, but the most desperate forms of poverty awaited widows.[56]

Our interest in the economic condition of widows lies chiefly with the experience of women in the working and middle classes. Among the latter, those who had a shop, farm or other business left them by their husbands were far more secure than the widows of members of the new professional class. When a husband of a woman in this last group died, his income disappeared at once.[57] The lower classes in Victorian England were far from monolithic themselves, marked instead by a socio-economic diversity that many historians simplify into two main groups, the respectable and the rough. Nor were they united politically. The working classes were replete with division and contradiction, and together they comprised about three-quarters of the total population.[58]

The work experience of married women might differ considerably by region and age as well as by class. In northern factory districts such as Lancashire, wives continued to work after marriage, while women wedded to London tradesmen did not.[59] Although women's participation in the workforce declined with age, at every age level more widows worked than married women.[60]

The 1834 New Poor Law was coloured by Malthusian worries about the population exceeding its ability to support itself and by Evangelical concerns that located responsibility for poverty not in the economic, social, political or cultural realms, but in the perceived moral failings of the poor. It introduced a regime much harsher than the one it replaced, abolishing allowances in aid of wages (i.e. 'outdoor relief') and promoting the notion that every able-bodied person should work. The law was designed to make relief an unappetizing prospect for the poor and it succeeded, in that it encouraged the mobilization of the wage-earning capacity of every member of the family, in part, as a strategy they themselves pursued to avoid the workhouse, in part, because the authorities separated them on entry into it. Widows were at a supreme disadvantage here, in that they lacked a key asset, the earning power of an adult male. Many had to depend on private charity, mutual aid (including assistance from other widows), or begging in order to avoid the dreaded workhouse.

For a time the law was unevenly applied. Outdoor relief continued for a time: in 1846 over half the recipients in England and Wales were widows.[61] Overall, a tougher line was taken from 1871, which seems to have encouraged the poor to view the assistance it offered all the more only as a last resort. They instead preferred poor-to-poor charity, if waged labour and other forms of assistance could not meet their needs. Widows and their children were among the most vulnerable to the miseries of the workhouse system. Even where parish relief was available to widows, as in London, it was meagre. At best, the effects of the Poor Law were to mitigate but not eliminate the differences in income available to married women and widows. The association of widows with abject poverty was so close that some local authorities simply assumed they could live on a subsistence level, an attitude that sparked contemporary criticism.

Over time the role of the state increased in the area of material support, as it offered unemployment, health and housing benefits. Working men's friendly societies were in the early twentieth century transformed into compulsory government insurance programmes, a development without parallel in the United States in this period. Eligibility for benefits, in a manner consistent with the ideology of the family wage (see below), typically centred round males. The 1911 Insurance Act, for example, guaranteed unemployment insurance to families with an out-of-work (male) breadwinner. Interwar legislation focused solely on widows whose decedent husbands had enjoyed a type of employment that was insured. An exception to this trend was the 1897 workmen's compensation statute, which, unlike most of its American descendants, was gender-neutral. This law did allow for post-accident election of remedies by injured employees, so that they could choose to file a lawsuit in tort instead of a claim for workmen's compensation. In this point of detail many American statutes followed this legislation as a model.[62]

During the First World War the national government began to assume

4. Modern England and the United States

a more aggressive posture in support of widows, orphans and other needy persons, working more closely than ever with a private organization called the Charity Organization Society. This was an important transitional period in the development of the modern welfare state. In 1925, the Widows', Orphans' and Old-Age Contributory Pensions Act was passed, an important development in the provision of material assistance to the elderly (here defined as 65 and older).[63]

This piece of legislation was profoundly stamped by the ideology, economics and gender politics of the period. Feminists, joined by some Labour Party politicians, had insisted on a governmental subsidy for all mothers, to compensate them for their poor wage prospects and tendency to leave the paid workforce on marriage. The ruling Conservatives passed a bill that instead provided for pensions for all widows, with or without children, whose husbands had been insured. The successful proposal lent assistance on the premise that its beneficiaries had been deprived of their 'breadwinner', thus ratifying women's dependence on men in the wake of their achieving the franchise, but both ideas supported the (post-)Victorian ideal of female 'domesticity', the ultimate guarantor of which the state now emerged.[64] All the same, many failed to receive adequate support and it is difficult to exaggerate the difficulties faced by some widows in the period between the two world wars.[65]

That many women had to work to support themselves, in fact, were compelled to do so in order to avoid starvation, was a fact recognized as early as 1842 in a report by the Royal Commission on Women's and Children's Work.[66] The lesson appears to have been soon forgotten. Many married women preferred factory work because it was free from interruption by the demands of childcare and housework, paid them for their efforts and offered a chance to socialize.[67] In fact, there are today two main views on women's labour in the industrial sector, a negative one that sees them as exploited by it, and a positive one that emphasizes the opportunities it offered. Both have some validity, although much of women's work remained seasonal or casual, with many working-class girls and women in the 'rough' category moving in and out of prostitution, for example.[68]

Overall, relatively few working-class women worked in factories, although their proportion rose in the nineteenth century. Most were involved in homework (a term that refers to non-domestic waged labour performed in the home, such as the manufacture of cigars or items of clothing), resort to which also increased in this period. It was especially favoured by mothers with small children, including widows. The much-vaunted separation of the spheres of home and work was never complete in actual fact, for all its repeated ideological assertion. Some widows were able to use older children or neighbours as sources of childcare while working. Pay was low, in and out of the factory, while working conditions could be wretched in either case.[69]

For many working-class women work was a necessity. Even among those in the skilled sector, husbands and wives often both worked. It has been estimated that only 15% of skilled male workers (that is, the ones with the most favourable prospects) earned enough to support the entire family.[70] Women's work was hardly marginal in the sense that it assured family survival in many cases.[71] The late nineteenth-century ideal of the father and husband as the sole family breadwinner was an impossibility for most workers, owing to a number of factors, including low pay and under- or unemployment.[72] The evidence suggests that most working-class married women worked at some point in their lives, which meant effectively taking on a 'double shift', as described above.[73] Many were the major or even sole support of their households, which was true of the vast majority of widows. Widows tended to receive the very lowest wages, often working for less than subsistence earnings. Oral histories testify to their experience of desperation.[74] Paradoxically, it was often working-class widows who achieved the ideal status of sole breadwinner for the household, but they were hardly rewarded for this achievement.

The experience of working women in this period was shaped in large part by a well-developed sexual division of labour. This was characterized by policies of gender segregation, sex-typing of jobs and women's exclusion from the workplace, pursued in different measure and at different times by capitalists, male unionists and the state. The latter intervened conspicuously through legislation ostensibly aimed at the protection of women by banning them entirely from a field, such as with the 1842 Mines Regulation Act, or placing limits on their participation, for example, the numbers of hours they were permitted to work. Sometimes factory owners resisted such regulations, although they were often content to exclude women from work, not on the basis of a rational pursuit of self-interest, but because they subscribed to the prevailing ideal of the male as sole breadwinner, who earned the 'family wage', rendering a wife's contribution to family earnings superfluous. Union workers were even more inclined to this perspective than factory owners, taking pride in their role as breadwinners and fearing the consequences for themselves of women's entry into the labour market. This attitude reflected more than a concern with lower wages, but also anxiety over submission to female authority in the workplace and corresponding male dependency. 'Maintaining order' often meant excluding women from work with men. These workers were not, however, as successful as the early modern guilds in the effects their hostility to women workers had in the end.

As in other periods, a woman's experience of marriage and widowhood was at least in part a function of her personality. Many wives from the 'rough' elements of the working classes were formidable characters, more adept at managing the household finances than their husbands.[75] There is no denying all the same the role of socio-economic status as an influence on the variety of woman's experience. From the mid-century, many middle-class women exercised authority in their realm of the family home, as the ideology of the 'angel in the house' grew dominant. This ideal was somewhat contradictory, in that it exalted wives as decorative in an economic sense and yet promoted their role as active household managers. The trend was most visible for the upper middle classes, whose absolute separation of family residence and place of work was both a material fact and a choice dictated by sentiment. But even lower middle-class households felt themselves under great pressure to keep up appearances, above all to distinguish themselves from the working classes, as they attempted to maintain a lifestyle associated with reliance on servants even in the face of an inability to afford them. They were not always successful in separating workplace and home.[76]

Increasingly throughout the nineteenth century, various critics, including some Evangelical Christians and middle-class moralists, denounced women's participation in the workforce as inappropriate. Their work came ideally to be identified with unpaid domestic service, rather than with that performed in the labour market, to the extent that, in the 1881 Census, women working at home were classed as unemployed. Charitable, social or political work was deemed far more socially acceptable than paid employment.[77]

Perhaps the most important concrete manifestation of the 'angel in the house' and 'male breadwinner' ideas was the decline in the numbers of married women workers in the second half of the nineteenth century. There were far fewer of them in 1900 than in 1850, with their estimated rate of employment dropping to perhaps half of what it had been a half-century before. The working classes had begun to join the middle classes in this exodus.[78] This meant that wives were not well placed to benefit from the 'widening sphere' of female work in the late Victorian period. New types of positions such as nurse, teacher, typist and clerk offered women better pay, enhanced status and greater security than previous options.[79] They still fell short relative to men's wages, however. In the event a husband was disabled, unemployed, deceased or simply missing, a wife could not hope to make up the economic loss to the household.[80] Women were typically assumed to be temporary workers, pending matrimony, an assumption that had a negative impact on both pay and job content.[81] The lower prestige and pay of 'women's work', in fact, propelled many to marry, and also encouraged a condition of dependency for women in marriage.[82]

During this period a broad, although not universal, social consensus developed over the evils of married women's labour. By 1900 motherhood was asserted as a duty not just to the family but also to the nation. Waged work was thought to injure femininity. Happiness for women was to lie in sacrifice for the happiness of others. Middle-class advocates of these ideas believed they should hold for the working classes as well as for themselves, and so supported not just the exclusion of married women from the workplace known as the 'marriage bar', but the campaign, prominent in

Widows and Patriarchy

the late nineteenth and early twentieth centuries, for the 'family wage', the idea that a working man's pay should support his entire family, and so render it unnecessary for his wife to seek employment. These Reformers, influenced by Evangelicalism, viewed the exigencies of working-class life as evidence not of economic need, but of moral failure. Protective legislation and the anti-woman bias of male unionists did their part to exclude women from work.[83]

Widows were perhaps the biggest losers in these developments. When women's work was discounted, even though the focus was on married women, this had negative implications for their rates of employment and pay. They did not benefit from the 'family wage' campaign, and in some cases, when they had children, they were excluded from jobs on the (skewed) logic of the 'marriage bar'. They were largely ineligible for the greatest single field of employment for women and girls in the late nineteenth and early twentieth centuries, domestic service. Instead widows were fortunate to find work as landladies or operators of schools for girls.[84] Respectability for them came in the workplace typically with jobs that mimicked traditional domestic responsibilities.[85]

Older women (and men) in general found entry into the workforce difficult.[86] Widows were often driven to very marginal types of employment such as commercial baby nursing.[87] As a rule, they took whatever work they could get. And work they did: one survey of a town in Nottinghamshire in 1881 shows 77% of widows were employed. Women, widows or no, were responsible for the care of their children, with little prospect of help from the state or from anyone else except as a last resort, apart from some exceptions in the years toward the end of this period. Working-class widows were vulnerable to fall-out from the infanticide scares of the Victorian age, which were in great measure generated by middle-class fears about a working-class failure to live up to their ideal of non-working motherhood.[88] Widows, as ex-wives, were hardly immune from the effects of the prevailing domestic ideology.[89] Dependent persons like widows were often poor and in this period grew poorer.[90] Most of the women on the Poor Relief rolls were widows, ranked, as ever, among the deserving poor, but the poor nonetheless.[91]

The First World War opened up working opportunities for women as never before. But the return of (male) veterans as well as the massive rates of unemployment in the immediate postwar period led to resentment of women workers, who were vilified as prostitutes and in many if not most cases forced out of the labour market. The result was a return to the prewar sexual division of labour, although the largely successful experience of women as workers during the war helpfully illuminates its status as a social construct.[92]

In recent years a controversy has raged in the scholarship on Victorian widows. A pessimistic school asserts that many, if not most, women, even in the middle classes, experienced serious financial hardship after the

4. Modern England and the United States

death of their husbands. Low average wage income discouraged accumulation of savings and investments, as noted above. Insurance benefits were available only to a few and were even then often inadequate, as were those provided by professional societies.[93] The optimists maintain that many widows were able to live comfortably on the wages from a job in a respectable profession, on income from investments, and/or on the returns from a business they operated themselves; indeed, some were able to look after not only themselves but other persons as well.[94] One can criticize the pessimists for moving too hastily at times from the plane of ideology to that of lived experience – much of their case is moreover highly speculative. On the other hand, although the optimists are able to depend on a solid evidentiary base composed of documents such as census returns and wills, the scope of such research remains limited. This means that more work is required before any great amount of certainty is possible on this matter.

Modern English widows and freedom of movement

Aristocratic women played by their own rules. Secure in their enjoyment of property under the rules of settlement and trust, many wielded great power within the family. Mothers by and large played a key role in arranging the marriages of their daughters. In this way they influenced the transmission of enormous amounts of property settled at time of marriage. Separate estates for wives were criticized as creating separate interests for spouses, a complaint possibly to be taken as a sign of their effectiveness.[95] Deprived of political rights, upper-class women possessed great political influence through access to wealth and patronage.[96] They were free to ignore their children, develop outside interests and friendships with men, and, within certain limits of discretion, conduct extramarital affairs. Elite women had a realistic view of marriage, without high expectations of romance or fidelity from a husband, and were not always immune to bad treatment from him. They were nobody's 'angel in the house'.[97] Widowhood for such women was no particular challenge, and no liberation either, which they scarcely required. This is not to say that some elite widows were not so emotionally dependent on their husbands that they were miserable without them. The most famous example from this period is Queen Victoria after the death of Prince Albert in 1861.

Matters were different for the less privileged in society, of course. Recent research suggests, however, that at least some middle-rank widows were able to live comfortably on independent terms, and in some cases were even responsible for the welfare of others, as we saw at the conclusion of the previous section. At all social levels, force of personality counted for a great deal. At the same time, it seems clear that urban women were not so much in thrall to husbands and fathers as women in the countryside appear to have been. Among the working classes in particular great flexibility and contingency in domestic arrangements came to prevail.[98] All women, married or not, were compelled to navigate the implications of the contemporary marriage ideal.

In the early nineteenth century, a fierce anti-marriage polemic arose. In part this had its origins in the shabby treatment accorded Queen Caroline by George IV, which outraged wide sectors of lower- and middle-class opinion, even as it seemed to characterize a certain contemporary style of male behaviour. By the same token, the positive example of Victoria and Albert raised expectations of proper conduct by husbands, at the same time that Evangelicals attacked the dominant double standard of sexual behaviour.[99] As the example of Queen Caroline demonstrates, even socially prominent women might experience disastrous marriages, a fact that helped spawn a polemical literary tradition criticizing marriage for women.[100]

Contemporary feminists did not hesitate to identify marriage as a form of slavery for women, or women and wives as slaves, a tradition that dates back at least to the seventeenth century, and that can ultimately trace its pedigree to antiquity. Mary Wollstonecraft, in her *Vindication of the Rights of Women* (1792), a work that enjoyed a broad influence, made effective use of the analogy. Wollstonecraft further identified marriage with prostitution. Even some conservatives came to agree, at least with the first analogy, and both were to form a recurrent feature of feminist rhetoric throughout the nineteenth century. Around 1800 there was much hostility on display to the religious practices, laws and secular customs surrounding marriage. In 1825 a utopian tract advocated its abolition as the preferred path to gender equality. These reformers viewed changing the law as inadequate: as long as men and women enjoyed unequal powers in free competition, the results would be unequal. Ambivalence toward conventional matrimony generated both asceticism and antinomianism, as, for example, with Shakers and Mormons. By the 1830s critics were both claiming that all women were slaves and loudly equating marriage with prostitution. A decade later, some radicals were rejecting marriage in favour of free love.[101] It has been easy for some historians, confusing the ideal with the reality, to overstress the contrast between the family characterized by the tradition of patriarchal severity and the newer, individualistic and affective model. Husbands could still be violent and brutally so.

Out of this criticism arose the idea that marriage could, and should, be improved, rather than abandoned. By the 1850s even the most radical elements had for the most part turned away from their opposition to conventional marriage. Economic, political and social change tended in a more conservative direction.[102] Earlier, Owenites had expressed concern for abused wives and went on to claim that the female sex possessed a unique moral vision, which was also a position adopted by some anti-feminists. This view bears close resemblance to the Evangelical ideal of a special mission for women in the home, a mission bearing on the restraint

4. Modern England and the United States

of men and their proclivities that were viewed as baneful. In other words, they regarded women as the moral superiors of men. Methodists in particular advocated a broad role for women in religious practice as preachers, stewards and teachers. An ideal of equality between spouses had arisen much earlier among dissenters, especially Quakers.

Over time the struggle for the moral improvement of society became increasingly secularized. Owenite socialists preached the value of women's equality in the ownership of property and in their full access to education and employment. Followers of nineteenth-century French socialists like Saint-Simon and Fourier idealized women, proclaiming not their equality with, but their superiority to, men. This association with socialism for a time slowed the efforts of legal reformers, even as the exaltation of woman's nature bore full fruit in the 'angel in the house' ideal. The practical consequences of these assertions of women's moral superiority were limited. Women, as wives, were still by and large dependent. The nineteenth-century ideal of women as passionless wives was a reversal of an earlier view that saw them as sexually avid. 'Superior' did not necessarily mean 'equal', of course. The virtuous woman was now as much as ever before emphatically held to be necessary for the preservation of the social order.[103]

The continuing value placed on a woman's domestic role somewhat paradoxically encouraged their entry into the public sphere in the second half of the nineteenth century, even as many women, especially married ones, retreated from the world of work. Although they tended to accept the gendered division of labour within the household, many (not all) nineteenth-century feminists believed that women's oppression was grounded in their relegation to the private domain.[104] At the same time, theories about women's superior nature legitimized their participation in social programmes and in a sense demanded it, as the extension of domestic virtue on a broader front was deemed a social good. Elite women were active in the campaign to repeal the notoriously anti-female Contagious Diseases Acts. Passed in the 1860s to check the spread of sexually transmitted disease in the armed forces, these laws, repealed in 1886, allowed police great discretion over women alleged to be prostitutes. To take another example, upper-class women were also prominently engaged in the women's suffrage movement.[105] This involvement was a sign that the boundaries between the public and private spheres were porous and subject to constant renegotiation. In fact, it is now persuasively argued by scholars that the ideology of 'separate spheres' was very far from being perfectly realized. English women in this period were in no real sense secluded and confined, any more than were their Athenian counterparts in antiquity. Many viewed marriage as a Christian mission that obligated women to fight, not for their emancipation, but for the moral regeneration of society, a conviction that brought them into the limelight in many cases.[106]

Given the legal disabilities, material inconveniences and bad reputation of marriage, it is not surprising that some women avoided it entirely. A tradition of marriage refusal dates as far back as the 1840s, and many women throughout the nineteenth century who could afford to do so remained resolutely single. It was the only way they could even attempt to live the life of a full adult citizen, although in reality this was an option available only to males. The companionate ideal was rarely achieved in real life, a fact that held true especially at either end of the social spectrum, among both the elite and the working classes. Difficulties were not confined to these sectors, however. By the 1890s rejection of marriage on various levels of the middle and upper classes was so widespread as to cause concern, which in turn generated more pressure for reform.[107]

Most nineteenth-century never-married women (or 'spinsters') did not choose their fate, however, which was more the product of demographic exigency and social anxieties over female hypogamy than of hostility to marriage. Marriage remained the only realistic and respectable way for most women to rise – or at least to avoid falling – socially and economically. It also afforded a minimal level of legal protection to women. Aside from sheer economics, there were some inconveniences, such as social isolation, associated with the single life that made it a great burden for many. Most middle-class women (between one-fifth and one-quarter of the population) wanted to marry and did so. Marriage was more important for women purely as a status than it appears to have been for men, and there is some reason to think that male and female ideals of conjugal life differed from each other.

At all events, evidence suggests that in the early twentieth century the companionate ideal was rising in popularity. It is telling that, before divorce was (relatively) widely available, separated women would pass themselves off as widows.[108] By the mid-nineteenth century people were marrying in increasing numbers, earlier, and more often at that.[109] Unmarried women, namely widows and spinsters, were regarded as suspect on the ground that they were vulnerable both to economic hardship and sexual corruption, especially on the lower levels of society.[110] The idealized nuclear family model left no role for widows.[111]

Certainly widowhood was by itself no ideal state, to judge from contemporary literature, but only a very small window can be opened on this vast subject here. For the poet Gerard Manley Hopkins widowhood was an apt metaphor for (artistic) isolation, powerlessness and sterility.[112] A sampling of Charles Dickens turns up a series of bleak caricatures ranging from victim (David Copperfield's mother Clara) to predator (Mrs MacStinger in *Dombey and Son*). Anxiety and exhaustion are argued to be hallmarks of contemporary fictional characterizations.[113] Victorian prose literature liked to poke fun at widows who failed to live up to the high standards set for the etiquette of mourning, either out of an abundance of zeal or the reverse.[114] Rather than as true examples of the 'merry' type, these fictional

4. Modern England and the United States

representations may be viewed as satirizing the sentimentality surrounding the figure of the sorrowful widow, which appears to dominate representations of the widow in this period.

A more complex, if not more sympathetic, portrait is offered by a widow writing about widows, the Scottish Margaret Oliphant in *The Ladies Lindores* (1883). Two women, Mrs Warrender and Lady Markland, become widows at about the same time, and both experience this event as a liberation into a new life, with new opportunities. They become close friends, in a mother–daughter kind of way.[115] It is difficult to conclude that this type of portrayal is representative, however. Wives can be said to eclipse widows, even as a negative stereotype, at least in the case of the most prominent adaptation of the Widow of Ephesus tradition in the English language literature of the period. The character of Molly Bloom in Joyce's *Ulysses* stands forth as a failed Penelope and worse.[116]

English husbands and wives, over a long arc of time dating to the early modern period and even before, had been accustomed to act more like emotional partners than as master and servant, and women had typically enjoyed a certain amount of freedom in marriage.[117] Even among the working classes, a rough degree of equality often operated between spouses. Here personality mattered more than access to economic resources or the strictures of the law. Rebels against the middle-class ideal of marriage may have been admired by some, but they were not emulated by many.[118] Contemporary novels were filled with weak men and rebellious heroines, but these were an invitation to escapism, not an incitement to overthrow patriarchy. The extensive prescriptive literature praising the submission of wives does, however, suggest that many found such recommendations to be a challenge, and there is plenty of evidence indicating that for many married women the idea of the docile 'angel' was an ideal at best. Many entered marriage supremely confident of playing, with no small success, the uneven hand they had been dealt. In Victorian England 'husband-management', the control of inept and stupid, or even angry, violent or lazy husbands was a skill shared by many.[119]

Harriet Beecher Stowe confidently asserted, in a book published in 1866, that as a rule English matrimony was far more patriarchal in its insistence on wifely obedience than the American version. Such generalizations by contemporary observers are not without value, but there are limits to their usefulness all the same. It will be clear that, just as the experience of marriage, meaning in particular the precise balance of authority and/or the articulation of the gendered division of labour within the household, could vary greatly from one relationship to the next, so there were also several competing marriage ideals in play during the Victorian period for both England and the United States. In England, the sentimental or companionate model favoured by feminists, itself far from monolithic, shared much with the Evangelical one mentioned above, such as a disgust with the sexual double standard for men and women. At the same time, it emphasized spousal friendship and equality over gender hierarchy and wifely submission, although it must be emphasized that in such matters the Evangelical ideal showed some variation as well, since it sometimes emphasized the moral superiority of women over men. A patriarchal model of husbandly authority, sometimes (rather awkwardly) described in terms of the Roman institution of *patria potestas*, remained popular, certainly among many men.

Feminists frequently invoked the sentimental ideal as a means of criticizing the contemporary law of marriage and its inequalities. They were successful to a large extent in promoting reform of that institution on the level of law. The consequences of that reform and their version of the marriage ideal both enjoy a strong influence to this day. There is also important evidence of the impact of the latter on the lived experience of marriage, although this does not guarantee that the ideal was always or even typically realized. For many, marital harmony remained elusive. Ideals clashed with each other and with behaviour. Class differences show forth, both for men and for women. Middle-class men were more influenced by the Evangelical companionate ideal than were upper-class males. Such aspects as the separation of spheres, and the power and authority wielded by a husband, could be more nuanced and hotly contested among members of the lower classes. Expectations, above all on the part of middle-class women, seem to have risen in this period over the emotional rewards of matrimony.

As competing ideals, however, the patriarchal and companionate models were not, in a strict sense, opposites. The attempt to exercise traditional authority in this period often gave rise to compensatory pressures encouraging more egalitarian marital relations. The protection of women was frequently invoked as a defence of patriarchy. A more subtle deployment of power than mere invocation of male authority was thought by some to be better disposed to secure gender hierarchy. The sentimental marriage ideal was useful toward this end. At times the assertion of one ideal spurred recourse to another. Victorian marriage was an institution so riddled with contradictions that one can easily describe it as both 'patriarchal' and 'companionate'.[120]

By 1900 the womanly ideal had shifted in emphasis, so that a married woman's exalted position depended ever more on her status as a mother. In other words, marriage had become matrifocal and children conferred a newly valued status. The state responded warmly to this trend, for example, by establishing from 1907 'schools for mothers'. One might have expected never-married mothers, common-law wives and widows with children to benefit from this trend, but they did not.[121]

A study of the 1851 Census in Birmingham as well as in Essex and Suffolk counties shows that 68% of the widows listed were heads of household, while in Lancashire it was rare for young widows with small children to reside with other family members.[122] A study of two villages in

4. Modern England and the United States

nineteenth-century Nottinghamshire shows a majority even of poor widows as heads of household, both among the young and elderly (over 65), while very few lived alone.[123] Overall, from 9% to 14% of all English households had widows or spinsters as heads during the second half of that century.[124] The data from a study of contemporary middle-class households in a city in Scotland, namely, Glasgow, show significantly higher proportions, that moreover continued to rise in this period. In other words, between one-third and one-half of the households under study had female heads at different points, suggesting a limit to women's economic and social dependency on men at this level of society, despite the ideology that favoured this.[125]

The vast majority of such women were widows, although their percentage, as opposed to that of spinsters, declined over the same period. A greater number lived with their daughters than with sons, but living with adult children of either gender appears to have been a last resort for widows.[126] Despite controversy in the scholarship, examination of the residence patterns of elderly widows and widowers in late nineteenth-century England and Wales suggests that the introduction of means-tested old-age pensions in 1910 for persons over 70 years old had scarce influence on these preferences, at least in the short term. More important were general trends, such as the decline in the numbers of servants and the incapacity of younger adults to set up their own households, in influencing the frequency of widows' co-residence. This phenomenon increased slightly in this period, certainly with married children.[127] In a society where the nuclear family form dominated, the loss of a husband and father, as a key source of income, often had devastating effects, leading in many cases to the termination of the household.[128]

Most middle-class feminists were gradualist reformers and not revolutionaries. Even so, they were disappointed in the results of their efforts at law reform, which they viewed with clearer eyes than do some modern scholars. In large part the explanation for their failure is that legal change was inadequate to redress the basic injustices confronting women.[129] Marriage remained as before, by and large, a private institution, although never completely so for women, and there is little doubt that privatization favoured the male interest.[130] Ideals of marriage counted for a great deal beyond the legal rules themselves. What is more, at any one time, whatever the marital ideal, most adult women were unmarried.[131] This is not to deny the extent of the feminist achievement in eroding status distinctions at law among women, as we saw above.

Sympathy for widows appears to have been both genuine and widespread, but this did not translate into a general improvement in their condition. Widows began and ended the period under study with none of the social and economic benefits accruing to marriage. Over the course of 75 years they saw the legal advantages of their state gradually eroded by the gains of married women, who were also the beneficiaries of a widely shared complex of values elevating them to the status of angels, in and out of the house.

Modern English widows and remarriage

Nearly half of mid-nineteenth-century marriages lasted less than 25 years before interruption through the death of one of the partners.[132] The low remarriage rate for widows and widowers, much lower than in the sixteenth century, when it was as high as 30%, dated back to the seventeenth and continued through the second half of the nineteenth and into the early twentieth century. In 1851, the proportion of such persons remarrying was only 11.27%. Even so, the percentage of men remarrying was higher than that for women, and rose in this period, as they increasingly wed much younger, never-married women.[133] Less than 10% of widows who remarried were over 45 years of age, and rarely did these women find second husbands among never-married men.[134] Widows with property left to them by their deceased spouses often found themselves in conflict with their new husbands over its disposition.[135]

Among the working classes, motives for remarriage included financial stability, companionship and/or affection and the wish on the part of women to avoid the imputation of immorality or prostitution.[136] The anti-marriage polemic of this period was a discouragement to remarriage, as in some cases both widows and widowers feared subjection to a new tyranny.[137] A number of widows chose not to remarry, in part motivated by fear of losing their financial independence.[138] Elite widows holding on to property in trust were under no great pressure to find new husbands.[139] Rural widows, on the other hand, were quite prepared to remarry when they could. It was a better alternative to poverty.[140] Some widows simply cohabited short of marriage with new partners when such were available.[141]

United States widows and private law

As late as the 1840s, relatively little of fundamental importance regarding the rights of women had changed in the system of private law that the United States had by and large inherited from England. The position of never-married women and widows remained superior in many important ways to that of married women, who continued to labour under coverture and its implications. In legal terms a wife remained, as before, identified at law with her husband, ever dependent on his will. A husband administered the marital property, acquiring ownership outright of a wife's personal property and a life interest in her real property that continued even after her death, if he survived her. Agreements between spouses were a legal nullity. Husbands had, in principle, a duty to support their wives, and wives to provide services to husbands. A wife owed her husband

4. Modern England and the United States

obedience in exchange for support, which the law, however, could not compel him to provide, while he controlled all property, had the power to determine marital domicile and held exclusive rights to custody of children, to the point where he could appoint as guardian someone other than their mother on his death. He was bound by a wife's contracts, even when the pair were separated; criminal, as well as civil, liability for her acts remained his responsibility. The rights of a husband to physical and sexual possession of a wife were manifested in the rules for *habeas corpus* and criminal conversation (a tort action against a wife's lover). The status of a wife as property was a legal fiction often (mis)taken as fact. As in other historical periods, the legal status of wives continued to cast a long shadow over the relative independence they enjoyed, under the law, as widows.[142]

All the same, it is worth observing some of the differences in the experience by region of women in the colonial and early Republican periods. Such differences resulted in large part from the fact that no optimal solution to the challenge of providing for widows was discovered. The Puritans in New England were intent on perfecting a version of patriarchy in which male heads of households reigned supreme and their wives were submissive to them. One result was that the laws, for example, of Massachusetts and Connecticut altered English law to place widows under a severe disadvantage with regard to conveyances, dower and separate estates. Similar motives held for the Quakers in Pennsylvania, with somewhat distinct results. Their idea was more or less to take coverture to its logical extreme by reducing the chance for separate spousal interests to arise. The motive behind these innovations was not only religious but also commercial, in that simplified legal rules stripping women of their rights facilitated the circulation of property and therefore (male) enterprise. Puritans and Quakers had great faith in the ability and willingness of male relatives to provide for the women of the family. Southern colonies such as Maryland, Virginia and South Carolina were more obliging to women in these areas of the law, conceding widows and even wives greater autonomy. Maryland and Virginia allowed widows to claim a share of the husband's personal property even though this benefit was by now denied to English widows.

One should not exaggerate the overall significance of these differences, however. Relatively few women benefited from separate estates in late eighteenth and early nineteenth-century America, although they were popular with the well off in some areas of the country, for example, with remarrying widows in South Carolina. The very purpose of separate estates has been argued to serve the male interest, by protecting property from a husband's creditors, providing support for widows who might otherwise strain community resources, and ultimately guaranteeing male-to-male transfer of patrimonial assets. Separate estates might benefit husbands directly, as the courts well knew. Regional variations in legal rules, the fruit of a bundle of social, economic and ideological factors, did not efface a dependency forced on widows that was common at first to every colony and subsequently to every state.[143]

Like English common law, Christian doctrine was part of the source code of nineteenth-century marriage law in the United States. The dominant religious and legal culture lent marriage the flavour of a coercive institution for women, a tradition destined to withstand many a reform. It was supported by the notion that spouses were 'one flesh' in a union that was ideally eternal in the prevailing Protestant ideology.[144] The black letter of the common law often spelled disadvantage to widows, especially in states like Massachusetts, Connecticut and Pennsylvania, which lacked equity jurisdiction from the start. This disadvantage was heightened in Pennsylvania, which alone gave preference to an estate's creditors over widows and moreover did not permit a widow to cash out her interest in real property, allowing the heir to sell it instead.[145]

Financial security in widowhood typically required good legal planning. A widow had, generally, a right to one-third of a life interest in her husband's real estate as dower, or one-half if there were no children, and in a few states one-third or one-half of his personal property. These shares were available to her on her husband's intestacy or if she chose to reject the terms of his will ('widow's election'). Dower served as a kind of extension of coverture in that it preserved a wifely economic dependence on a husband past the point of his death, protecting the community from the need to provide support. Dower, unlike bequests, was proof against the claims of creditors everywhere except Pennsylvania. Jointures, available in more jurisdictions than were separate estates, offered an alternative to dower, but seem to have been less popular in America than in England. Widows also recovered their own real property on a husband's death as well as some personal items dubbed 'paraphernalia'.[146]

A husband might leave more than the legal minimum in his will, and there is evidence that many did so, for example, increasingly in Pennsylvania after 1830. Many husbands in this state allowed their wives to retain their personal property and/or dowry during marriage and bequeathed it to them in their wills. In a number of states before 1850, in fact, there is evidence that widows often did better under a husband's will than the law by itself would imply.[147]

For the period under study, just as in the years preceding 1850 described above, well-to-do women, especially remarrying widows, might protect their interests through resort to jointure or a separate estate established through a trust. Many, if not most, married women, however, had no way to maintain their property separate from their husbands. Some elite husbands were not above persuading their wives-to-be that prenuptial agreements violated the companionate ideal of marriage. Others saw advantage precisely for themselves in such agreements. A wife kept her property intact, while her husband was freed from the burden of

4. Modern England and the United States

dower. A wife's property was protected from her husband's creditors while he had the use of it.

In general, marriage settlements gave women more rights than they possessed under the common law.[148] The courts were often inclined to protect the interests of husbands, however. An 1817 case rewrote the law of trusts, relying on English precedents that allowed a wife to convey her property to a husband, unless the terms of the trust expressly forbade this. The court, in its holding, exulted in the (anti-woman) common law and the traditional ideal of marriage, asserting that separate estates for wives materialized marriage to the point of 'legalized prostitution'.[149]

Widows might be named as executors of a will, although husbands were, to judge from the evidence of early nineteenth-century Pennsylvania, reluctant to impose what some viewed as a burden. At the same time, many widows did not hesitate to assume the status of sole executor, even where this might have easily been avoided.[150] One motive for renouncing a role as executor was that this excluded one from acting as guardian of one's children. Although some widows also refused this, most husbands preferred to leave this option open for them and refrained from appointing a guardian by will. In general the design of a will was motivated more by a desire to protect the interests of children than to tie the hands of widows.[151]

Unmarried women enjoyed a status that in private law closely approximated that of many males, in that they could make contracts, write wills, dispose of property and assume the guardianship of children.[152] This is one reason why legal reform centred round the rights of wives. Another is the idealization of wife and, increasingly over time, mother in the American version of the Victorian cult of domesticity. The virtuous woman was expected not only to abstain from political and economic activity but also to demonstrate her incompetence at such matters. Wives and their marital dependency loomed so large in the popular imagination that single women (perhaps as former or future wives) were often assimilated to them in debates over policy.[153] The high valuation placed on married women led to concerns with their material welfare, especially after marriage ended through the death of a husband. After losing a husband, the best even a well-provided widow could look forward to was in many cases adequate maintenance and not genuine economic autonomy.[154] There were three principal areas of concern and contestation regarding the legal rules for women's marital status: property, custody and guardianship of children, and divorce. The cumulative impact of changes in these areas helped create a new, distinct marital identity for American wives, with both direct and indirect consequences for widows. Eventually, the heft of the legal distinction between them disappeared.

There were several factors helping to promote change in the legal status of wives in the early to mid-nineteenth century United States. One was the rise of Evangelical Christianity, which generated a measure of tension with a dominant religious culture promoting the submission of women to their husbands. Another factor, overlapping with the first to an extent, was the emergence of a feminist movement. Both Evangelicals and feminists criticized the diversity and complexity of the American system of private law, which they perceived as inherently unfair to women, especially the poor and vulnerable among them.[155] As early as 1837, feminists identified the law of marriage with that of slavery, a principle restated with vigour at Seneca Falls in 1848, partly because both were oppressive institutions defined by rules that were articulated and enforced by the state.[156] They protested the incapacity of wives to make a will, to sue or to be sued. The expense, inefficiency and anti-democratic nature of the equity courts, where they existed, were another spur to reform.[157] Status as a wife was important for women, but, when this appeared to have degraded, many demanded changes in the law.[158] One reformer, Marietta Stow, was able to rely on her own adverse experience as a widow in composing an attack on contemporary law entitled *Probate Confiscation: Unjust Laws Which Govern Women*, whose second edition appeared in 1877.

While reformers' complaints about the unjust effects of the American system of multiple jurisdictions were in important respects well founded, this system also became an engine of change in its own right, as states competed with each other to offer new and improved versions of the law. This trend is perhaps most remarkable in the diversity of legal regimes regulating divorce, separation and remarriage, but can be seen in other areas as well. The movement for revision of state constitutions in the period from 1845-60 was a strong force in itself, prompting a re-examination of the legal status of women. Mississippi enjoys the distinction of being the first state, in 1839, to pass a MWPA that allowed wives ownership and control of their own belongings whether acquired before or during a marriage. It was followed by a handful of others and then, significantly, New York State in 1848 (and 1849, and later). Although the state legislature made it increasingly clear that a wife enjoyed independent legal status regarding her property, the New York courts placed limits on a wife's capacity to convey property to her husband out of a concern with her vulnerability to coercion, a rule accepted by the United States Supreme Court in 1889. Several other states followed New York's initiative with statutes similar in design but that were susceptible to diverse treatment in the specific legal culture of each. In order to prevent the defrauding of his creditors, these laws typically made it difficult for a husband to transfer property to his wife.

The MWPA yielded an important indirect benefit for widows, since such statutes reduced their exposure to the consequences of a decedent husband's financial mismanagement, especially his accumulation of debt. Wastrel husbands benefited by having a wife's assets available on which to subsist, if necessary. The political circumstances behind these laws as well as their actual content differed from state to state (so that some, for

4. Modern England and the United States

example, have questioned the status of the Mississippi statute as an MWPA, arguing that it was simply a measure for debt relief). All the same, protecting women (and men) from the effects of male irresponsibility was a major theme of these laws. Granting women financial independence was far less important, to the extent it was important at all. More desirable was the goal of better equipping married women to fulfil the role already allotted to them in the context of the family.[159]

New York State followed in 1860 with a law designed to allow wives ownership of their earnings as well as their property.[160] The courts interpreted this law, like its predecessors, restrictively, on the ground that husbands had the right to wives' domestic services, a principle destined to endure another century, as both courts and legislatures resisted feminist demands for the recognition of a joint property regime for spouses.[161] In fact, the effects of these statutes have been the subject of great controversy among scholars. By 1900, women in a number of states had accumulated significant rights to their own property.[162] Research into women's share of wealth shows a notable increase in this toward the end of the nineteenth century, suggesting some measure of success for the laws over the long term.[163] A link has even been claimed to exist between passage of the laws and the rise in registration of patents by women.[164]

On the other hand, it has been argued that the financial dependence of wives on husbands was little attenuated by these laws. Most women did not own property of significant economic value, and worked in their homes or family businesses. Only under very specific conditions could such work give rise to a claim under the new rules. The legislation failed to address the question of the labour relation at the heart of the marital relationship, one that very much resembled that between master and servant. Courts still regarded a woman's domestic labour as an obligation imposed on her by her status as a wife, rejecting all attempts at enforcing an interspousal contract that would remunerate her for such services.[165] Aside from the very rich and the very poor, married women remained for the most part financially dependent on their husbands.[166]

Both optimists and pessimists have an effective argument to make in this debate. Even so, we do well to keep in mind the power of the law to create the basis for claims, and so rights, to legitimize a new (or an old) ideology, in short to define what a husband and wife should be. In this sense the MWPA represent an achievement for women, if only a partially realized one. Their civic status was, and remains, a field of contestation.[167]

In 1849, just prior to achieving statehood, California, in drawing up its constitution, adapted an institution that derived from Spanish law, and ultimately from the Visigoths, a regime of community property for married couples. This was a radical departure from common law principles. One motive seems to have been that these rules were thought attractive to prospective women settlers, who were then in short supply, granting them a claim to one-half of the common marital property. For similar reasons the constitution defined a category of separate property, real and personal, acquired through inheritance or gift, for married women. Some widows were to benefit a great deal from these rules.

These provisions were in fact directly borrowed from the 1845 Texas constitution, in this respect heavily indebted to the Spanish legal tradition. Such arrangements had a precedent in Louisiana, which had been ruled by the Spanish and French. Spanish-Mexican women in New Mexico traditionally owned property during marriage. It is worth observing that in California the idea of benefiting women was for a time undermined by subsequent legislation that gave management not only of the common but a wife's separate property to her husband, resulting in some disadvantages for widows in succeeding to their husbands.[168] At any rate, the underlying principle was to prove popular, at least in the West. By 1890, eight territories or states, meaning the four just mentioned plus Arizona, Idaho, Nevada and Washington, had adopted community property rules.[169]

Utah, first as territory and later as state, had its own peculiar history in coming to grips with the legacy of polygyny, as in the late nineteenth and early twentieth centuries the widows and half orphans of subsequent (and contemporaneous) unions to a first marriage were now disadvantaged, and now privileged on intestacy.[170] In the same period, widows in Arizona, thanks in part to the implementation of a community marital property regime, found themselves enjoying rights in inheritance law that were as generous as anywhere else. A widow was entitled to one-half of marital community property plus other benefits, a liberality mirrored in the interest shown in granting women suffrage on Arizona's achieving statehood in 1912. Some widows were able to live relatively prosperously as a result. Widows had the right to act as husband's executor and the guardian of all minor children.[171]

The law for widows in the American Southwest in this period has been relatively well studied. It shows an interesting contrast in legal systems between the civil law in Arizona and New Mexico and the common law in Colorado and Utah. Under the civil law, a community marital property regime prevailed, in which each spouse was entitled to one-half on the death of the other, thereby possessing a vested and equal interest in the marital estate. The husband was the manager of the common property and he was allowed to dispose of it without his wife's consent, until legislation in the early twentieth century made it necessary to secure this. Dower rights were abolished during this period (with the effect of giving widows a right to ownership rather than a life interest in a husband's real property), while both Arizona and New Mexico passed an MWPA in the late nineteenth century. The community property system was a legacy of the Visigothic conquest of Spain, which explains why so much of the legal detail and ideology surrounding this institution resemble more the marital property law of late medieval and early modern Germany rather than, say, the ancient Roman system strictly and completely separating the property

4. Modern England and the United States

of wife and husband.[172] The common law jurisdictions in this sample, Utah and Colorado, enforced the rules for coverture as described above, although with the difference that they allowed spouses to opt for a modified separate property regime, which gave widows benefits similar to those in the civil law jurisdictions. Both Colorado and Utah abolished dower and passed MWPA in this period.[173]

The law on marital property and succession was not alone in showing considerable variation from place to place. The various factors of multiple jurisdiction, competition among the states and the revolution in transportation helped complicate the law on divorce, separation and remarriage to the point of confusion and contradiction. From almost the beginning, all states, except South Carolina, allowed absolute divorce but did so under a variety of rules. One could without difficulty find oneself married and divorced in different states at the same time. Some states operated as divorce havens, for example, Indiana and later Nevada. In general terms, the law might often seem almost random and randomly oppressive. Courts sometimes found it difficult to distinguish who was the true wife, or widow. In an 1854 New York decision on a suit launched by a widow to recover her dower, the Court of Appeals ruled against her because her late husband had been previously married and divorced for adultery, which barred remarriage under the law of that state. By the 1880s, the courts relied on a statutorily defined presumption of death when a spouse disappeared without a trace for five years.[174] Abandonment, or self-divorce, might be even more prejudicial to a wife than loss of a husband to death. So it is not surprising to see the legal authorities treat deserted wives as constructive widows. By the same token, the widespread acceptance of common-law marriage made it difficult for many widows to establish their rights to a decedent husband's property. Presumption of marriage typically trumped lack of proof, at least where alarms about polgyny and free love were not in the air.[175]

At the start of the nineteenth century, American courts accepted that a man could enforce his rights to custody of his wife and children through a writ of *habeas corpus*, in part because English courts of the time also viewed a father's authority as absolute. This began to change in the early part of the century, as a new legal standard emerged, 'the best interest of the child', that came to be identified in principle with maternal, not paternal, custody. This was asserted as early as 1809 in a South Carolina case. A key moment in this development occurred with a 1842 New York decision regarding a plaintiff named John Barry. The court recognized Barry's theoretical right under coverture to recover his wife and children after a separation, but refused to enforce it in fact. A man who relied on the judicial system to assert his rights in this way was liable to be deemed undeserving of them.

What emerged from this case was the effective extinction of a husband's right to recover custody of his wife and the transformation, slower to take hold, of a father's absolute power over his children into consideration of their best interest, which might, and often did, result in maternal custody. A failed male, meaning an abusive or negligent father, or husband, risked losing his rights. Mothers were thought to be endowed with a special capacity for the moral and religious training of children, who especially required maternal care during their 'tender years'. This principle, although contested in the courts, came to be ratified by state statute, for example in New York in 1860, although as late as 1868 a legal treatise asserted the absolute nature of paternal power and courts continued to favour fathers over mothers in custody disputes, often for economic reasons.[176]

Legal authorities showed even greater hesitation over granting women guardianship of their children, and when they did concede this they tended to limit the exercise of maternal authority. Widows were often assumed to lack financial independence, and were thus viewed as persons in need of protection rather than possessed of valid claims at law to the custody or guardianship of their children. Remarriage did not help a widow's case, however, since it impaired confidence in her dedication as a mother. In 1910 only nine states and the District of Columbia granted equal rights of guardianship to men and women.

Change, when it did occur, could sometimes be long in coming. For example, an 1850 law in California allowed a mother to act as her children's guardian only when she was a widow, requiring not only that her husband was dead but also that she did not remarry. Even so, her husband could appoint someone else instead in his will. After many years of feminist struggle, by 1900 mothers in California finally enjoyed rights of guardianship equal to those of fathers.[177] As in England, such changes should be viewed as part of a general, although decidedly non-linear, trend toward the erasure of differences in marital status among women.

Not all legal changes benefited women, or did so in a straightforward, evolutionary way. A wife's dower rights often posed problems to a husband who wished to alienate property. He might negotiate a release with his wife, threaten her (or worse) with violence, or simply ignore her interest. Complications that followed a widow's assertion of her rights often provoked concern that dower was too great a restraint on the market in real estate in an increasingly mobile country. To many, the plight of widows mired in economic difficulty suggested that dower did not fulfil its basic purpose. A perception followed that new rules were necessary.[178] The courts refused to accept a provision of the 1860 New York earnings statute that authorized wives to carry on business under their own names until a new law was passed in 1884 granting them the right to contract with third parties.[179] Some husbands were quick to grasp the beneficial (to them) aspects of a separate property regime for their wives' property, in that it protected such assets from their own creditors, as we saw above.[180] So an 1858 New York decision interpreting the MWPA that forbade married

4. Modern England and the United States

women from using their property as security for husbands' debts might seem to shield it from exploitation, but in fact cut both ways with respect to the male interest.[181]

An important factor prompting action for change in the law by courts and legislatures was perceived failure by the relevant male authority figure, the husband. There was growing concern with the implications of his potential for waste, incompetence and cruelty. Patriarchy, as in other cultures, sought moral justification as a means of legitimization, so that defining (and condemning) a bad husband served to validate the exercise of authority by good ones. Some authorities conceded that husbands had no really effective way to secure wifely obedience through coercion, and could only aim for cooptation and cooperation. Others feared that a failure to support impoverished wives might impose undesired costs on the community.

As we have already seen, a husband might rule supreme in principle, but dishonourable and untrustworthy behaviour could cost him his rights. The state reserved a right to intervene in egregious cases to preserve the dignity and status of a wronged wife or widow. The villain who prevented his wife from worshiping as she chose inspired many an advocate of change. Large numbers of widows required community support, that is, Poor Relief, suggesting a pattern of failure on the part of decedent husbands.

Reformers advocated an ideal of marriage as a partnership that was very far from reflecting the law in force, as an 1861 case affirming that a husband was under no obligation to share property with his wife demonstrates. Some played on the traditional conception of marriage as a private realm to argue for reform, for example in the area of dower. But limits on a husband's power did not automatically spell new rights for a wife, as the continued existence of coverture legitimized an unequal structure of power. Marriage may have been based on contract but it remained very much a status. Reform of coverture reflected a basic concern with safeguarding transmission of property between males. The MWPA are a prime example of this anxiety. The financial inadequacies of many husbands encouraged critiques of the social adequacy of law. Law could ultimately do little to make men better husbands, but it could better position women in the service of their interest.[182]

Policy makers sought to reconcile two conflicting aspects of the ideal of wifely, and ultimately widows', dependency. There was, as ever, a fear that women of any status might become too independent. This was matched by a concern that wives, and especially widows, become too dependent on the resources of the community. Many thought that the right solution was to configure women's dependency within marriage so that when they were widowed they could rely on the provisions made by decedent husbands. Ideals of subordination and protection stood in stark tension with each other.[183] As the difficulties inherent in this policy were revealed the state played an increasingly important role. All the while it seems that during this period sympathy for the widow came to outweigh suspicion of her.

One further change in the law of importance to widows was the passage in a number of states of wrongful death statutes, modelled on the 1846 Lord Campbell's Act in Britain. New York followed this law almost word for word, but dropped husbands as potential beneficiaries. Only the wives, i.e. widows, of victims and their next of kin were eligible (husbands did not qualify as 'next of kin' under common law). Most of the states that enacted such laws followed suit, excluding widowers from their benefits. Courts supported the legislative will by rejecting legal challenges launched by widowers. Wrongful death statutes constructed a new model for personal injury litigation, to the favour of widows and other dependents suing for support denied by the loss of the family breadwinner.[184]

Toward the very end of this period, workmen's compensation laws began to appear in a number of states. These laws, the product of a horrific crisis, provided support in case of death or accidental injury. Their popularity spread quickly. As early as 1917, they already covered some 68% of workers in the United States.[185] The crisis had a disproportionately large impact on women and children, relatively young in either case, who depended exclusively on the male breadwinner of the family for their material support. When this resource was suddenly removed through his death or serious injury, dependent women and children were reduced in most cases to a pitiable state of penury, all the more serving as objects of sympathy because deemed wholly undeserving of their dramatic reversal of fortune. The crisis generated a grave challenge to society's ability to maintain the ideal of the family wage. Like the majority of the wrongful death statutes passed earlier in this period, most of these statutes adopted asymmetrical gender-based death benefits, in which only widows or next of kin, not widowers, were automatically eligible for support due to the lost wages of a decedent worker, here, most decidedly, *workman.*

Widespread resort to compensation laws reflects in part a failure of other solutions attempted through the law of torts, workmen's cooperatives and employer-financed funds. By 1925, only five states, all in the Deep South, lacked compensation programmes. Soon after their enactment, rates of industrial accidents began to decline. As widows interacted with the government bureaucracies charged with administering the programmes they tended to grow more assertive. Benefits were transformed into entitlements and came to form the basis for new claims on the system.[186] We can see how widespread support for the family wage had helped aggravate the economic effects of the nuclear hardship scenario described by demographers. Great efforts were made in the field of public policy and other areas of social life to ameliorate its impact, although this is hardly the sole explanation for the new direction taken. In an important sense, the American version of the welfare state was constructed on a foundation of assistance to widows and orphans.

The second half of the nineteenth century witnessed a great change in the rules determining women's legal status. Contemporary feminists

4. Modern England and the United States

hailed the MWPA as signifying the end of slavery for the female sex. By the 1890s two waves of statutes were being consolidated into Married Womens' Acts. But this was in the end no revolution. For years, judges had been accustomed to blunt the impact of much pro-woman legislation in order to maintain the tradition of the common law, to the point of sometimes rejecting the explicit language of a statute. For the law on separate property to matter, women needed to have a separate source of income. Equality at law was not equality in fact, and there were limits even to theoretical equality. Gendered marital status continued to matter for some time even after the disappearance of dower. Coverture was in important respects 'modernized', not ended. Legal protection for women was derived in essence from a theory of female helplessness. Certain deviations from the norm might meet with challenge, but not the basic principle of gender hierarchy.[187] For this reason, the virtual disappearance of distinctions of marital status for women did not spell the end of patriarchy.

If revolution is to be rejected as a model for change in this period it is perhaps more important to reject the alternative of evolution. This model is more tempting in that a facile reading of modern women's history based on some indisputable landmarks, chiefly legal in nature, of the era encourages the conclusion, reached by some historians, that all or most of this has been a steady march of progress, at least in the United States and England, from the Dark Age of the reign of Victoria to the Golden Age of the present. These landmarks include the passage of the MWPA, the repeal of anti-woman legislation, the assertion of women's rights to custody of children and the grant of suffrage. This theory is hardly persuasive even on the level of law, although its inherent dubiousness is perhaps more clearly illustrated in the sections that follow.[188] By the same token, the history of this period marks no 'descent from paradise', postulating a mythical Golden Age in the early modern or pre-modern eras.

United States widows and economic privilege

The rise of the middle classes in both England and the United States helped bring about a broader distribution of property ownership in these societies than in any of the cultures studied so far. It is bracing all the same, however, to reflect on how irrelevant the rules on property ownership discussed in the section above were for large sectors of the population in the United States. On one estimate, in 1890, nearly 85% of persons over 60 years of age living in rural areas owned their farms, while only about one-third of those living in the 11 largest cities in the United States were homeowners and not tenants. Rural widows might thus appear privileged, but they tended to cede the role of household head to an adult child, often under the terms of a maintenance arrangement dictated by a husband's will. Worth noting is that the nation's urban population doubled from 20%

in 1860 to 40% in 1920. Real wealth remained inaccessible to most of the nation's elderly, including widows.[189] There is no reason to think that the situation of younger widows was on the whole far superior.

One partial but notable exception is found on the western frontier, where many widows benefited from the Homestead Act of 1862 and the Kincaid Act of 1904 in the acquisition of landed property. The Homestead Act was particularly beneficial. It offered 160 acres of government land to any citizen who was the head of a family, over 21 years of age, and lived on the property for five years. This was a highly attractive prospect for many single women, namely, widows, divorced women and abandoned women with children.[190]

During this period, employment opportunities for women were highly circumscribed, workers' pensions as well as insurance policies were rare and private charities of little assistance. As ever, economic dependency within marriage tended to spell even greater dependency after it ended. The economic power and autonomy of widows depended once again to a large extent on the demographic facts they confronted and the assets bequeathed to them by their husbands. Women, largely disadvantaged in or excluded from the labour market, relied a great deal on marriage for their material well-being. Financial dependence of women on their husbands often continued even after the marriage ended by the death of the latter. Widowhood for many meant economic dislocation at best, destitution at worst. Employment for women was, as ever, problematic in terms of availability, pay and quality. Although there was some improvement especially in the early twentieth century in the forms and amount of external assistance available to widows, a crucial development, as we shall see below, had to wait until 1939, when Congress amended the 1935 Social Security Act to embrace elderly wives, widows and dependent children in its benefits.[191] Even then the 1939 amendments prescribed the same gendered ideology of the family wage that law makers had previously adopted in wrongful death statutes and workmen's compensation legislation. This tradition was to last until the mid-1970s, when the United States Supreme Court began to take action against rules now regarded as unconstitutional on the ground that they promoted inequality between the sexes.[192]

Generalization about women's, or widows', economic status and opportunities is often difficult insofar as conditions not only varied over time, but by region, class and race.[193] Women's participation in the labour force was influenced by a variant of the male breadwinner ideology that was just as strong, if not stronger, than its English counterpart. This ideal, imperfectly realized as it was, reinforced a highly developed gendered division of labour.[194]

As we have seen, many husbands left their widows, in their wills, more than the bare minimum required by the law. Even those without a will or administrative inventory of their property might be generous, to judge

4. Modern England and the United States

from a study of early nineteenth-century Pennsylvania. Poorer men left a higher percentage of their estate to their widows. At the same time, husbands who wrote wills or whose estate was settled out of court were especially likely to leave more than the legal minimum. As a result, inheritance law governed a relatively small number of estates. In Chester County and Philadelphia in this period only a minority of widows received as little as the legally mandated one-third. In the decades just before 1850 entire estates increasingly went to widows, a practice well suited to changing economic conditions that augmented the value of assets available at least to some women who had lost their husbands. In the city, personal property typically amounted to a greater share of the husband's assets than real estate. The usual practice in any case was to bequeath a share of or the entire estate as a life interest rather than with absolute ownership, which does not seem to have been intended, nor to have served, as an impediment to the prosperity of widows.[195]

By the late nineteenth century most husbands in Bucks County, Pennsylvania left more than the minimum dictated by intestacy, a departure from practice earlier in the century. Greater numbers of husbands named their wives as executors of their wills. Women were entrusted with administering estates, certainly when these were of a modest size. Fathers, at least on the level of the middle classes, began to treat daughters and sons equally in their wills, evidently out of newfound confidence that the MWPA would allow the former to retain their bequests.[196] In late nineteenth-century Arizona, with its community marital property regime, the widow's minimum share was one-half. Although more generous than the common law third, it was still difficult to live on half of what was previously available, a fact that encouraged many husbands to leave more than the minimum.[197] The same held true for Los Angeles in this period, where, it is worth noting, the percentage of wives named by their husbands as executors was as high as 80%. In the early twentieth century, common law states like Pennsylvania (1917) passed laws reforming the rights on intestacy of widows, bringing them more into line with contemporary practice and the rules in community property states.[198] The mid to late nineteenth century trend away from the relative stinginess shown to widows in the early Republic prefigured the practices of the late twentieth century, when spouses tended to receive all or most of an estate.

Although a few widows increased their share through illegal means, many were skilled at providing for their families using entirely legal methods, for example, by prudent exploitation of real estate or shrewd handling of other resources, such as stocks.[199] The family, still strongly identified with the household in the early nineteenth-century United States, remained for the most part a unit of production as well as consumption, until increasing industrialization helped promote a separation of these spheres.[200] As in England, however, the development of industrial capitalism was uneven. Even as late as 1895, as contemporaries were well aware, while some industries had largely relocated to a factory setting, others remained in the home.[201]

The latter phenomenon is perhaps most obvious in the case of the family farm, which served as both a home and a business. Wives might play a key role in household production, sometimes by taking on a variety of jobs. A widow could influence the share she received from her deceased husband while he was alive, to the point in some cases of participating in the writing of his will. Widows took over shops in the city and farms in the country that had been operated by their husbands.[202] They were often highly competent executors of their husbands' estates, suggesting they had played an active role in managing family finances during marriage. Testamentary practice responded over time to changes in the economy and social values, as seen just above.[203]

Wives among the elite were typically well informed about the details of investments and family income. Men, with good reason, trusted the economic skills of their wives, who often went on to become expert financial managers during widowhood. In defiance of cultural stereotypes and legal restrictions, widows participated in the world of work, and with no small success in a number of cases. A widow, no less than her deceased husband, might be described as a 'man of business'.[204]

While some women did not experience an economic decline on widowhood, for others their new status simply intensified their existing marital poverty.[205] Widows who did not prosper may have been financially incompetent, but were even more likely to have received less than what their husbands intended, in early nineteenth-century Pennsylvania, for example, thanks to the claims of creditors to the estate.[206] As in Victorian England, rhetoric about the family wage helped depress women's pay and discourage their entry into the workplace.[207] Central to the ideal of the family wage were the male worker and sole earner himself as well as the wife and children who depended on him for their sustenance.[208] Employment opportunities for women, as in contemporary England, were limited by the practices of gender segregation in the workplace and sex-typing of jobs.[209] Women as a consequence were concentrated in low-paying jobs in the manufacture of clothing and textiles, for example.[210]

It has long been recognized that widows worked as boarding house operators, shopkeepers, day nurses, laundresses and seamstresses, that is, largely in jobs that functioned as extensions of their ideal domestic role. Homework, as defined above, was a popular option, especially for widows with small children. Recent research suggests the range of jobs they held might be broader than once assumed, although still for the most part informal, poorly paid and demeaning, while offering no chance of advancement. Above all, poor widows wanted to avoid the almshouse. For many the only option was to string together more than one ill-paying, casual job at a time. Some found no alternative to prostitution. Economic demands outweighed the reigning ideology of (non-working) womanhood among

4. Modern England and the United States

working-class widows, just as they did in a different way for elite women. Some widows resisted, however, because they considered themselves still to be wives, and so refused to enter the labour force, or, as middle-class women confronting downward social mobility, regarded some tasks to be beneath their dignity, such as housecleaning or factory work. Older widows frequently found their options foreclosed – a disadvantage of entering the workforce at a relatively advanced age – and were compelled to accept inferior jobs, in other words, whatever menial drudgery was available.[211]

Some historians have argued for a decline in women's employment opportunities around the turn of the twentieth century.[212] It does seem likely that by the end of the nineteenth century, the ideology of 'separate spheres' for men and women was having more of an impact on lived experience than ever before. This has implications for both the supply of and the demand for women workers. In the first decades of the new century, participation by adult women, especially married women, in the workforce was low, especially compared with contemporary European levels.[213] Certain regions, like the Southwest, simply had few job opportunities for women of any marital status.[214] Prejudice against all but the neediest of wives working outside the home was highly durable. Only 12% did so as late as 1930.[215] A wife's status that laboured under both the marriage contract and a wage contract was viewed as a conflict fraught with difficulty for husbandly authority.[216] Evangelical Christians and others deplored the loss – to a husband – of a wife's domestic services and compared the free labour market to the antebellum slave market, arguing the need for protective legislation.[217] Members of the elite often had great difficulty understanding that the reality of working-class life often required a financial contribution from a wife's labour outside the home.[218]

Dire need drove many to work, and worse. Seventy per cent of widows in early nineteenth-century Pennsylvania, on one estimate, had dependent children when they lost their husbands.[219] Some did not hesitate to exploit their children economically, as stepfathers routinely did.[220] Others sought a way to lighten the financial burden placed on them. Widows placed their children in orphanages only with great reluctance, and most who did retrieved them as soon as they could. Still, for an unlucky few loss of a husband also meant loss of their children.[221]

Not that long ago, scholars tended to argue for the independent residence of widows in this period. On this view, relatively few widows shared their residence with one or more of their children, although some shared a dwelling with other widows. In recent years the dominant opinion has shifted, with most scholars now holding that in the nineteenth and early twentieth centuries most elderly widows and (in smaller percentages) widowers (elderly here means those over 65) lived with or next door to their children if they had any still living. A typical scenario was that adult children stayed on in the parental home. The multigenerational pattern occurs most frequently in the higher economic levels of society. Rural widows tended to be dependents while urban ones acted as household heads. Throughout this period this multigenerational residential phenomenon was in a state of gradual decline, which sharply accelerated after 1920.[222] On the frontier, nearly all single women lived in multiple-person households, composed of their children, other relatives or women friends.[223]

Adult sons were expected to support their widowed mothers, including sharing a residence, but, as in nineteenth-century England, there were widows who preferred relative hardship to residing with their children, either out of a desire for independence, or to avoid burdening their offspring, or both.[224] In late nineteenth and early twentieth-century Denver, where widows were especially numerous and most families did not have the resources to care for them, widowhood meant the end of an independent household for many older women, while younger widows usually continued as household heads.[225] A similar pattern is attested by the 1880 Census for Arizona, where widows found job opportunities scarce.[226] While most widows on public relief in early nineteenth-century Philadelphia lived with their adult children, others entered the almshouse rather than turn to their children.[227] In late nineteenth-century Arizona, many widows worked as housekeepers for their adult children, although fewer of them by 1900, when a good number listed themselves with the census as heads of households.[228]

As in other periods, a few widows provided financial support to other widows, sometimes by performing charity work themselves, sometimes in writing their wills.[229] Private charity was sometimes available to those deemed 'worthy'. Widows were highly likely to qualify, above all, those who were prepared to conform to upper- and middle-class notions of proper behaviour. Such charity thus exacted a price and inflicted a stigma, representing for many an absolute last resort.[230]

Public assistance, rare and problematic, was considered in this period to be a hard-won privilege and not an entitlement. For the Victorians, charity was transformed into a punitive contractual agreement in which aid was exchanged for work. The English New Poor Law of 1834, severe as it was, served as a model for American reformers, although their adaptations tended to be even harsher than the original. It is possible to trace signs of this austerity even earlier. In early nineteenth-century Pennsylvania as elsewhere public assistance came in two main forms, outdoor relief and the almshouse (also known, outside of Pennsylvania, as the poor house). Widows, especially downwardly mobile ones, were deemed particularly deserving of support. But even they were thought by many to merit severe treatment, not because they were thought to have deserved their fate, but because, otherwise, in the current thinking, the threat of moral laxity loomed.

Older widows preferred to receive outdoor relief, augmenting the often inadequate funds provided by the authorities with whatever proceeds

4. Modern England and the United States

arose from work and savings. Friends, family or others might be paid to house a widow. Not only did entry into the almshouse curtail independence, it required the surrender of all assets, making it a last resort for many. In principle, dependency abrogated common law rights, which was true enough of marriage itself for women, so that in this sense nothing much changed. The typical widowed inmate was a young woman drawn to the city by the illusion of economic opportunity. A change in the Pennsylvania Poor Law in 1828 encouraged a dramatic rise in their numbers. In 1813 widows were only 2% of the adult females in the almshouse, a proportion that increased to over 20% after 1828. Outdoor relief was eventually abolished in nearly half of major American cities, removing an important option for the impoverished widow.[231]

In 1910 Denver County widows were recorded as 14% of charity recipients, a figure likely to understate the reality. Most were young or middle-aged mothers. Here outdoor relief was regarded as an extraordinary measure, designed to be partial and temporary in nature. The authorities were overly optimistic, however, about the capacity of families and friends to support widows financially.[232] In late nineteenth-century Arizona, the law on marital property and succession was relatively favourable to women, allowing some to live well and reducing the numbers on relief. Widows requiring public assistance had to depend on qualifying thanks to the petition of neighbours or a physician, and offer proof of both need and worthiness.[233] Local programmes dominated the scene for most of this period. As late as the start of the twentieth century, social welfare programmes were practically non-existent on the state and national levels.[234]

Mormon widows in this period might look to a variety of sources of aid. Beyond what their husbands bequeathed them, crucial assistance was provided by children, especially sons, who offered not only financial, but also social and psychological support. Those who took over a deceased husband's business or were able to make use of their own skills in such fields as teaching, midwifery or bookkeeping tended to fare the best. Church and community support was available only for the short term, functioning as a temporary and partial expedient. Widows were encouraged to regard assistance from the Mormon Church as a privilege, not a right. The church provided a kind of default welfare insurance for them, a failsafe against destitution. Between 1882 and 1907 plural wives and children (those from unions following, but contemporaneous with, a first marriage) were excluded from rights to inheritance from their husband and father, with consequences that may have been as much psychological as material, especially given that in other years they were eligible for only a diminished share.[235]

The position of Hispanic widows in Santa Fe during this period was far less privileged. Adult women without husbands, including the divorced, separated and deserted, were at the bottom of the social scale in terms of income and jobs, limited for the most part to labour as domestics and paid less than others for the same work. Single mothers were in the worst situation of all. Few owned farmland, a chief economic asset in that area. They had no real access to poorhouses and other charity. As bad as it was at the start, the economic status of unmarried women in Santa Fe declined in the late nineteenth century.[236] Hispanic widows in the Mesilla Valley in southern New Mexico do not appear to have been appreciably more prosperous. Some depended on charity from the Catholic Church in the form of money, medicine, food and clothing, as well as support from family and personal resources. Many found themselves in serious hardship, however. Some relied on male 'friends', trading financial help for a potential drop in status. Younger widows might return to their parents' homes, and older ones might reside with their adult children. The available jobs were few in number and limited in range, such as teaching, keeping a store or boarding house, farming, midwifery and domestic service. For many, an informal, casual basis of support was the best they could manage.[237]

As noted a number of times, the financial status of a widow typically depended to a great extent on her situation as a wife. Great difficulties persisted for many women throughout this period. Contemporaries feared that extending public assistance to wives, even those in desperate straits, converted them into a family's chief breadwinner. Ideally, the household was set apart and protected from the corrupting effects of the marketplace. But as perceptions flourished of male failure to provide and its consequences, criticism followed. The unwillingness or inability of husbands to sustain their wives financially was viewed by some as a breach of the marital contract entailing a forfeiture of rights, above all those to a wife's labour. The MWPA themselves had not compromised those rights except in drastic situations. By 1887 some two-thirds of the states had promulgated wives' earnings statutes, some dating to the antebellum period. Feminists envisioned these laws as recasting marriage along egalitarian lines and striking a blow for the economic independence of wives. They were often indifferently designed and sloppily drafted, however. More importantly, they did not end a husband's claim to his wife's services as a matter of law. Enforcement by the courts of pro-woman statutes was an enormous problem, as we have seen. Without underrating the achievement of feminists in altering the law of marital status, or the increased prosperity enjoyed by some women in its wake, it is impossible to be very sanguine about the impact of this legislation in some fundamental respects. The laws, after all, amounted to little more than an expedient to shore up, by co-opting women, a patriarchy put to the test by a widespread male failure that threatened its moral legitimacy and financial base. Rather than fostering the independence of women it bound many of them to a double shift of work outside and inside the home.[238]

Direct financial assistance promised better at first. As early as the beginning of the nineteenth century, some pension funds were available for a very small number of poor widows, such as those who had been

4. Modern England and the United States

married to war veterans. In 1862, Congress voted a generous pension programme for the widows (as long as they remained unmarried) and other dependents of Union soldiers killed in the Civil War, or from a related cause (Confederate widows were at best eligible for less generous state programmes). Over the course of the century, wives of some workers, such as police officers and firefighters, became entitled to spousal death benefits. In 1890, Congress extended pension benefits to widows of virtually all Civil War veterans, rendering many more women eligible. Even so, many found themselves forced into the workforce. Fraternal organizations might offer an insurance programme for some, while unions were one more potential source of assistance.[239] In 1882 Congress approved pensions for four widows of presidents, implicitly acknowledging the vulnerability of all widows.[240] The Arizona Pioneer Society, which typically benefited the Hispanic widows of decedent European males and their children, deserves particular mention, although members rarely resorted to its widows' and orphans' fund.[241]

By the late nineteenth and early twentieth centuries widows, especially the poor, ill and elderly among them, were increasingly deemed a public responsibility.[242] Just as law makers sought to improve the lot of well-off widows by junking the system of dower in favour of improvements to the law of succession, over time they came to address the needs of poor widows through programmes such as 'Mothers' Pensions'.[243] A White House conference on dependent children in 1909 was a stimulus for a series of Mothers' (or Widows') Compensation Acts that passed in a number of states after 1911. These were not aimed at widows per se but at the widowed mothers of young children. In fact, their main purpose was to encourage widows to care for their children at home and stay out of the workforce. In a sense, 'widow' was redefined for the purposes of this body of statute law as widow with child or children. The distribution of benefits, never very generous, might be broadened to embrace abandoned wives and others provided they too met a standard of moral 'worthiness'. Recipients had to qualify as morally blameless, as did workers under the new rules for workmen's compensation.

Widows formed the majority of single mothers in this period and remained the main objects of sympathy among this group, although even they might arouse suspicion.[244] As with dower reform, which was aimed primarily at assisting better-off widows, advocates of Mothers' Pensions sought to address the challenge posed by women's financial dependency within marriage. In the former, a privatized solution, recourse to a decedent husband's patrimony, was preferred; in the latter, the state came to the rescue. One driving concern, especially in the former instance, was with prospective loss of status – an ancient anxiety – the notion that any woman, or at least any wife, could end up a poor widow. Marriage remained, both ideally and in actual fact, as much an economic status as a legal one for women.

Although relatively few benefited from these statutes nationwide, providing aid to women without husbands no longer seemed to pose a threat to the ideology that insisted wives be dependent on them. One can trace the events leading to statutory reform in Colorado, for example, where, as elsewhere, the assistance provided under the act was inadequate to the needs of the state's widows. In Arizona, a 1914 statute providing aid to widows with dependent children was declared unconstitutional not long after passage. Its successor in 1916 allowed each county to develop its own policy, so that they varied considerably in terms of generosity. Aid was not always distributed equitably by ethnic group, as Europeans were typically preferred to Hispanics. Nonetheless, given the hostility to government assistance encouraged by the American tradition of voluntarism and individualism, the mere existence of such laws was a significant development. State aid was – in theory – enforceable at law, while informal assistance from friends and family remained as aleatory as ever. Other solutions came to the fore with the passage of time. Charity Organization Societies sprang up in many cities toward the end of the nineteenth century in order to assist better the 'worthy' poor, including widows.[245]

Despite these developments, great differences persisted among the states.[246] In the early twentieth century they increasingly began to pass legislation authorizing unemployment insurance, in addition to the laws on wrongful death and workmen's compensation, described above.[247] In these years the economic insecurity of widows and others was more and more viewed as a threat to the health and welfare of the entire population. Decisive material change for most widows had to await the amendment to the Social Security legislation benefiting them in 1939, provided they did not remarry. The failure of the state-based assistance programmes meant, however, that widows in some areas were far worse off in 1940 than they had been half a century before. The economic dependence of wives, and so widows, on husbands long survived the theoretical achievement of political and legal equality by women with men.[248]

United States widows and freedom of movement

Many widows relished the release from coverture set in motion by the death of their husbands. The actual implications of wives' legal status were liable to exaggeration, although not without real-life consequences for married women. The quotidian demands of subordinating oneself to a husband, the loss of a voice both within the marriage and in the public sphere, were easily re- or misinterpreted into an ideal of total submission to a husband's legal and religious authority. Radically different views prevailed about a wife's ideal role and identity, as can be seen in the various marriage ideals popular at the time. Some even viewed coverture as a denial of a woman's independent moral identity.[249] Widowhood was then all the more valued for the opportunity it offered of legal inde-

4. Modern England and the United States

pendence and personal autonomy, a desire reflected in some widows' preference to remain heads of their households. A number of widows, in short, found the experience liberating.[250]

In this period the ideal of companionate marriage, a relationship based on a reciprocity of rights and duties, even if ultimately contracted between individuals of unequal status, was widespread and deeply felt. On this theory, marriage was a permanently binding contract, creating a new status for the parties, especially for the wife. On the other hand, many felt its consensual basis loomed so large that a lapse of agreement should be accommodated through the possibility of divorce.[251] The link between idealized, contractually based marriage and legally recognized divorce had been made by the Puritans many years before.[252] For many Christians, as well as conservatives in general, however, the status aspect of marriage exalted it above contract in a moral sense.[253] Southern apologists for slavery had by mid-century developed an analogy between marriage and slavery, justifying both as relations of inequality that supposedly benefited all parties involved. Anti-slavery activists attacked this view, characterizing slavery as a perversion of the marriage bond, if sometimes ignoring the existence of coverture.[254] Post-Civil War implementation of traditional gender roles among freed slaves reveals the extent of their ambivalence. A freedman's authority over his wife was regarded as essential to his own autonomy, not only by abolitionists, it seems, but by freedmen themselves, who were able to cite to good effect a scriptural authority, verses from a letter attributed to St Paul that counselled wifely submission.[255]

The idea that women were passionless and morally purer than men was based on a sexual double standard. This made it easier, nonetheless, to hold men accountable for the spread of immorality and disease, which in turn encouraged the assertion of a single standard of sexual behaviour for men and women. An impact was felt also in the development of public policy on abortion, illegitimacy and child support.[256] It would be difficult to overemphasize the role of Christians and Christianity, especially Evangelical Protestantism, in both defending the status quo and advocating reform. Christian influence on social attitudes was pervasive, even among feminists and scientists. Nevertheless, a secularizing trend can be discerned that grew stronger in the late nineteenth and early twentieth centuries. Scientific authority gave the appearance of being apolitical, universal and objective. This lent it an enormous prestige, even as it validated time-honoured beliefs and practices concerning women. Social policy was increasingly left in the hands of medical experts and other social welfare professionals. Patriarchy found here a formidable new justification.[257]

As in England, there was a flourishing tradition of criticism of matrimony and even an anti-marriage counterculture, with many of the very same influences at work. Feminists accepted the analogy drawn by apologists for slavery between marriage and slavery, although with the twist that neither institution was morally legitimate.[258] In the 1850s, radical critics of marriage emerged in the form of the 'free love' movement. Socialists criticized the legal inequality of the sexes. Celibate Shakers in a sense offered an even more extreme alternative.[259]

Polygyny was widely perceived, however, as the biggest threat to conventional marriage. Many critics viewed it as a form of sexual slavery, arguing that Christian monogamy was what emancipated women. The tradition of the Enlightenment connected polygyny with coercion, and even despotism.[260] Anti-marriage radicals across the board provoked a strong conservative reaction, expressed above all in a defence of coverture.[261] But concern with male failure persisted, and marriage criticism formed a staple of popular novels and magazines in the early twentieth century. At the same time the ideal of companionate marriage flourished in the very same literary genres.[262]

The status of widow was in social terms highly valued. In late nineteenth-century Santa Fe, for example, where marriage was a means of upward mobility for many Hispanic women, widowhood was a highly respectable condition.[263] In a bid for respectability some women who did not technically qualify claimed it for themselves nevertheless. It facilitated remarriage better than the status of the deserted or that of the divorced woman, which were regarded as far less socially desirable.[264] The status of widow was asserted by some women to shield their children (and themselves) from the stigma of illegitimacy. It was sometimes simply easier to invent a dead husband and father. A claim to widowhood was deemed so effective in hiding sexual behaviour otherwise liable to criticism that widows are perhaps over-represented in some of our sources.[265] Upper- and middle-class women benefited in many places from the projection of the asexual ideal onto widows, which created new opportunities for their participation in social life.[266]

One great challenge, all the same, was social isolation. Widows' letters offer poignant testimony of their loneliness.[267] Aside from family, widows tended to live with, or near, other widows. The company of other widows offered an easier transition into their new status for many, breaking their social isolation in an acceptable way.[268] Children were a similar source of emotional and sometimes financial support. In a sense, this was especially true of eldest sons, who were expected to serve as examples of proper behaviour and as advisers to the younger children, although daughters could also be a great help to a widow.[269]

Some widows resorted to memorialization, or even idealization, of their dead husband's memory as a means of coping with their loss.[270] By the mid-nineteenth century public manifestations of mourning became more socially acceptable. Widows dressed 'as widows' (meaning in black at first, often with a veil, then tending towards shades of violet) for as long as two years after a husband's death. Books of etiquette prescribed at least a year

4. Modern England and the United States

of mourning.[271] In the Southwest, the custom among Hispanic widows was to don black for a year and respect limits on socializing with others.[272] In an unintentional tribute to Juan Luis Vives, however, Mormon widows were encouraged to think of their husbands as still alive, and so avoid mourning their deaths.[273] But a young widow who seemed to emerge too quickly from mourning might occasion scandal.[274] For the financially well-off who did not lose their husbands too early in life, mourning might be relatively restrained.[275]

As in other cultures, religion could be a great source of emotional comfort for a woman who had lost her husband.[276] For widows in New Mexico, involvement with the Catholic Church was often vital in this regard.[277] But the promise of an eternal life with a deceased spouse was sometimes inadequate to the trauma of loss, as we see with some Mormon widows who resorted to forms of 'subversive mourning', ignoring the dictates of their religion and grieving for a dead husband despite the prohibition against doing so.[278]

Belief in the afterlife did not discourage everyone from pursuing success in this world.[279] Nineteenth-century widows could be fierce litigators, engaging in what often turned out to be lengthy (that is, lasting several years in some cases) legal battles to settle a husband's estate. Their adversaries might be executors of the will, recalcitrant sons, and in an important sense a sluggish legal system.[280] Once again, force of personality mattered a great deal in dealing with challenges that arose both in and out of the family. Some widows did not hesitate to use provisions either of their husbands' will or of their own to command the obedience of their children. Often their own wills served as a corrective to the perceived unfairness of their husbands'.[281] The MWPA increased the share of the family property available to them and encouraged more women to write wills, typically in favour of daughters over sons.[282] Others were more subdued in their behaviour, such as many Mormon widows, whose accounts of their lives after the deaths of their husbands are characterized by an extreme self-effacement.[283]

Throughout this period, widows gave the lie to a basic premise of the 'separate spheres' ideology intended to keep women out of public, namely the theory of womanly incompetence. Many were called on to play a number of different roles, some of which were utterly inconsistent with this idea.[284] Some found a measure of independence in life on the frontier.[285] Like other women, they participated in various reform movements of the day, such as temperance, abolitionist, environmental and local voluntary associations.[286] There is evidence to suggest that widows, like other American women in this period, were geographically mobile. For example, of Mormon widows who survived their husbands by at least 20 years without remarrying, more than half moved across county or even state lines.[287]

Literary portrayals of widows in the late nineteenth and early twenti-

Widows and Patriarchy

eth centuries can receive only the briefest notice here. On the whole, they seem to have been sympathetic.[288] The nineteenth-century feminist Elizabeth Cady Stanton could appeal to a flourishing stereotype of the suffering widow in making an appeal for the improvement of women's rights to property.[289] Even so, such depictions can blend into caricature, as with Mark Twain's Widow Douglas in *Huckleberry Finn.* Elsewhere, as in the short story *The Widow's Protest*, Twain seems simply to appeal to the prejudices of his readership. Worth noting is the unflattering, and rather roughly so, portrait of a widow in the work of a woman sometimes compared with Twain, Frances Miriam Whitcher and her Widow Bedott.[290] It is possible that with both Whitcher's and Twain's work, we have a reaction to the culturally dominant figure of the sorrowing widow, a reaction that both parodies and incorporates elements of this representation.[291] The result is perhaps more a caricature of this type than a shift to the 'merry' widow type, although Whitcher does come close to the latter at times.

Widows receive more favourable treatment in the tradition of the late antebellum southern novel, where, however, for all the sympathy expressed for them, they are shown to be weak, vulnerable, and – before too long – dead. In general, their characters are conceived and presented exclusively in terms of prospective marriage partners for the males, in the context of a narrative that is nothing if not male-centred, and extremely so perhaps even by the standards of the time.[292]

These portrayals are belied by the actions of some Southern widows during the Civil War, in which they took on great responsibilities caring for the sick and wounded in hospitals. Others sought any work they could find, motivated by sheer necessity. Some, especially among the many younger women who lost husbands to the war, showed greater initiative than deemed socially acceptable in seeking remarriage, a notable instance where concerns with the 'merry' widow arose.[293] Perhaps the most egregious, however, are the Florida widows who provoked a scandal through alleged war profiteering.[294] One should not conclude, however, that widows living outside the South were entirely free from reproach. For example, the Union veteran widows' pension programme was notoriously rife with fraud and corruption.[295]

A woman's response to the loss of a husband might depend to an extent on her level of education and work experience.[296] In the post-Civil War era, women attended college in increasing numbers. Only in the early twentieth century, however, could women become attorneys. By the 1920s some appear as judges and legal writers, although they were few in number.[297] Access to formal education or job training may have been greater for some older women, who had acquired skills elsewhere, as we see, for example, in Arizona after 1900. Over time, however, this advantage disappeared.[298] In general, the social respect conceded widows helped open up, for some of the well-placed among them, previously unknown opportunities in the public sphere.

4. Modern England and the United States

Glenda Riley has developed the thesis of the 'female frontier'. This holds that women's experience on the western prairies and plains was shaped far more by considerations of gender than by region, time period, class, race, religion or marital status. The ideal of domesticity and the gendered division of labour outweighed these other factors by a good deal.[299] This argument seems, however, more relevant for the thesis of the overall historical continuity of women's experience than for conditions peculiar to the nineteenth-century American West. Losing a husband in the unsettled conditions of that time and place had serious consequences for many women, as an abundance of evidence suggests. Riley acknowledges that many Western widows were rendered destitute and that widows and orphans were often regarded as the worthy objects of charity.[300] Others, as we have seen, achieved a measure of independence. One can stress the vulnerability of all women while conceding that some were more vulnerable than others. There is a sense, all the same, in which the experience of frontier life began to efface the distinctions of marital status. Widowhood was, in the late nineteenth and early twentieth centuries, undergoing a transformation that would eventually lead to its disappearance as a separate, identifiable status and role for women.[301]

United States widows and remarriage

A minimum period of mourning of one year was prescribed by contemporary books of etiquette, as we have seen, and remarriage that seemed precipitous, especially of younger widows, might provoke criticism. The zeal of widows and widowers to find new marriage partners certainly did seem excessive to some observers. No law, however, barred such unions.[302] In early nineteenth-century Pennsylvania, husbands would sometimes insert a prohibition on widow's remarriage into their wills with a penalty in case of breach, curbing legacies, restricting widow's access to children's property or providing for reversion to children of the property made available to the widow as a life bequest. The motive was to all appearances, however, grounded in a concern for the children's welfare rather than in a desire simply to constrain widows from finding new husbands. Widows were thought vulnerable to the designs of unscrupulous men who might impoverish stepchildren. Rather than accept such treatment, widows could reject the will with its anti-remarriage provisions and opt for benefits on intestacy. In any case, such provisions declined significantly after 1830.[303]

Evidence for rates of remarriage aligns broadly with that from other periods. Data from mid-to-late nineteenth-century Utah show that of widows under the age of 40, at least 37% and as many as 65% remarried, while few widows over 40 did.[304] There is some suggestion that the practice of polygyny in Utah encouraged widow remarriage, at least in theory. All the same, these figures are supported by data from the 1910 Census for the northeastern United States, where polygyny was largely absent, which show half or more of widows under age 40 remarrying. Marriage among older widows was again much less common.[305] As noted above, the proportions of elderly widows were steadily increasing during this period, a factor that by itself suggests an overall decline in the rate of widow remarriage.

An exception to the general trend occurs in the years after the Civil War, in which a large number of young women became widows with little chance of remarrying.[306] As ever, remarriage for widowers was more common, swifter, and to younger women.[307] An explanation has been sought in the gendered division of labour that rendered it imperative for widowed men to seek the household services of a new wife.[308] Whatever the reason, this pattern is roughly consistent with what can be recovered concerning a number of other societies in past time.

When possible, some widows, especially older ones, seem to have preferred independence to remarriage, independence not just in financial terms but in setting the course of their own social life, as suggested by recent evidence.[309] But many had little choice in the matter, as economic pressures compelled a new marital union or the lack of a prospective husband prevented this. When opportunity presented itself, as with the gender imbalance in many areas of the late nineteenth-century West, we sometimes find a greater incidence of widows remarrying, as on the Oregon Trail, where some remarried more than once. The prospect of material support, as well as avoidance of the social isolation that the single status often imposed, played a role in these decisions.[310] While there is evidence that many widows availed themselves of the preponderance of single males over single women in the far West to remarry frequently and with ease, numerous others seem to have relished their newfound independence and remained single.[311]

Assuming a widow's identity facilitated remarriage for divorced and deserted women. In principle, remarriage after divorce was problematic both for society and the courts, especially for persons divorced on account of socially disapproved behaviour such as adultery. Some critics went as far as identifying freedom to remarry after divorce with 'free love'. At the same time nineteenth-century Americans tended to assume they had a right to remarry, whatever the law said.[312]

Widowhood as a vanishing status

No one doubts that the grant of suffrage to women was a necessary and salutary step. It certainly played a decisive role in the levelling of distinctions of status among women. All women were placed on an equal footing regarding this important aspect of (male) citizenship, and it was no longer possible to argue, for example, that married women did not need the vote because their husbands voted for them.[313] But it is easy to overestimate its importance. In the end it proved easier to treat women for some purposes

4. Modern England and the United States

as males than to recognize their independent and equal status as women. Granting married women many of the rights previously enjoyed by widows and never-married women helped create a new civic category that accommodated all women. This did not by itself guarantee equality with men, however. To the extent that married women were assimilated to widows this was a positive development; to the extent that widows were assimilated to wives it was a negative one. Moreover, the reform was an imperfect one. Traces of coverture, the principle of wifely subordination, still lurked in the fabric of the law and of social life.

One problem was that marriage continued to function as much as an economic as a legal status for women. The challenge of widows' poverty demonstrated the hollowness of family wage rhetoric. The problem of female dependency, in and out of marriage, seems almost an inherent feature of patriarchy, essential to its operation as a system of gender hierarchy but with great potential to undermine and disrupt it. Tinkering with the legal apparatus of marriage and the economic relationship between spouses at its core has long been a preferred solution.

Widowhood can trace its disappearance as a discrete status to more than just changes in the law. If anything, the widespread sympathy for widows and their plight, shared by both policy makers and broad sectors of the public, emerged as strong as ever in this period and sustained for a time their social identity.[314] This state of affairs was not permanent, however. The government economic programmes designed to meet the needs of deserving recipients such as widows and orphans that arose in the first half of the twentieth century severed over time the enduring and to all appearances virtually inevitable link between widowhood and poverty in both England and the United States. In a sense, this outcome marks the triumph of one side of the ideal of dependency that held for widows. But the long-term effects of demographic change were perhaps even more dramatic. Concentrating widows in the upper age brackets of society made them all but invisible, and had the important if secondary effects of rendering age-old concerns with their freedom of movement and remarriage largely moot.

5
Conclusion: Widows in history

Do widows have a history? The simple, unsatisfactory answer is, yes and no. The question is difficult, indeed in the end impossible, to disentangle from similar inquiries revolving around the historical experience of women in general, patriarchy and the family. It should occasion no great surprise that these matters are deeply controversial. Some historians emphasize continuity from the past to the present, albeit in radically different ways. Others have seen fundamental shifts from antiquity, the late Middle Ages or the early modern period. There is ample material in this book to support a case either for continuity or for change, a fact that suggests caution in generalizing about the preponderance of one or the other.

Patriarchy's progress has been far from linear. The economic opportunities enjoyed by many women in the late Middle Ages were eclipsed in the early modern age. The more recent modern period has seen such rapid changes in family life that searching for signs of stability may seem futile.[1] To an extent the answer to the question of whether continuity or change predominates in the experience of widows depends on which arena of experience (economic opportunity versus family life, for example) and which women (upper versus lower orders, for example) are at issue.

One can argue that the historical events that mark one period from another in our mapping of the past have had few direct and profound consequences for many widows. They were, for the most part, poor and vulnerable both at the start of their widowhood and at its close, a principle that holds true from culture to culture over time. It is also persuasive that the lived experience of widows has been almost as diverse as their number, so that the idea of a 'typical widow' is elusive at best. The inadequacy of the two typologies cited in the Introduction, the sorrowing and the merry widow, to describe the vast majority of widows in past time is an illustration of this point.[2] And yet both of these points, if pursued to their logical conclusions, seem guaranteed to lead to an ahistorical dead end. The diversity of widows' experience does not prevent certain deep structures from lending a basic shape to this for most of them. At the same time those structures allow for a discernible periodization that defines developments in widows' status and role over time.

These results are compatible with the view that much if not most historical change does indeed affect women, although often in ways different from its impact on men of similar socio-economic backgrounds. This is why it is entirely legitimate to question the application to women's expe-

5. Conclusion: Widows in history

rience of traditional chronological categories such as 'Renaissance', 'early modern', or the division into 'medieval' and 'modern' – one might also question their application in some ways to men – and at the same time difficult to escape them. The effects of change on the experience of gender differ over time, so that no traditional turning point in history can simply be assumed to have a great meaning for women or to have been irrelevant, for that matter.[3]

The underlying patterns that influence widows' lives begin with the facts of demography. These differ in significant ways from culture to culture and over time and yet a few basic points carry over. Gender-differentiated mortality does not appear to have played nearly the same role in any of the periods under study that it does today. The same holds for divorce, although antiquity may form a partial exception to this principle. Much more important in determining the numbers of widows and the length of widowhood is the age gap between spouses at first marriage. This varies considerably from society to society, but in every culture under study the husband is on average older than the wife. This makes for more widows than widowers and longer periods of widowhood for women from the start. Of great significance for numbers is the proportion of women who marry in a culture. Another important element is remarriage practice. The widespread tendency for widowers to remarry sooner, more often, and to younger partners than widows forecloses remarriage as an option for many of the latter. Poorer widows are less likely to find new partners and wealthier ones often find an obstacle in the loss of important economic benefits if they do. Age and class, or at least wealth, are the most important factors affecting widows' remarriage chances across time.

Family structure is a demographic factor that can have a major impact on widows' financial well-being. The nuclear form is liable to leave them ill-situated at critical moments of the life cycle, as the exponents of the nuclear hardship scenario point out. The cultures we have studied that had the nuclear as the dominant family form – that is to say all of them in this book except Greece and Rome – tended to develop compensatory mechanisms that provided assistance at these times of peak vulnerability. This does not, of course, guarantee that these have always been adequate to the purpose.

The married state itself has traditionally represented a limit on women's freedom, the more so the less public and more privatized it is. At the same time, marriage has never been strictly private in nature for most women. Even today, to the minds of many policy makers, it serves an important mediating function, helping to define women's role as citizens and providing a financial buffer against claims on public resources.[4] It has offered many women a basic level of economic protection plus companionship, often in exchange for the submersion of a wife's legal personality under that of her husband. The only exception, in all of the periods under study, is ancient Rome, and its non-*manus* form of marriage, which is

Widows and Patriarchy

perhaps enough by itself to suggest that Rome was the most self-confident of all the patriarchies we have examined in this book.

The vast majority of never-married women were, for a time at least, in a similar position of identity submersion with respect to their fathers. Moreover, most were prospective brides, contemplating the loss of whatever independent status they enjoyed. Widows, except when they remarried, of course, stand out as women whose status in important respects resembled that of men, if that is indeed the inevitable standard to which they are to be compared. Of course, the status of men has hardly been a unitary one either.[5] At the same time the connection between marriage and citizenship, that is, the right to marry, should not be undervalued. It is obviously a necessary precursor to civic identity as a widow.

Statute law is often written without explicit reference to gender, and the significance of this is difficult to dismiss. Law is in a sense a theory of proper conduct, not to be confused with actual behaviour, but at the same time it is more than a theory. Law uses language as an instrument of power and its normative force depends on it. Of course, there are limits to the implications of this fact. For example, gender-neutral law on the books does not necessarily mean gender-neutral law in application.[6] As a result, discriminating against women in theory might even seem in some respects pointless. In a situation where women were effectively barred from pursuing legal claims, the law on the books could afford to affect a high-minded generosity.[7] Rules were sometimes based on the questionable premise that women both knew their own self-interest and were capable of acting on it.[8] The inexperience of widows in business matters often rendered their equality before the law a moot point, just as their ignorance of the law proved costly in financial and/or emotional terms. In sum, inexperience, lack of knowledge and social constraints on women's assertiveness can easily negate law's ostensible fairness to both genders.[9] At the same time, law on the books can give rise to claims on society not otherwise available to women.

Enlightenment theories about the role of reason and natural law in the discovery of legal rules did not directly translate into new rights for women. Nor did the assertion of equality motivated, for example, by the ideology of the French Revolution, although it 'politicized' women, lead to full civil rights for them. And yet such developments were necessary precursors of real change for women in the modern period.[10]

It is revealing that when gender-specific rules are developed they seem more likely to be designed for the protection of widows than their outright exploitation. There is a long tradition of legitimizing power by offering protection to widows as a category, an emblematic class, of the weak and the vulnerable. Even so, protection may objectively constitute no advantage, such as legislation that effectively ratifies the sexual division of labour by lending it the approval of the state.[11] Another example can be

5. Conclusion: Widows in history

found in the rules of property law that defined a new type of ownership for women.[12] Legislative intent may be distinctly noble, such as the motive to protect women from the consequences of particularly egregious male failure. The outcome of protective law making tends, however, to confirm women's vulnerability rather than to end it. The general principle is, bluntly put, one of unequal equality.

This is not to deny that changes over time in the law, economy and society now benefited, now harmed, the interests of widows and women in general. Widows, wives and never-married women must be viewed, not in isolation, but in line with each other, in order to understand the real impact of such changes, not just on the welfare of widows in broad terms, but on the deep structures in patriarchal society that at all times have operated to uphold male superiority and female subordination. In other words, it is often very difficult to be certain if developments in either legal rules or custom effectively free women from the control of male family members.[13] Patriarchy sometimes appears to operate on a principle of homeostasis. It was only in the nineteenth century that the implications of gender for social life began to cease to be structured by marital status. This was precisely when the insistent exclusion of women from the 'public sphere' reached a high pitch, both negatively in terms of explicit prohibitions that prevented them from voting and holding elective office and positively in the sense that the household was firmly relegated to the private sphere.[14]

Discriminating against females has sometimes been revealed as counterproductive in that it obstructed their usefulness to patriarchy, for example, by hindering their role in the transmission of property from male to male.[15] In this way the interest of the widow and that of her family might not be construed as radically different from each other.[16] The extension of legal rights to women, whatever the motive, still created scope for women's agency and a reduction of male power, however slightly, given its sheer scale.[17]

Changes in the law significantly affected the economic status of a number of individual widows and even propertied widows as a class, albeit in different ways. Two examples from England are the repression of the more extreme judicial presumptions of intent to bar dower toward the end of the eighteenth century and the widespread disappearance of the right to dower in fact long before it ended in theory in the early nineteenth century.[18] Changes in the economy have been equally varied in their effects. The advent of capitalism had a highly ambiguous and contradictory impact on women's fortunes, assisting some, but perpetuating and indeed refining the sexual division of labour.[19] Viewed in the long term, material provisions for women have been out of balance with male property rights.[20] So, for example, the rights of married women to separate property did not automatically translate into genuine power.[21] This is not to deny the existence of a material benefit for many.

Widows and Patriarchy

More than any other factor, a woman's economic status has defined her experience of widowhood. In other words, although the categories of class and gender are separate and separable in analytic terms, it is impossible to understand either apart from the other.[22] The vast majority of female workers in past time encountered a workplace that was structured against their interest, especially in terms of segregation by sex and sex-typing of jobs. The economy itself, not just the dominant gender ideology, has often helped generate these sexual divisions. All women have been disadvantaged in this way, although married women and widows have traditionally fared the worst.

The sexual division of labour shows enormous differences over time and from place to place. Each of the cultures under study has had its own organization of male and female work. Although the sexual division of labour predated the rise of capitalism, this phenomenon was sharpened considerably in the early nineteenth century, marginalizing women at the same time it offered many of them new economic opportunities. This division of labour, with its characteristic practices, such as sex-typing of jobs and segregation of the genders, can usefully be described as one of the deep structures of patriarchy.

Marriage, in the sense of the relationship of husband and wife as defined at law, must seem fair to function properly, which is to say, from a traditional perspective, in order to guarantee the subordination of women within it.[23] The implications of this proceed far beyond the legal rules themselves. The 'patriarchal code', which justifies male power (and women's lack of it) often depends on an ideological justification that is in large part moral in nature.[24] We have seen much evidence in this book of a marriage ideal that stresses an affective relationship between spouses, an ethic of equality and mutual regard, to a greater or lesser extent. Every culture under study in this book has had its own interpretation of this ideal, which often sits at odds with any number of legal rules and received social customs. One cannot assume such variants to be monolithic within a culture. There is even evidence of differentiation by gender in some cases.

Changes that have occurred over time have not always been in the direction of warmer, more egalitarian relations between spouses. The Reformation, for example, introduced a good measure of authoritarianism. Some of its longer-term effects can be distinguished from its shorter-term ones, however. New developments in religious thought and practice, above all, the emphatic proclamation of the spiritual equality of men and women, helped create new opportunities for the latter. From the seventeenth century it was recognized that husbands, like kings, had a responsibility to wield their power justly. This was the era of increasing challenge to regal authority, which broke the bond, once indissoluble in appearance, between patriarchal authority and legitimate government. Eventually, the principle was extended to parents, usually fathers, in the sense that

5. Conclusion: Widows in history

abuse or neglect meant they no longer deserved obedience and also forfeited other rights.[25] By the same token, a husband who mistreated or deserted his wife might not be thought to qualify as a husband at all, a point granted increasing recognition in the nineteenth century.[26] The companionate ideal that flowered in the Victorian age allowed women to make claims on the system that were unimaginable in the early modern period, and before.

The cult of domesticity that, on a conventional estimate, arose in the eighteenth and flowered in the nineteenth century, helped create a separation of public and private spheres that was always more ideological than real, except perhaps that it tended to disguise the impact of governmental and economic forces on the family.[27] This ideal division was assisted by developments connected with industrial capitalism, such as the separation (a long time in coming for many workers) between home and workplace. Nineteenth-century capitalism was far from bringing an end to patriarchy, as some have thought (or hoped) but it did introduce important transformations. One of these was, paradoxically, an increased participation by women in the economy, even if this often meant substituting supervision by males in the workplace for supervision by males at home.[28] Theories of sexual difference justified a gendered division of labour both between home and workplace and within each.[29] The reigning ideology played out very differently according to class, while the principle of male control was preserved overall. The entire experience renders more persuasive the argument of scholars such as Judith Bennett that changes in the European economy associated with pre-industrial capitalism did not make for a radical improvement in women's lives.[30]

The economic impact on women of industrial capitalism is overall consistent with the ideology of New Patriarchy that came to supplant the early modern version, once class differences are taken into account. This new model of gender hierarchy offered some powerful positive incentives to wives, above all in the form of a marriage ideal based on sentiment and reciprocity. Increasing access to education helped promote women's role as companions to their husbands. In the wake of the Enlightenment's celebration of (male) rationality, however, the (re)construction of the feminine as the gender of sensibility over sense, together with women's relegation to what was termed the private sphere, effectively subordinated them. Moreover, the wife was now, in place of the husband under the old regime, responsible for the home and all that was supposed to take place there. She was even made responsible for her husband, a dramatic switch in role.[31]

Responsibility does not always spell power, however. There was a strong public interest in promoting the family. A corollary of this principle was to promote good behaviour by family members. The courts were prepared, within limits, to enforce the duties society stipulated for spouses. In part they acted to shore up the position of the male heads of household, who continued, at least ideally, to wield true influence. For them, greater privatization of the family meant greater freedom of discretion to assert their authority.[32] This trend met with a significant reaction, however. An important part of New Patriarchy's history is the attack launched on it by feminists in the nineteenth century.[33] While patriarchy in the past had hardly been free from criticism, there was no precedent for this assault. To downplay its significance is to deny women an important part of their history.

Some Roman historians have advanced the case that family life in antiquity, at least for the upper-class Romans, was, if not quite 'modern' in its lived experience, far less harsh than it was once argued, or simply assumed, to be.[34] For us this raises an important question. Can there be a question of continuity, in any obvious way, with the ancient world for the modern family, the status and role of women, or patriarchy itself? Much of the evidence we have surveyed in this book encourages scepticism. The tradition on widows that formed in late antiquity dominated the medieval period, but underwent a significant transformation in the early modern age. Even the apparent connections with the distant past can be illusory in an important sense. The 'cherry picking' from Roman law and other aspects of the ancient tradition, so characteristic of the early modern period, actually represents an important break with antiquity, because these aspects were instrumentalized in a manner that rendered them far more anti-female once they were taken from their original cultural context.

Even so, despite periodic difficulties, patriarchy has proved remarkably durable. It survived, if notably transformed, the transition from the early modern to the modern period, a transition marked by difficulties that are perhaps better described as chronic rather than acute.[35] More remarkably, it overcame challenges that were, I would argue, even greater in the period that preceded it. The term 'crisis' then, if ever, characterizes the experience of gender relations in the passage from late medieval to early modern, a transition from which patriarchy emerged stronger than before. Historians have persuasively insisted that the history of the modern age reflects no 'descent from paradise'. The gendered division of labour, with its sex-typing of jobs, segregation and exclusion of women, and pay differentials, existed as surely in the sixteenth century as in the nineteenth, albeit with important differences that flow in both positive and negative directions.[36] The history of patriarchy has been, on the long view, a troubled one, and its historiography, not surprisingly, remains a site of controversy.[37] One good reason for this is its sheer complexity. As we have seen, there were more than just two forms of patriarchy in past time, the classical and the modern.

Such shifts help confirm an important truth. The experience of widowhood could vary considerably over time and from culture to culture, as well as within a culture. It is not unusual for compensating pressures to arise when the balance of interests tilts too far in one direction or another. One

5. Conclusion: Widows in history

of the few constants we have seen is that the economic situation of wives is, more often than not, superior to that which they enjoy as widows. So there tends to be a loss of status, however slight in some instances, attendant on widowhood. Marriage, for all of its inequalities and difficulties, offers at least a modicum of legal and economic protection to most women in most cultures. Living alone often presents difficulties of various kinds for women. Little choice has been typically granted to widows, or women in general, in the matter of seeking employment.

The weakness and vulnerability of widows is a cultural construct, and an enduring one at that. Representations of widows as passive and dependent are belied by much evidence to the contrary. Reality and representation are not always so easily disentangled, however. Concerns with the social and economic welfare of women living outside the married state continue to be felt to this day.[38] The figure of the impoverished widow resonates from culture to culture in the everyday lives of many. Even wealthier widows have often found that losing a spouse signifies financial loss and perhaps a reduced standard of living. The construct described here has been a curiously self-reinforcing one, which has helped shape the lived experience of countless women in a number of cultures. The vulnerability of widows is both literary topos and lived experience.

There are of course too many exceptions to this trend to ignore. Wealthy and powerful widows have emerged again and again across cultures to challenge the tralaticious stereotype of vulnerability. Many have had ample resources bequeathed to them, above all, by decedent husbands. Unfettered ownership of property, where possible, grants a widow power, a point that has also generally held for men. Many have prospered through the force of their personality. One way that widows have typically taken action is in providing assistance to other widows.[39] In all of the societies under study women lacked the 'public' rights of citizenship that until relatively recently were the exclusive attributes of males. Our examination of widows shows, however, that women's status has hardly been monolithic and that it is an error to lump women into a single category as has been commonly done. Despite the primary importance, above all economic, of marriage for women in past time, this has been repeatedly revealed to be the most disadvantageous in its implications for legal status. Widows, for all the challenges they face, have often fared better in terms of property rights than wives, and sometimes in terms of civic status as well.

The tension explored throughout this book between the deep and abiding structures of patriarchy on the one hand, and change in women's status and role that has been significant enough to delineate different historical periods on the other, emerges as of primary importance. Such phenomena suggest that the history of patriarchy is in essence non-linear, in other words, not the product of evolution, legal or otherwise. For women's status and role the historical record reveals no simple trajectory in one direction or another.[40] This does not mean it is completely random. One can detect a similar pattern for both England and Germany during the late medieval and early modern periods, for example. This is a cycle that, put very simply, commences with a steadfast form of patriarchy, followed by a loosening, then a re-imposition of male authority in even starker terms.

What all the periods examined in this book have in common is the abiding strength and durability of the underlying structures of the patriarchal order, above all, the means to secure transfer of important property between males. These structures are perfectly compatible with a great deal of significant change. We have here, as in so many other cases explored in this book, an example of how patriarchy tends to generate compensatory pressures favouring women. When these threaten to undermine the very premise of male dominance, however, a kind of counter-compensation sets in, restoring matters to what has aptly been described as the 'patriarchal equilibrium'.[41] A great deal of engaging and useful history, to my mind, can be written in describing such a balancing of competing influences and interests.

It is clear that much work remains to be done. A number of other areas of analysis have the potential to contribute to our understanding of patriarchy in past time. These include women's informal political influence, economic power and reproductive rights, for example. The question of ideology continues to loom large. Various justifications for gender hierarchy show surprising continuity for all of their apparent differences. Marital status also remains a crucial subject for investigation. Never-married women have only just begun to receive attention in the scholarly literature, but this does not mean that the study of wives or widows has progressed as far as one would like. One important aspect of the latter that merits further exploration in my view is the representation of widows in literature. Or one might choose to apply all or part of the theoretical framework of the spectrum of statuses to other cultural contexts, above all, non-Western ones.

I express the hope that this monograph might point the way toward a more complete and comprehensive understanding of the history of gender hierarchy, but must also warn of its limited predictive value. As an historical form, patriarchy is complex, varied and resistant to broad evolutionary trends. It is anything but an evolutionary trend itself, to judge from what I have been able to learn about it. Far from proceeding in a straight line, it is highly unpredictable, almost infinitely flexible and adaptive. All the same, there is hope our understanding of it can improve.

Notes

1. Introduction

1. For these verses, see Lovell 2006: xiv.
2. For the idea of a spectrum of statuses in classical antiquity, see Finley 1999: esp. 35-61. Historians of gender relations in the early modern period have recently discovered the utility of such a concept for understanding the status of men: Shepard 2003. For discussion of the contrast between the radical feminist view and the liberal argument, which to my mind invests too much significance in the grant of the public rights of citizenship to women in modern times, thus exaggerating the continuity of their experience both before and after, see Baker 1984; Dietz 1987; Patterson 1987; Pateman 1988; Walby 1997: 166-79. All the same, it will be clear that I agree with the liberals on many points of detail.
3. See Pateman 1988: 3, 9-16; Bradley 1989: 28; Fletcher 1995: xvi. By 'universal' I do not mean consistent in form and content between cultures, an idea that has been rightly criticized: Bradley 1989: 51, 53, 58.
4. Bradley 1989: 60.
5. See Pateman 1988: 3, 29-30, 219; Bennett 1989: 260-2; Wiesner-Hanks 2001: 12-18.
6. Bradley 1989: 23-4, 35, 50. The debate over the role of companionate marriage in the transformation of patriarchy is of more recent vintage, originating with Lawrence Stone in 1979: Bradley 1989: 53.
7. Harris 2002: 12-15.
8. Hufton 1995: 25.
9. For the Greeks, I much prefer the approach of Patterson 1987, who shows that a gender-differentiated conception of citizenship existed at Athens, to that for example of Nicole Loraux, who simply assumes that only a male-centred definition of citizenship was current.
10. Bennett 1989: 266.
11. See Baker 1984; Dietz 1987; Walby 1997: 166-79.
12. See Bradley 1989: 61; Spring 1993: 100 on the dangers of feminist Whiggery.
13. See Wilson 1992: 1.
14. Nelson 1988: 25.
15. Laslett 1995: 61.
16. Rose 1992: 166.
17. Schattkowsky 2003: 11. One must be on guard against universalizing the experience of widows regardless of location, social class, or historical period: cf. Wilson 1992: 22-3.
18. Moscucci 1990: 5, 88.
19. Spring 1993: 100.
20. See Jussen 2000: 22.
21. Koch 1991: 11.
22. Stretton 1998: 2.

Notes to pages 4-8

23. Fletcher 1995: xvi.
24. Bradley 1989: 38; Wiesner-Hanks 2001: 61.
25. Bradley 1989: 51; Fletcher 1995: xix, 191; Harris 2002: 10-14.
26. See Wiesner 2000: 5.
27. DiGiulio 1989: 9; Buitelaar 1995: 8; Dubler 2003b: 1644; Ingendahl 2003: 267.
28. See Weiler 1980: 161.
29. Schattkowsky 2003: 16.
30. See McGinn 2004b: 4-7.
31. Jussen 2000: 321.
32. One way to make for a more economical presentation is to place some bibliography on a website: see the Preface.
33. See Scadron 1988b: 6, 12; Dubler 2003a: 803-6; Dubler 2003b: 1673.
34. Scadron 1988d: ix.
35. Scadron 1988d: x. Data on non-Western widows are particularly difficult to obtain: Nelson 1988: 22; Schlegel 1988: 42.
36. Wiesner-Hanks 2001: 32. Legal sources, particularly some types such as the records of medieval manorial courts, can considerably exaggerate the role of males: Goldberg 1992b: 13, 85.
37. Erickson 1993: 223.
38. Scadron 1988a: 308; Fletcher 1995: xix, xxi-xxii.
39. Fischer 2002: 14, 24, 55.
40. See Wiesner 2000: 8.
41. Goldberg 1992b: 37.
42. Taylor 1980: 8; Beecher et al 1988: 119; Scadron 1988a: 308; Wilson 1992: 177; Amtower and Kehler 2003: xii.
43. Fletcher 1995: xxii; Fischer 2002: 18-19. On rare occasions when widows seem over-represented in the sources the suspicion of historians is rightly raised: see Goldberg 1992b: 144; Hartog 2000: 325.
44. Bradley 1989: 32; Miller 1998: xiii; Harris 2002: 10-14.
45. See Wiesner-Hanks 2001: 7; Fischer 2002: 24.
46. See Taylor 1980: 8, 104-5; Wiltenburg 1992: 4; Jussen 2000: 319.
47. See the useful survey, with discussion, at Bradley 1989: 50-6.
48. For this reason, I avoid resort to euphemisms and/or alternatives, such as 'male dominance' etc.: see Bennett 1989: 260-2; Bradley 1989: 53-6.
49. See Bennett 1997: 90; Miller 1998: xiii. For an exception to my general practice, see Chapter 5: Conclusion.
50. Finley 1999.
51. Buitelaar 1995: 4.
52. See Bennett 1997: 90; Shepard 2003.
53. See Wiltenburg 1992: 3-5.
54. Wiesner 2000: 52.
55. Wiesner 2000: 306.
56. The threefold division of women's status according to marital state is not limited to the West. For an application from Confucianism see Wiesner-Hanks 2001: 121.
57. Scadron 1988b: 1.
58. Schlegel 1988: 42; Morgan 1991: 2.
59. Dubler 2003b: 1646 uses this term to describe the normative framework marriage establishes for widows, but it arguably has broader implications.
60. Ingendahl 2003: 267.

Notes to pages 8-10

61. Dubler 2003b: 1654.

62. See, for example, Hartog 2000: 343, on the nineteenth-century United States.

63. Thus the term 'grass' or 'grace widow' from an earlier time: Gillis 1985: 204, 210, 251. Lopata 1996: 1 includes divorcées who have lost ex-husbands to death, which makes some sense from a strictly contemporary perspective. Sometimes another type, such as spinsters in Victorian England, can overshadow widows in popular discourse: Hahn 2002: 35.

64. Buitelaar 1995: 1-4; Schattkowsky 2003: 31.

65. Beecher et al 1988: 123; Scadron 1988a: 307; Stretton 1998: 181; Cavallo and Warner 1999: 6; Hartog 2000: 322-3. In developing countries the identification of a woman as a widow can present genuine, even painful, difficulties in the context of practices such as concubinage, polygyny and customary marriage: Owen 1996: 3, 58.

66. Laurence 1994: 53-5.

67. Erickson 1993: 112, 127; Laurence 1994: 54; Harrington 1995: 260.

68. Staves 1990: 178.

69. Cavallo and Warner 1999: 4; Fischer 2002: 59-60.

70. Crick 1999: 36 on pre-Conquest England.

71. Fischer 2002: 265, on the widow as 'hinterbliebene Ehefrau' or 'left-behind wife'.

72. Buitelaar 1995: 12.

73. See Taylor 1980: 9.

74. Sharpe 1999: 229.

75. See Stretton 1998: 104-6. Demographers define never-marrieds as persons over fifty who die without marrying: Hufton 1995: 255.

76. Scadron 1988b: 3.

77. Fischer 2002: 266.

78. Jussen 2000. See Fischer 2002: 21-3.

79. Scadron 1988b: 2; Schlegel 1988: 43.

80. Fischer 2002: 88-9.

81. Lopata 1996: 6. Components of the experience of widowhood such as relative age (old versus young) and role (active versus passive) are also somewhat elusive: see the considerations of Taylor 1980: 100-1. 'Old' and 'young' are of course culturally determined concepts: see below.

82. Scadron 1988b: 2-3. For a threefold division of the typology into the merry, poor and ideal, see Cavallo and Warner 1999: 6. The latter two can however be subsumed under the 'sorrowing' rubric.

83. See Stretton 1998: 228-9; Hahn 2002: 41-4.

84. The German word for widow, *Witwe*, derives from the notion of sorrow, according to Freist 1999: 164; cf. Taylor 1980: 7, who emphasizes the ideas 'to become empty', 'to lack (something)', as well as the modern definition 'the one left behind' (similarly, Hahn 2002: 35). Both are consistent with the root meanings of Greek *chêra* (χήρα) and Latin *vidua*. See for example, Hunter 1989a: 308, who cites as the basic meanings of the verb *chêreuein* 'to be bereft', 'to be bereaved of a husband'; this terminology can also refer to a divorced woman, as can Latin *vidua*.

85. See Lopata 1996: 6.

86. Buitelaar 1995: 4; Amtower 2003: 120.

87. Buitelaar 1995: 6. For an example from early modern England that conflates the two types, see Amtower and Kehler 2003: xiii.

88. Amtower and Kehler 2003: xix.

Notes to pages 10-14

89. Amtower 2003: 121.
90. Panek 2004: 3.
91. Stretton 1998: 214, 223-4.
92. Buitelaar 1995: 13.
93. Stretton 1998: 46, 222, 228-9.
94. Roberts 1999: 26, 44.
95. Laurence 1994: 55-7.
96. Buitelaar 1995: 15; Cavallo and Warner 1999: 18, 22.
97. See Wiesner 1998: 129; Dubler 2003a: 802.
98. See Hufton 1995: 144; Wiesner-Hanks 2001: 94; Schattkowsky 2003: 21.
99. Nelson 1988: 23; Scadron 1988b: 3; Cavallo and Warner 1999: 3; Pelling 1999: 43.
100. Schlegel 1988: 43.
101. Nelson 1988: 24.
102. See Taylor 1980: 7; Buitelaar 1995: 4; Roberts 1999: 25; Wiesner-Hanks 2001: 28. The first example of 'widower' given by the *Oxford English Dictionary* is from 1362, over five centuries after the first cited usage of 'widow'.
103. Buitelaar 1995: 4-5; Fischer 2002: 63-4, 255-6.
104. See Hufton 1995: 223; Wall 2002b: 3.
105. Historical demography, which arose in the context of the study of the European family, is still a relatively new field: Hurwich 2006: 3.
106. Palmore 1987: 94-7; Mineau 1988: 150; Wiesner-Hanks 2001: 124. It is important to remember that 'old' and 'old age' are culturally determined concepts that show great variety from time to time and place to place: Rose 1994: 272-3; Hahn 2002: 34-40.
107. Laslett 1995: 8-9, 40.
108. Walker 2003: 258.
109. Dubler 2003b: 1646.
110. Cott 2000: 8; cf. Grossberg 1985: 302; Salmon 1986: 13.
111. Salmon 1986: xi; Stretton 1998: 1; Wiesner-Hanks 2001: 87. Law makers – almost invariably male – have until recently tended to treat women as a monolithic object of regulation: Wiesner 2000: 36; Wiesner-Hanks 2001: 90.
112. Bradley 1989: 39; Wiesner 2000: 36. See the statement of Cott 2000: 8: 'Marital behavior always varies more than the law predicts'.
113. Grossberg 1985: 155.
114. Fischer 2002: 25.
115. Wiesner-Hanks 2001: 89.
116. Bradley 1989: 59; Staves 1990: 6; Laurence 1994: 8, 16; Cott 2000: 1.
117. Pateman 1988: 3, 6, 10-12; Wiesner 2000: 6.
118. Patterson 1987; Cott 2000: 3-5.
119. Barrett 1977: 858-9; Wall 2002b: 11.
120. Bradley 1989: 1, 8, 38-9.
121. Bennett 1989: 266; Bradley 1989: 68-70.
122. Wiesner-Hanks 2001: 64.
123. Hill 1993: 16.
124. Wiesner 2000: 133-4; see Bennett 1992a: 147, 150, 164; Bennett 1997; Offen 1997.
125. Taylor 1980: 103.
126. Barrett 1977: 860.
127. Buitelaar 1995: 6, 11.
128. Schattkowsky 2003: 18.

129. In this sense, my work connects with the study of *mentalités*, an important approach taken in recent years to the study of the family in past time. See Hurwich 2006: 3 for a recent overview.
130. Buitelaar 1995: 13.
131. Scott 1999, with Bennett 1989: 258; see also Hahn 2002: 45; Ingendahl 2003: 278.
132. Bennett 1989: 267.
133. Taylor 1980: 38, 104; Hahn 2002: 43-44.
134. Barrett 1977: 864; Lopata 1996: 123; Chen 2000: 344.
135. Hufton 1995: 266.
136. Nelson 1988: 24.
137. Pateman 1988: 15; Lopata 1996: 33.
138. Rose 1992: 11; Wiesner 2000: 8.
139. Goldberg 1992b: 290-6, 309; for a counter-example from Tuscany in 1427 see 343.
140. Palmore 1987: 93, 102-3.
141. Wall 2002b: 8.
142. Buitelaar 1995: 12-13.
143. Barrett 1977: 861.
144. See DiGiulio 1989: xvii, 2. It would be useless to challenge the eloquence of Joan Didion on this subject. See, for example, the distinction she draws between grief and mourning: Didion 2006: 143. For a broad contemporary perspective, see Gilbert 2006.

2. Classical antiquity

1. Hunter 1989a: 303-5. Some of these are of uncertain marital status and may be divorcées: Hunter 1989a: 294, 308. The Greek word *chêra* has a broader range of meaning than the English 'widow', and can signify any type of unmarried woman, although there are texts where it not only can but must mean 'widow'.
2. Golden 1981: 322, 329; Sallares 1991: 148-51; Pomeroy 1997: 5-6.
3. Golden 1981: 323-8, rightly discounting, in my view, the conclusions drawn from skeletal evidence. See also Sallares 1991: 107-29.
4. Golden 1981: 329; see also Hunter 1989b: 40; Pomeroy 1997: 169.
5. Pomeroy 1997: 184-5; Cox 1998: 212.
6. Golden 1981; Pomeroy 1997: 120, 161-2.
7. See Cox 1998: 71.
8. Casualty rates spiked, for example, in the campaigns of the mid-fifth century, the disastrous end of the Sicilian Expedition, and the final years of the Peloponnesian War and its aftermath: see Golden 1981: 321. The widow at Aristoph. *Thesm.* 446 lost her husband in Cimon's Cyprus campaign of 450/449, and evidently never remarried. All the same, one should be wary of exaggerating the numbers of casualties: see Corvisier 1999.
9. Diog. Laërt. 2.26, sometimes understood to refer to polygyny.
10. Thuc. 2.45.2.
11. See Andersen 1987.
12. Frier 2000: 788-97.
13. Frier 2000: 795-6.
14. See McGinn 1999: 623-5, adducing the suggestion by Saller and Shaw that non-senatorial members of the elite may have fallen toward the extremes for both men and women, thus opening up potentially the largest age gap of all.

Notes to pages 20-23

15. Krause 1994b: 73 estimates that as many as thirty per cent of adult Roman women were widows. This result is much more convincing for the mass of the population than for the upper orders: see McGinn 1999: 618-19.
16. Parkin 2003: 222.
17. Frier 2000: 799-800.
18. McGinn 2004a.
19. Sogner 1994: 10-12; for a discussion, see Chapter 4. From an early period, widows (or at least unmarried women), together with orphans, formed a category of their own in the census: Treggiari 1991: 498.
20. Most soldiers, however, were probably unmarried over the course of the period under study, so that their deaths did not, at least technically, produce widows: see Weiler 1980 184.
21. See Treggiari 1991: 473-82. Evidence from Roman Egypt suggests we cannot assume a very low rate: Frier 2000: 800.
22. Cox 1998: 212; McGinn 1999.
23. They could receive bequests through a will: Schaps 1979: 21-2; Hunter 1989a: 295.
24. See Ste. Croix 1970; Schaps 1979; Hunter 1989a: 293-4, 300-3; Just 1989: 26-7; Pomeroy 1997: 15, 186; Cox 1998: 104; Gagarin 1998.
25. Just 1989: 26-7, 74.
26. Lysias 32, with Just 1989: 32-3, 130-1.
27. Weiler 1980: 178.
28. See Patterson 1998: 79-83.
29. Patterson 1998: 73-9.
30. Aristot. *Pol.* 2.6.11 (1270a).
31. Hunter 1994: 36, 53; Cox 1998: 143, 211-12; see Lysias 32 and Isaeus 8, for example. The first point is conceded by Pomeroy 1997: 185 (cf. 110) but not lent nearly as much emphasis.
32. Hunter 1989b: 45; Hunter 1994: 21-3, 30.
33. Hunter 1989a: 300-1; Parkin 2003: 205-10.
34. See, for example, the self-interested presentation at Aeschin. 2.148.
35. Cox 1998: 100-1.
36. Hunter 1989a: 299, 302; Hunter 1989b: 43-4; Hunter 1994: 21-2, 30-3; see also Pomeroy 1997: 185.
37. Hunter 1994: 28-9.
38. Cox 1998: 103, 143.
39. Hunter 1989a: 302; Hunter 1994: 22-3, 197, 200; Cox 1998: 103.
40. Acknowledged for example by Hunter 1989a: 291; Hunter 1994: 5.
41. Compare the advantages accruing to Spartan women from the legal capacity to own land: Ste. Croix 1970: 277; Patterson 1998: 76-7.
42. Pomeroy 1997: 15. An exception to the general rule of powerlessness was the wealthy, brotherless, quasi-heiress known as the *epiklêros*: see Schaps 1979: 36-8 (see also 76).
43. Ste. Croix 1970: 275; Schaps 1979: 75; Weiler 1988: 30.
44. See Lysias 19, 32.
45. See Schaps 1979: 84.
46. Although caution is expressed at Cox 1998: 104. One may note the pessimism of Pomeroy 1997: 16: '... the Greeks considered the family in all its manifestations too important to turn over to women'.
47. Hunter 1989a: 298.
48. Hunter 1989a: 299. Sources that present rural women as engaged in

domestic rather than agricultural tasks seem to reflect more an upper-class sensibility than a sub-elite reality: see Just 1989: 108, 113.

49. See Xen. *Oec.* 7.22-5.
50. Blundell 1995: 145.
51. Weiler 1980: 177; Hunter 1989a: 299; Hunter 1989b.
52. *Suda* 4.369, with Weiler 1988: 29.
53. Hunter 1989a: 299.
54. Gagarin 1998.
55. Athenians, unusually, felt compelled out of regard for their own ideology of equality to explain women's unequal status, even as they were satisfied to the point of complacency about such explanations: see Schaps 1998: 185.
56. Hunter 1989a: 292; Cox 1998: 101.
57. Hunter 1989a: 303-5.
58. Pomeroy 1997: 189; Cox 1998: 101, 193.
59. Aristot. *Ath. Pol.* 56.7.
60. Hunter 1989a: 303; Hunter 1994: 195.
61. Hunter 1989b: 39. Out of the forty-eight women in the sample, twelve we know to have lived with an adult son: Hunter 1989b: 47 n. 43.
62. Cox 1998: 100-1.
63. See Cohen 1991: 133-70.
64. Pomeroy 1997: 169; Cox 1998: 100-1.
65. Pomeroy 1997: 168; Cox 1998: 182.
66. Weiler 1988: 30. Older women in general enjoyed greater freedom of movement: Bremmer 1987; Just 1989: 112.
67. Humphreys 1993: 47-9, and the section above.
68. Bremmer 1987; Henderson 1987.
69. See Günther 1993, against Weiler 1988. 'Old' is of course a culturally relative concept, so that widows were typed as such in some societies where we think this was biologically unlikely: Hahn 2002: 34-5.
70. See Watson 1995: 20-91.
71. Henderson 1987: 118-19, 128. I take the presentation of the widows in these plays to reflect male upper-class anxieties about, in the main, elite women, whatever the putative socio-economic status of the characters portrayed. But the sheer numbers of unmarriageable widows of all social classes generated by the war will have made an impression overall. The later comic writers Philemon and Menander wrote plays entitled *The Widow*, which unfortunately have not survived: Bremmer 1995: 34.
72. Of course, much of this material ultimately derives from Homer's *Iliad* and stories associated with the Trojan War: see Weiler 1988: 16-21. Evadne merits particular mention because she kills herself in grief over loss of her husband (Eur. *Suppl.* 990-1071), as does Laodamia in the lost *Protesilaus*. There is no evidence that contemporary Athenian widows followed their example. Alcestis, who avoids widowhood by the ultimate sacrifice, is perhaps in a class by herself (*Alc.* 280-325).
73. See Dem. 18.259-60 with Dillon 2002: 158-9 (cf. 217).
74. Hunter 1989a: 291, 293, 298, 303; Just 1989: 66-7; Hunter 1994: 192. One index of the ease of remarriage for elite widows is the evidence that suggests this was feasible even with a reduced dowry: Hunter 1989a: 295-6; Cox 1998: 102. Remarriage of a widow was not in every case unproblematic, to judge from the controversy over an alleged incident at a wedding ceremony mentioned by Hyper. *Lyc.* 5-6, although the circumstances seem unusual, and the truth of the matter is beyond recovery.

75. Schaps 1979: 41; Weiler 1980: 180; Weiler 1988: 32; Pomeroy 1997: 169, 171, 187; Cox 1998: 193; Hanson 2000: 149.
76. Hunter 1989a: 294; see also Schaps 1979: 82; Golden 1981: 329-30; Weiler 1988: 31-2.
77. See Plut. *Solon* 20.4.
78. Hunter 1989a: 296-8; Hunter 1994: 16; Pomeroy 1997: 27, 126-7, 130, 188; Cox 1998: 93.
79. Hunter 1989b; Pomeroy 1997: 169, 172, 184-5; Cox 1998: 193.
80. Hunter 1994: 30.
81. See e.g. Hunter 1989a: 298; Günther 1993: 315; Pomeroy 1997: 169, 188-9; Cox 1998: 17, 19-20, 26; for optimism, Weiler 1980: 179-80; Andersen 1987: 43.
82. Cox 1998: 181-2.
83. Weiler 1988: 29.
84. Widowers with children were cautioned against remarriage because of the difficulties associated with introducing a stepmother: Watson 1995: 5-6, 48.
85. Henderson 1987.
86. See Just 1989: 116-17.
87. For a glimpse of what life may have been like for some such women, see the freedwoman-nurse at [Dem.] 47.55-6, who returns as an elderly widow to live in the household in which she had served as a slave.
88. Saller 1994: 49, 55.
89. Gardner 1986: 5-29.
90. Gardner 1986: 163-203.
91. Treggiari 1991: 366; Treggiari 2003: 162-3.
92. Treggiari 1991: 365-6.
93. Gardner 1986: 170-8; McGinn 1998: 77.
94. Gardner 1986: 74-7; Treggiari 1991: 366-74; Treggiari 2003: 164.
95. Gardner 1986: 163.
96. Gardner 1986: 97-116; Treggiari 1991: 323-64; Hanson 2000: 154-5; Frier and McGinn 2003: 84, 128-9.
97. Gardner 1993: 111-18.
98. McGinn 1998: 70-84.
99. See Gardner 1986: 52-3; Hanson 2000: 158.
100. McGinn 1998: chs 5 and 6.
101. Treggiari 1991: 498.
102. See Dixon 2001: 70, 104.
103. Hemelrijk 1999: 98; Dixon 2001: 75, 78.
104. A mass of evidence is collected by Krause 1994c: esp. 47-122, whose perspective on the effectiveness of such means of support is too pessimistic for the upper orders.
105. Dixon 1988: 47-67; Cokayne 2003: 138, 160, 178; *contra* Krause 1994c: 103; Krause 1995a: 113-29, 220-47, 251; cf. Parkin 2003: 246.
106. Dixon 2001: 85, 99; Vuolanto 2002: 208-11, 224-6.
107. Vuolanto 2002: 208.
108. Tac. *Agr.* 4.2-3.
109. Vuolanto 2002: 232.
110. Frier and McGinn 2003: 461-2.
111. Frier and McGinn 2003: 235-7.
112. Parkin 2003: 217, 221.
113. Cokayne 2003: 165.
114. Dixon 2001: 90, 92, 96-7, 106. Plutarch's Cato the Elder tells his son that

a widow ideally maintains inherited wealth while men should add to it: *Cato Maior* 21.8. This may suggest that a more conservative approach toward profit was deemed appropriate for widows in particular, although Cato's views were often deemed extreme, or at least peculiar.

115. For another view, see Pölönen 2002.
116. For the evidence, and a very different view of it, see Krause 1994b: 133-8; cf. 1994a: 85.
117. Krause 1994a: 95-6; Dixon 2001: 38-9.
118. Apuleius' wife Aemilia Pudentilla was a widow before her remarriage to him. See Apul. *Apol.* 70.4, 87.7, 93.4.
119. Krause 1994c: 123-219; for some possible examples of widows engaging in business see Treggiari 1979: 76-80.
120. McGinn 1997: 107-12; McGinn 2004b: esp. 62-71.
121. McGinn 1999: 619-20. The Romans recognized that experience of old age was conditioned to a great extent by economic status: Parkin 2003: 224-6.
122. Corn. Nepos *Praef.* 6-7.
123. Hemelrijk 1999: 307 on Mart. 4.31.
124. Hemelrijk 1999: 244.
125. Apul. *Apol.* 1.5.
126. Hemelrijk 1999: 10-11.
127. Hemelrijk 1999: 265, 268.
128. Parkin 2003: 246, 259.
129. Mart. 2.32.
130. Plin. *Ep.* 2.20.1-6.
131. Treggiari 1991: 500-1.
132. Hemelrijk 1999: 100-1, 116-22; see Apul. *Apol.* 69.2.
133. Treggiari 1985. For attributions of drunkenness and superstition, see Krause 1994a: 97.
134. See Dixon 2001: 33, 146-7.
135. Iuv. 6.405-6.
136. Plin. *Ep.* 7.24.
137. See the comments of Krause 1994a: 90-1; Hemelrijk 1999: 15, 88.
138. McGinn 1998: 150-1.
139. Krause 1994a: 91, 102.
140. Phaedrus *App. Per.* 15; Petron. 111-12.
141. Eumolpus introduces the story as exemplary of 'womanly weakness' (*muliebris levitas*: Petron. 110) and avoids the word for widow (*vidua*) throughout, suggesting that, whatever interpretation we prefer, it is meant to be generalized to all women, and not just widows.
142. Without question Petronius exploits the negative portrayal of Dido in Vergil, as does Ovid for his Dido, and Apuleius for his Charite, with some interesting differences, to be sure: see May 2005: 140, 148. Most scholars think that Vergil's predecessor Naevius invented the love story between Dido and Aeneas, to set aside an earlier tradition that has the queen of Carthage choosing death, and so loyalty to her decedent husband, over remarriage. If so, Vergil made this version his own and at the same time shaped it as the dominant one: La Penna 1985: 50-2. On the theme of a widow's sexual availability at her husband's funeral, see Ovid. *Ars* 3.431-2.
143. See Huber 1990: 12-81; Courtney 2001: 165-73; May 2005: 134, 138-42.
144. Huber 1990: 83-91; Jussen 2000: 282.
145. Parkin 2003: 69, 76-81, 86, 115, 128-30. Romans were not only ambivalent

Notes to pages 33-35

about old age but vague about it as well, employing a notably inexact terminology in its regard, a fact that underscores its status as a cultural construct: see Parkin 2003: 19-22.

146. Krause 1994a: 94-6.
147. Hemelrijk 1999: 252-3; Cokayne 2003: 134-52; Parkin 2003: 347, 350.
148. See, for example, Plin. *NH* 28.48 on the use of widows' names in magic spells.
149. See Watson: 1995 92-222.
150. Krause 1994a: 80; Krause 1994c: 244-51, but cf. 252, where the class distinction disappears.
151. Hanson 2000: 156.
152. Worth noting is the (non-Roman, in origin) tradition on Isis as a widow and her search for her lost husband: Weiler 1980: 173.
153. See Krause 1994a: 74, 78-80; Dixon 2001: 89-112. Even so, here is a difference with Athens: see above.
154. Dixon 2001: 22.
155. See Dixon 2001: 97.
156. On the difficulty of distinguishing widows from divorcées in the census records from Roman Egypt, see Hanson 2000: 152.
157. See Krause 1994c: 6-46, with McGinn 1999: 627; Hanson 2000: 152, 156; Parkin 2003: 10, 53.
158. Apul. *Apol.* 67.3, 72.6, 93.4.
159. Watson 1995: 170.
160. Treggiari 1991: 467.
161. See McGinn 1999: 619, 621-2; Treggiari 2003: 174; cf. Jussen 2000: 156.
162. Plut. *Ti. Gracchus* 1.4-5.
163. See, for example, Lab.-Iav. D. 50.16.242.3.
164. Worth noting is that the religious calendar seems to have placed far fewer restrictions on the remarriage of widows than on the weddings of first-time brides: Shaw 1997: 64.
165. Treggiari 1991: 501; Hemelrijk 1999: 134.
166. See Apul. *Apol.* 68-71.
167. Gardner 1986: 50-6; Treggiari 1991: 494-5. A widow might be released from the obligation to respect the time period either through petition to the emperor or by giving birth: Paul. D. 3.2.10 pr; Pomp.-Ulp. D. 3.2.11.2
168. Hemelrijk 1999: 138.
169. Weiler 1980: 182.
170. Ovid. *Fasti* 1.35-6.
171. See XII Tables 10.4.
172. Treggiari 1991: 489-98; cf. Jussen 2000: 31, 178-9.
173. See Treggiari 1991: 486-9 and the story of the Widow of Ephesus above.
174. Astolfi 1996: 84-5.
175. These rules regarding upper and lower age limits applied to divorced and never-married women and a similar set existed for men as well: Astolfi 1996: 41-3.
176. Astolfi 1996: 161-71.
177. Apuleius has Aemilia Pudentilla at first contemplating remarriage on the advice of medical professionals, to combat the negative effects on health thought to arise from a lack of sexual activity: *Apol.* 69.1-3.
178. Krause 1994b: 108-13; cf. Hanson 2000: 150.
179. See Treggiari 2003: 177-82.
180. See the essays by Hawley, Braund, Smith, Pollmann, May and Feichtinger in Smith 2005a.

181. McGinn 1999: 618-19; Hanson 2000: 150-1. Rathbone 2006: 102-3 sees a higher rate of remarriage for lower-status widows in Roman Egypt, but the (slender) evidence does not encourage such optimism. See Bagnall and Frier 1994: 113 (figure 6.1), 120 and below.

182. McGinn 1999: 625.

183. Hemelrijk 1999: 109-12.

184. Treggiari 1991: 125-38; Steininger 1997: 33, 38.

185. Jens-Uwe Krause argues age thirty as the watershed for widows' remarriage chances, and/or five years after becoming a widow: 1994b: 74-85. For these and other factors which I take to be far less important, such as loss of virginity and/or presence of children through prior marriage, see Krause 1994b: 114-32. The low remarriage rate for Egypt has been challenged, but unpersuasively: above.

186. So Bradley 1991: 162 against Krause 1995a: 47. Presumably, widows did not remarry much younger partners as often as widowers did. Pliny the Younger's union with Calpurnia was marked by an age gap of as many as twenty-five years: see *Ep.* 4.19.

187. Hemelrijk 1999: 265.

188. See Krause 1994a: 87, 95.

189. Frier 2000: 800.

190. Watson 1995: 5-6, 152.

191. Tertullian comes close to ranking widows above virgins for this reason: Tert. *Uxorem* 1.8.1-3 *CCSL* 1.382. See Jussen 2000: 54-60. According to Clement of Alexandria, some people ranked widows higher than virgins precisely because they rejected sex after experiencing it: Clem. Alex. *Strom.* 3.16 (101.5) *GCS* 52(15).243.

192. For innovations in late antique law regarding widows, much of which turns on issues of disposition of property and remarriage, see Arjava 1996: esp. 167-77; Evans Grubbs 2001.

193. Weiler 1980: 168-73; van der Toorn 1995: 19-20; Norrback 2001: 23-80; Bennett 2002: 26-31. For an exploration of particular reasons why widows in the ancient Near East were vulnerable, see Matthews 2003: 22-4. For ancient Israel, see Block 2003: 71-2.

194. Exodus 22:21-3.

195. See Bennett 2002: 38-48. Norrback 2001: 9 (cf. 198-9) defines 'widow' in Deuteronomy as a woman whose husband has died and who has no other male supporter.

196. Deuteronomy 14:22-9, 26:12-15.

197. Deuteronomy 16:9-12.

198. Deuteronomy 16:13-15.

199. Deuteronomy 24:19-22.

200. Deuteronomy 24:17-18; cf. 10:18.

201. While all widows may not have been poor, most, if not virtually all, were perhaps regarded as at least potentially vulnerable, at least to downward mobility, something more to be feared perhaps than poverty itself, at least by some: cf. van der Toorn 1995: 20-3.

202. See Exodus 22.21-3; Sirach 35:14-15.

203. See Job 22:5-9, 24:2-4, 29:12-13, 31:16-18; Psalms 68:5-6, 146:9; Isaiah 1.17; Jeremiah 22:3, 49.11; Ezekiel 22:7; Malachi 3:5. For another view see Bennett 2002, who argues that the Deuteronomic rules on widows and the rest are intended to exploit and 'dehumanize' them. Cf. van der Toorn 1995: 19. For comparative evidence from pre-Columbian American cultures, see Weiler 1980:

Notes to pages 38-41

164. Repetition of the theme may suggest the problem was intractable: Taylor 1980: 7. On the ambiguous, and in later ages highly popular, Hellenistic-era figure of Judith, see van der Toorn 1995: 27.

204. Brown 1997: 273-4, 279, 662-8. Widows and orphans are assumed to be vulnerable and needy (and so worthy of assistance: see Luke 18.1-8) in the Gospels, but otherwise receive little attention in their own right (e.g. Mark 12.38-44; Luke 20.45-7, 21.1-4): see Thurston 1989: 21-8; Krause 1995b: 5-6.

205. *Acts* 6.1-7. Brown 1997: 293.

206. Winter 2003: 127.

207. See also *Acts* 9.36-43.

208. *1 Timothy* 5.3-16. Most scholars do not accept Paul as the author: Hunter 2007: 92. Worth mentioning is the roughly contemporary letter attributed to the apostle James, which identifies looking out for widows and orphans with purity of worship: James 1.27 with Brown 1997: 726.

209. So that it means both 'show respect to' and 'provide support for': Bratcher 1983: 46; Bassler 1996: 92; Johnson 1996: 173; MacDonald 1996: 163.

210. Thurston 1989: 49-50; Wagener 1994: 203; Bassler 1996: 93-4; MacDonald 1996: 157 see a reference to a vow of celibacy; see also Bratcher 1983: 49; Davies 1996: 85; Winter 2003: 123-40. In my view, the 'pledge' more likely signifies simply loyalty to a first husband. Vow or no vow, the 'real' widows are of course celibate, not to say chaste.

211. On the difficulty see Bassler 1996: 96, and also the discussion at Wagener 1994: 223-7.

212. Taylor 1980: 12.

213. For more analytical approaches, see Thurston 1989: 54; Bassler 1996: 92-8; Davies 1996: 85; cf. Johnson 1996: 177.

214. See Cardman 1999: 304.

215. See Bassler 1996: 96-7; Winter 2003: 137; despite Johnson 1996: 180; Hunter 2007: 95, celibacy is clearly preferred to marriage. The sexual motive for the latter is very strongly implied.

216. MacDonald 1996: 160.

217. *1 Corinthians* 7:8-9, 39-40.

218. Heid 2000: 48. MacDonald 1996: 156 points out that whereas Paul was attempting to deal with specific contemporary issues in the Christian community at Corinth, the author of *1 Timothy* lays down a series of general precepts primarily designed to avoid problems in future.

219. See Bratcher 1983: 47; Fee 1988: 118.

220. Taylor 1980: 12.

221. See Thurston 1989: 38; MacDonald 1996: 155-6.

222. This view cannot receive here the attention it merits: see the detailed treatment in Wagener 1994.

223. Krause 1994b: 157-91 has a useful survey. See also Krause 1995b.

224. See the discussion in Krause 1995b: 5-51.

225. See now Hunter 2007: 87-129, with whose analysis I sometimes differ, although he rightly recognizes the diversity of the encratite tradition.

226. Krause 1994b: 157-91.

227. Laurence 1997: 280; Jussen 2000: 162-3; Hunter 2007: 116-20.

228. Krause 1994b: 190.

229. Heid 2000: 250. Like Augustine's treatise, composed in the form of a letter addressed to a prominent widow, Jerome's letters were intended for circulation well beyond their addressees, but still largely within the relatively small circle of the upper-class ascetical community: see Feichtinger 1995: 210; Hunter 2007: 75. To judge by what survives, Jerome wrote to many more widows than married women and virgins combined: Laurence 1997: 270-1.

230. Feichtinger 1995: 3, 6, 21-3, 39, 89-90, 99; Cooper 1996: 113-14; Laurence 1997: 292; Steininger 1997: 77, 135-6, 196, 207; Jussen 2000: 30-4, 47, 314-20. Elizabeth Clark points out that Jerome's anti-marriage views were received much more unfavourably in the West than those of John Chrysostom were received in the East, a fact that partially explains the subsequent development of Augustine's more moderate position on the subject: Clark 1989: 30-1. It also makes the later influence of Jerome's views in Western Christendom all the more remarkable.

231. Hier. *Adv. Iovin* 1.3 *PL* 23.213-14; *Ep.* 22.15 *CSEL* 54.163; *Ep.* 66.2 *CSEL* 54.648; *Ep.* 123.8 *CSEL* 56.82. The idea derives ultimately from the parable of the sower in Matthew 13.8, 23. On its earlier uses, see Bremmer 1995: 45-6. The Priscillianists had stipulated a differential reward in heaven on the basis of John 14:2. They were an influence on Jerome: Hunter 1987: 59. In the early third century, the unknown author at Carthage of a sermon on this scheme of differential reward in heaven ranked martyrs first, then virgins, and finally continent spouses, while at mid-century Cyprian accepted the first two categories, but discreetly omitted the third: Hunter 2007: 114, 122.

232. Heid 2000: 259. On the evidence of Tertullian and Clement of Alexandria, see above in the notes. Some ambiguity on the issue can be detected during Jerome's lifetime. As late as 374-375, Basil of Caesarea felt obliged to clarify their relative standing: Elm 1994: 139; cf. 143. About a decade later, John Chrysostom postulated that some widows were superior to some virgins because more committed to a sanctified lifestyle: Ioh. Chrys. *Non Iter. Con.* 6 *SC* 138.198.

233. Late in the fourth century, both Helvidius and Jovinian argued for the spiritual equality of virgins and married women. Although attacked as heretics, their thinking was closer to the mainstream than has been often assumed: Hunter 2007: 31-5, 41-3, 188.

234. Feichtinger 1995: 22-3, 90, 96; Laurence 1997: 292; Jussen 2000: 52-61, 71, 331-2.

235. Feichtinger 1995: 90, 207; Cooper 1996: 113; Steininger 1997: 111, 128, 136-9, 145-7, 196, 205.

236. Steininger 1997: 104-9, 113-14, 122, 135-6, 196; cf. Elm 1994: 181.

237. Feichtinger 1995: 17, 36; Steininger 1997: 90-1, 117, 133, 204, 208-9.

238. Steininger 1997: 128, 204-5.

239. Feichtinger 1995: 173; Steininger 1997: 112.

240. Jussen 2000: 36, 76.

241. Feichtinger 1995: 101-2, 155, 178, 197, 207-8, 261, 295; Cooper 1996: 84; Steininger 1997: 114-16, 124-5, 134, 204.

242. Feichtinger 1995: 208; Cooper 1996: 81-2; Laurence 1997: 297-8; Steininger 1997: 114-16, 121, 130-5, 143.

243. *1 Corinthians* 7:8-9, 39-40 and *1 Timothy* 5:14-15.

244. Hier. *Adv. Iovin.* 1.14 *PL* 23.233.

245. Feichtinger 1995: 90, 94, 100-5, 149; Laurence 1997: 280-90; Steininger 1997: 122-7, 142-3.

246. Feichtinger 1995: 173; Steininger 1997: 129, 136.

247. Steininger 1997: 128-9.

248. See McNamara 1984: 18; Hunter 1987; Cooper 1996: 81-2; Steininger 1997: 125.

Notes to pages 43-47

249. Feichtinger 1995: 4-5, 11, 19-20, 40, 47, 99, 130, 170, 190, 200-3, 214, 223-30; Cooper 1996: 81-2, 93-4; Hunter 2007: 53-74.
250. Laurence 1997: 291-2; Jussen 2000: 79-80, 163-4, 213; Schroeder 2004: 429, 440; Clark 2005: 167-72; Feichtinger 2005: 188-9, 207.
251. Bremmer 1995: 46; Laurence 1997: 289. As noted above, the text can lend support to both pro- and anti-marriage arguments (although it hardly identifies marriage with prostitution).
252. Bremmer 1995: 50; Feichtinger 1995: 170-3, 183, 239-71; Cooper 1996: 80-7, 113-14; Jussen 2000: 33, 67, 72, 153; Hunter 2007: 3, 76-83.
253. Feichtinger 1995: 110, 245-9, 270-1, 297-9, 307, 316, 321-3; Jussen 2000: 34, 77-9, 210; Delarue 2001; Clark 2005: 156-67, 175; Feichtinger 2005: 182-9. Jerome, never one to be impeded by an austere standard of consistency, criticized Jovinian for citing pagan authorities in his work, claiming his own approach was a purely defensive measure: Hunter 2007: 20, 27.
254. Feichtinger 1995: 300, 321.
255. Feichtinger 1995: 73, 217; Steininger 1997: 197.
256. Steininger 1997: 182-6.
257. Steininger 1997: 182, 200; cf. Feichtinger 1995: 100.
258. Hunter 2007: 261.
259. Feichtinger 1995: 40, 73, 83; Steininger 1997: 197-201; Jussen 2000: 62; Hunter 2007: 264-8.
260. Feichtinger 1995: 38-40, 72, 79-81, 161-2.
261. Hunter 2007: 16-18.
262. See Hunter 2007: 243-83, whose perspective on Augustine differs somewhat from mine.
263. Feichtinger 1995: 38-51, 84-6, 68, 84, 99-108, 115-55, 255, 264, 272-83, 318; Cooper 1996: 69; Jussen 2000: 34-5. On the at times heated debate over the relative merits of monastic and clerical celibacy in the late fourth century, including Jerome's position, see Hunter 2007: 162-4, 202-24, 236-41.
264. Hanson 2000: 164; cf. Weiler 1980: esp. 192-3.
265. Krause 1995b.
266. Eus. *HE* 6.43.11 *SC* 41.156.
267. Ioh. Chrys. *Hom. in Matth.* 66(67).3 *PG* 58.630.
268. Krause 1995b: 22.
269. In the West these two institutions were often combined: Krause 1995b: 33-7.
270. Weiler 1980: 183, 189; Brown 2002: 32, 58-60, 65, 69. One law worth mentioning in connection with the themes of this section shows that Christian emperors were prepared to comfort, if only for a brief span of time, the vulnerability of widows, specifically by attempting to protect their property against depredation by (male, of course) monks and clergy: Valentin., Valens, Gratian. CTh. 16.2.20 (a. 370); cf. Valentin., Valens, Gratian. CTh. 16.2.28 (a. 390); NMarc. 5 (a. 455).
271. Jussen 2000: 152.
272. Jussen 2000: 321-7.
273. Bowersock 1978: 87-8.
274. Krause 1995b: 113.
275. Brown 1988: 147-8, who accepts the 'order of widows' thesis (above); Brown 2002: 58-9; cf. Bremmer 1995: 41.
276. It is important to avoid simply assuming that the vast majority of widows in past time could or did remarry: cf. Jussen 2000: 153, 167, 175, 256.

277. See Krause 1995b: 93-108. Salvian's radical position was that widows should hand over all of their property to the Church: Salv. *Eccl.* 2.14 *SC* 176.196, 25-7 *SC* 176.204-6); cf. 4.28 *SC* 176.329.

3. Late medieval and early modern England and Germany

1. For a clear and detailed exposition of the English legal system in this period, see Erickson 1993. Common and canon law jurisdictions might cooperate in dower cases: Walker 1993b: 88.

2. Beginning in the sixteenth century common law courts also dealt with sex offences (adultery, fornication, incest, and bigamy): Laurence 1994: 47.

3. The result was a collection of rules, for example on marital property, that were inconsistent to the point of haphazard: Stretton 1998: 38.

4. With respect to marriage jurisdiction, the pre-Reformation pattern of division of responsibilities between state and Church courts yielded in many Protestant areas to secular marriage courts (often called consistories) and in some places to a mixed jurisdiction: Harrington 1995: 153-4. Secularization of marital jurisdiction also occurred in Catholic Bavaria, which in important respects modelled its marriage laws on those of formerly Protestant, newly re-Catholicized, Augsburg: Strasser 2004: 29-34, 51-4.

5. On the piecemeal, uneven, and contested reception of Roman law in late medieval and early modern Germany, see Strauss 1986.

6. See for example Roper 1989: 17.

7. Wiesner 1986: 7, 17.

8. For law, see Koch 1991: 7.

9. de Vries 1994: 6-9.

10. For England, see Hinde 2003: 126-7. The population decline caused by the Thirty Years' War in early seventeenth-century Germany has been estimated to have been as high as forty per cent: Miller 1998: 8.

11. Goldberg 1992b: 7-11, 40, 210; see Nightingale 2005: 46-9.

12. Hufton 1995: 306, 493; Miller 1998: 7.

13. See de Vries 1994: 22; Laslett 1995: 46; Pfister 1996: 54-5; Wrigley et al 1997: 298-307.

14. Roper 1989: 32; Erickson 1993: 100; de Vries 1994: 30; Wiesner 1998: 136; Kowaleski 1999: 39, 56; Wiesner 2000: 71, 76, 268-70. Laslett 1972: 145 estimates that between the years 1574 and 1821, just over 32% of the female population were married while just under 60% were single.

15. Wrigley et al 1997: 122-48, 196, 352; Hinde 2003: 113-15; for a similar pattern from Germany, see Pfister 1996: 46, 50. For a broad sample of the European data for women, including both England and Germany, see Kowaleski 1999: 329-35. For differences between native urban and immigrant populations in early modern London, see Erickson 1993: 94. That Hajnal's demographic regime (Hajnal 1965) does not hold for all of Western and Southern Europe has been shown both for age at first marriage (see below) and household structure (which varies considerably from place to place and time to time): see McGinn 1999.

16. Goldberg 1992b: 208, 231; Erickson 1993: 120; Wiesner 2000: 73; Harris 2002: 18.

17. Spieß 2003: 87-91.

18. Hurwich 2006: 56-83, 248. Cf. Spieß 1993: 414-20 who, for a somewhat more extensive area of Germany in the late Middle Ages, shows a range of age at first marriage for men in this social group of 17-30, for women, 13-20, signifying a sizeable age gap for partners in a first marriage. This closed considerably in the sixteenth century, as women married later, bringing the pattern more in line with that described by Hajnal 1965.

19. Laslett 1972: 145; Froide 2005: 16.
20. See Bailey 1996; Hatcher 2003; Nightingale 2005.
21. See Goldberg 1992b: 7-20, 203-32, 263, 272-9, 324-61, 355; see also Rosenthal 1984: 38; Bennett 1992a: 149; Rosenthal 1992: 134; Bailey 1996: 18; Mate 1998: 29-33; Nightingale 2005: 66-8.
22. See Bailey 1996: 9-14; Kowaleski 1999: 58-60; Nightingale 2005: 63-4.
23. Hinde 2003: 126-7.
24. See Wunder 1998: 38.
25. Sogner 1994: 10-12.
26. Smith 1984; Wiesner 2000: 89.
27. As suggested above, a gender-specific mortality crisis like the Thirty Years' War in Germany would generate more widows and reduce their chances of remarriage: Freist 1999: 166.
28. Laslett 1988; Oris and Ochiai 2002: 40-51.
29. Bennett 1992b: 79-81, 91, 101; Hanawalt 1992: 37; Walker 1993a: 3-6; Stretton 1999: 193.
30. Amussen 1988: 78-80; Goldberg 1992b: 268-70; Hanawalt 1992: 39; Erickson 1993: 140, 204; Helmholz 1993; see Rosenthal 1993: 40, for an example from 1498.
31. Erickson 1999: 145; Stretton 1999: 196. Common law rules favoured the eldest son first, daughters in the absence of sons, then brothers or their offspring in the absence of children of either sex. In a stationary population, this meant that nearly 42% of women were heiresses and 25% of estates went to women: Spring 1993: 9-12, 66-7.
32. Most people died intestate and left only personal property: Erickson 1999: 152-3.
33. Brodsky 1986: 146; Hanawalt 1992: 24; Erickson 1993: 85. Widows also reacquired full ownership of land they had received independently through purchase, gift, or inheritance but that had been controlled by their husbands during marriage: Bennett 1992b: 91. The dowries of London widows tended to go to their children or to cover the expenses of the household or family business: Hanawalt 1996: 202-3.
34. Erickson 1993: 28; Loengard 1993: 73; Erickson 1999: 152. As to the dowry itself, a woman lost all right to movables, and could only recover leases as a widow if her husband had not while still alive disposed of them, which in some circumstances required a wife's permission: Erickson 1993: 24-5.
35. Brundage 1992: 193-5.
36. Compare the widower's right of curtesy, which gave him all of decedent wife's real property for life: Spring 1993: 121.
37. By the late Middle Ages lords of manors allowed tenants to alienate their holdings, as though they had rights of ownership, against payment of a fine: Smith 1991b: 45-6. Relatively few peasants appear to have owned land outright: see Cantor 2002: 123. On the potential legal complications of this system, see Walker 1993b: 93. It is a reminder that not all men were of equal status and that many lived in conditions of dependency: Shepard 2003: 210.
38. Todd 1990: 183-4, 188; Bennett 1992b: 72; Gates 1995: 19; Leyser 1995: 180-2; Mate 1998: 83-4, 91; Stretton 1998: 158-9. In the context of common law

dower, 'free bench' referred to the widow's right to remain in the marriage domicile for a brief period. In London, however, she held this right as long as she remained unmarried: Hanawalt 1992: 24; Barron 1994: xvii; Keene 1994: 6.

39. Loengard 1993: 72; Stretton 1998: 115-17; Harris 2002: 134-43; Lovell 2006: 28, 359-60.
40. Mitchell 1992: 182.
41. Walker 1993b: 99; Hanawalt 1993: 149.
42. Erickson 1993: 32-4; Stretton 1999: 195-6, 208.
43. Archer and Ferme 1989: 19; Hanawalt 1992: 33, 38; Mate 1998: 114.
44. Walker 1993b: 85, 96; Hanawalt 1996: 204-7; Stretton 1998: 180-4, 228-9.
45. Stretton 1998: 114, 129-54; Stretton 1999: 202.
46. Stretton 1998: 213-14; Stretton 1999: 197.
47. Harris 2002: 134.
48. Some widows pleaded to advantage their poverty, caused by the fact of their widowhood, in order to secure permission to construct cottages on commons and wastes: Walker 2003: 238. For complaints to the authorities about various forms of mistreatment, see Walker 2003: 242. On widows claiming war pensions toward the close of our period, see below in the notes.
49. Walker 2003: 247-9. Like other women, widows might resist the intrusion of authority as well: 254.
50. Archer 1984.
51. Clark 1990: 173-9; Rosenthal 1991: 193; Erickson 1993: 171; Mate 1998: 106-7; Harris 2002: 129; Hanawalt 2005: 139-40.
52. Todd 1985: 68-9; Brodsky 1986: 145; Amussen 1988: 81-4; Archer and Ferme 1989: 4-7; Todd 1990: 186-7; Rosenthal 1991: 191-2; Hanawalt 1992: 26; Erickson 1993: 156-61, 174-5; Barron 1994: xxix; Mate 1998: 105; Whittle 1998: 49-50; Stretton 1999: 200; Harris 2002: 129-30, 160.
53. The new rules operated to the disadvantage of heiresses as well, although the effects were graver for the daughters of the elite: Spring 1993: 17, 93-7, 183. Under Henry VIII's reign and later, the property of the heirs of landowners who had not reached the age of majority was taken over by the Office of Wards, to administer itself as guardian, taking the profits, or to auction or sell the guardianship to another party, usually a wealthy landowner: Lovell 2006: 483-4.
54. Erickson 1993: 25-6; Spring 1993: 35, 43-7, 120-1; Mate 1998: 76-91, 101-2; Stretton 1998: 26-7, 32, 119-20, 233-9; Harris 2002: 19-24.
55. Hanawalt 1992: 27.
56. The Statute of Uses laid down that prenuptial jointure barred dower, in effect linking the widow's portion to the size of the dowry, in a proportion that shrank over time. In this way the burden of the portion shifted from the husband to widow's family of origin. It set a precedent for limits on the rights of widows to succeed to personal property as well: Spring 1993: 31, 47-63, 118, 131.
57. The Statute of Wills allowed two-thirds of freehold land in military tenure and all other freehold land to be disposed of freely in a will; by 1645 all freehold land was at the disposition of the testator so that the common law rules held only for intestacy: Erickson 1993: 246. See also Spring 1993: 32; Mate 1998: 87-90, 101-3.
58. Erickson 1999: 153.
59. Even this discretion was limited by the rise of the strict settlement, a form of which appeared in the early seventeenth century, which hindered a man's ability to provide for his widow and children: Spring 1993: 17, 38, 74-8, 138-9.
60. Erickson 1999: 153.

61. Amussen 1988: 49; Erickson 1993: 72-7, 178-81, 185, 222; Stretton 1998: 233-9.
62. Spring 1993: 94-6, 145, 153-6, in criticism of Lawrence Stone.
63. Erickson 1993: 31, 114-16; Stretton 1998: 25-9.
64. Stretton 1998: 87-90.
65. Cavallo and Warner 1999: 14.
66. Erickson 1993: 129-30.
67. Erickson 1993: 123, 129-30; Foyster 1999: 114-15.
68. Erickson 1993: 132.
69. Erickson 1999: 152-7.
70. Walker 1993a: 4-5; Mate 1998: 195; Shepard 2003: 196.
71. Fletcher 1995: 225.
72. Botelho 2002b: 73. Land, like other property, might be alienated by gift, an act that would usually not be reflected in a will, and so is more difficult to trace: Erickson 1993: 67.
73. Walker 1993b: 84.
74. Hanawalt 1993: 146-8; Keene 1994: 17.
75. Erickson 1993: 19, 69-71, 77-8; Stretton 1998: 35-6; Whittle 1998: 43-7.
76. Hanawalt 1996: 202.
77. Whittle 1998: 63-7.
78. Mate 1998: 117.
79. Hufton 1995: 225.
80. Lovell 2006: 106-8.
81. Erickson 1993: 93-4; Stretton 1998: 120-1.
82. Rosenthal 1984: 46; Brodsky 1986: 148-52; Amussen 1988: 91-2; Harris 2002: 127-8, 167-72.
83. Barron 1989: 43.
84. Bennett 1992b: 72; Leyser 1995: 145-9, 180-2. Other studies show levels of 20% or slightly more: Todd 1990: 181-2.
85. Bennett 1992b: 92-4, 100; Leyser 1995: 153.
86. Bennett 1992b: 102, on Iver.
87. Leyser 1995: 180-2; Stretton 1998: 30-1, 161, 166, 177.
88. Todd 1990: 197-200.
89. Rosenthal 1984: 43; Barron 1994: xxi; Mate 1998: 117; Lovell 2006: 26-8, 71, 190-1, 369-71, 384, 402, 417, 459.
90. Mate 1998: 120.
91. Hanawalt 1992: 35; Barron 1994: xxi; Keene 1994: 7; Mate 1998: 111-13, 119; Stretton 1998: 237, 240.
92. Hufton 1995: 236; French 2003; Lovell 2006.
93. Levy 2003a: 161-4. One may compare the Roman widow Naevoleia Tyche, whose memorial to her decedent husband rather placed him in the shade: Chapter 2.
94. Erickson 1993: 12, 225; Fletcher 1995: 179-80; Leyser 1995: 166; Mate 1998: 72, 154; Harris 2002: 8-10; Lovell 2006: 52-63.
95. Archer 1992: 169.
96. Ward 1994: 45; Mate 1998: 179-80; Harris 2002: 144-52.
97. Todd 1990: 195.
98. Smith 1991b; Rosenthal 1993: 43; Leyser 1995: 181; Mate 1998: 115; Whittle 1998: 49, 52-3; Hanawalt 2005: 141.
99. Rosenthal 1993: 43.
100. Rosenthal 1993: 43; Laurence 1994: 34, 241.

101. Goldberg 1992b: 311-18.
102. Barron 1994: xxii; Kowaleski 1999: 49, 53, 57; Hufton 1995: 249.
103. Bennett 1992a: 160; Hanawalt 1993: 158; Barron 1994: xiii, xxvii-xxviii; Laurence 1994: 18, 116, 125-6; Leyser 1995: 178. Guilds were self-regulating associations of crafts- and tradesmen that were common features of European cities in this period. They varied a great deal in terms of their internal organization and civic status.
104. Barron 1994: xxviii; Keene 1994: 19-21, 25.
105. Barron 1989: 44-7; Rappaport 1989: 39-40.
106. Brodsky 1986: 141-2; Rappaport 1989: 41; Hanawalt 1992: 37; Barron 1994: xxix; Fletcher 1995: 229; Panek 2004: 17-18.
107. Brodsky 1986: 141-2; Bennett 1992a: 155-9; Goldberg 1992b: 93-157, 200-2; Laurence 1994: 109, 113-24, 130; Fletcher 1995: 224-7, 251; Leyser 1995: 145 argues against a rigid division for medieval peasants; Mate 1998: 12, 41-2, 58, 115.
108. Goldberg 1992b: 334-5.
109. Hanawalt 1992: 38; Laurence 1994: 126.
110. Bennett 1992a: 161; Leyser 1995: 148.
111. Graham 1992.
112. Goldberg 1992b: 113-14, 143; Keene 1994: 18, 22, 25; Laurence 1994: 117; Fletcher 1995: 242-4; Bennett 1996: esp. 37-59; Bennett 1997: 83-9; Mate 1998: 59-74.
113. Leyser 1995: 155.
114. Keene 1994: 2-3; Mate 1998: 12, 41-2, 58, 115; McIntosh 2005.
115. Goldberg 1992b: 7, 202-43, 336, 347; Donahue 1993: 205; Leyser 1995: 161; McIntosh 2005: 8-9; cf. Mate 1998: 38-42, who stresses the gender imbalance in towns as a discouragement to widows' remarriage. This imbalance, however, seems to have been present throughout the period; in fact it is a common phenomenon across historical cultures, in part because widows often migrate to urban areas: Oris and Ochiai 2002: 58-62.
116. Mate 1998: 15-17, 51-4, 73; McIntosh 2005: 37-40.
117. On the long-term 'rise of capitalism' see the statement by Wiesner-Hanks 2001: 65.
118. Goldberg 1992b: 7, 77-81, 360-1.
119. Goldberg 1992b: 312-18, 347, 361; McIntosh 2005: 31.
120. Wiltenburg 1992: 11.
121. Amussen 1988: 25-6.
122. McIntosh 2005: 252-3.
123. Mate 1998: 89-90; see also Whittle 1998: 37 on Norfolk.
124. Mate 1998: 196.
125. Erickson 1993: 119.
126. Erickson 1993: 52-3; Spring 1993: 13-17.
127. Erickson 1993: 66.
128. McIntosh 2005: 40-2, 252-3.
129. Wiesner 2000: 109.
130. Willen 1988; McIntosh 1998: 80; Froide 2005: 25-7.
131. Stretton 1998: 237-8; Foyster 1999: 118.
132. Stretton 1999: 199.
133. Willen 1988: 562-3; Mendelson and Crawford 1998: 180; McIntosh 1998; Sharpe 1999: 222; Amtower and Kehler 2003: xiii; Froide 2005: 34-5.
134. Willen 1988: 563; Mendelson and Crawford 1998: 179; Froide 2005: 25-6.

Notes to pages 64-68

135. Laurence 1994: 59.
136. See Botelho 2004.
137. See Herlihy 1990: 172-3; Leyser 1995: 164-5, 230.
138. Fletcher 1995: 3-4.
139. Amussen 1988: 93; Erickson 1993: 21;Walker 1993a: 2-5; Stretton 1998: 217-29.
140. Fletcher 1995: 107; Mate 1998: 5.
141. Bennett 1992b: 74, 77; Mate 1998: 133-4; Stretton 1998: 237-40; Lovell 2006: 146, 479.
142. Bennett 1992b: 78-9; Laurence 1994: 86; Hufton 1995: 253-4; Mate 1998: 173, 178, 198; Mendelson and Crawford 1998: 174-5; Wiesner 2000: 89-90; Froide 2005: 17-18.
143. Wall 1995: 88-9.
144. Todd 1999: 66.
145. Sutton 1994: 139-40; Mate 1998: 119, 167, 172.
146. Rosenthal 1993: 45; Barron 1994: xxvi; Ward 1994: 37-8; Erler 1994: 165-80; Leyser 1995: 155-6, 173.
147. Todd 1985: 76.
148. Hufton 1995: 405-8.
149. Mark 12.38-44; Luke 20.45-7, 21.1-4. Crawford 1985: 216-21.
150. Crawford 1985 (see 223 for women's participation in political activity at this time). Civil War widows, both parliamentary and royalist, could be relentless if not downright aggressive in pursuing their claims to state pensions, something not available again for over two centuries. Their skill and persistence were often rewarded with success: Hudson 1994.
151. Walker 1993b: 88; Stretton 1998: 192-7.
152. Hanawalt 1993: 159. Bess of Hardwick was able to invoke intervention by Elizabeth I to punish a scandalmonger: Lovell 2006: 197-8.
153. Carlson and Weisl 1999: 6.
154. Todd 1985: 77: Mate 1998: 74, 168.
155. Erickson 1993: 13; Mate 1998: 125, 130.
156. Gowing 1996: 68, 121, 158-9.
157. Rosenthal 1991: 230; Goldberg 1992b: 301; Erickson 1993: 176; Rosenthal 1993: 51-2; Laurence 1994: 262-3; Mate 1998: 152-3; Harris 2002: 137, 162; Walker 2003: 52-4, 62.
158. Walker 2003: 77, 111.
159. Laurence 1994: 83.
160. Carlton 1978: 124; Amussen 1988: 31-2; Hufton 1995: 278-80, 352.
161. Deal 1998.
162. Laurence 1994: 273.
163. Stretton 1998: 52-5, 67-8.
164. See Fletcher 1995: 124; Stretton 1998: 53-5, 91-2, 180-7; Sharpe, 1999: 232, 236, 238; Stretton 1999: 198, 205-15, 226-7; Todd 1999: 80; Harris 2002: 4, 25, 138.
165. See Sharpe 1999: 221, 231; Stretton 1999: 207.
166. See John of Salisbury *Policraticus* 5.8.
167. Whatley 1984; Jussen 2000: 326-7.
168. Koch 1991: 219-32; Leyser 1995: 139, 249-50; Wiesner 2000: 20-4; Feichtinger 2005: 198-200.
169. Erickson 1993: 227; Carlson and Weisl 1999: 8, 17.
170. Leyser 1995: 97.
171. Carlson and Weisl 1999: 18-19.

172. Carlson and Weisl 1999: 8-10.
173. Carlson and Weisl 1999: 4-5; see also Amtower 2003: 126-32.
174. See Amtower 2003: 126-7 (with bibliography); Moore 2003: esp. 133-8, 146; McCarthy 2004: 150-8; Feichtinger 2005: 201-2. Worth mentioning as evidence of Chaucer's later influence is the character of the Widow in an anti-marriage poem by the Scottish court poet William Dunbar. She boasts of her ascendancy over her departed husbands and revels in her independence in widowhood, much in the spirit of her model Alison: Bawcutt 2005: 101-5.
175. McMillan 1987.
176. See Feichtinger 2005: 194-5.
177. Huber 1990: 9, 83, 92-186; Carlson and Weisl 1999: 8, 17.
178. An important exception is Walter Charleton's mid-seventeenth-century *Ephesian Matron*, a sympathetic treatment of the Widow of Ephesus tale, deriving, as the title suggests, from the Petronian version: Huber 1990: 187-90.
179. Wiltenburg 1992: 7-10, 152-7, 214-15.
180. Carlton 1978: 119; Erickson 1993: 153; Chance 1992: 23-5; Stretton 1998: 56-65, 221-3. The evidence does not support the notion that English widows were in actual fact prone to sexual transgression: above.
181. Chance 1992: 25; Todd 1994: 425; Panek 2004.
182. Todd 1985: 54-5; Brodsky 1986: 125-6.
183. The difference with antiquity is that here the two stereotypes, of widow and stepmother, tend to merge each other, while in the classical period the stepmother's status as a widow was largely ignored. See Chance 1992: 26.
184. Panek 2004: 157-201.
185. Panek 2004: 86-9. Thomas Middleton's *Women Beware Women* (1621) also appears to refer to the story of the Widow of Ephesus: see Oakes 1990: 233.
186. Oakes 1990: 201-22; Chance 1992: 26-8; Fletcher 1995: 6, 71, 377. The sheer number of Shakespearean widows precludes an adequate survey here. '... of Shakespeare's 134 female characters, forty are widows, believe themselves to be widows, are considered widows, or have husbands who die in the course of the action': Oakes 1990: 5.
187. The 1995 film, which substitutes the corpse of the husband himself, is slightly more reminiscent of the Widow of Ephesus story.
188. See Oakes 1990: 153-99.
189. Chance 1992: 28-30; Panek 2004: 210.
190. Koch 1991: 203; Hufton 1995: 96-7; Fantazzi and Matheeussen 1996: xiv-xxiii; Stretton 1999: 207; Todd 1999: 67-70.
191. Vives, for example, justifies his views on a widow's suitability to provide moral training for her children by reference to Cornelia, mother of the Gracchi and Veturia, mother of Coriolanus: *De Institutione Feminae Christianae* 3.18.
192. Vives notes that absolute condemnation of remarriage is heretical, before reciting pagan Roman authorities (e.g. Tacitus) and examples (Cornelia again, among others) and, of course, Jerome to argue against it: *De Institutione Feminae Christianae* 3.25-6.
193. Vives certainly exaggerates the amount of control exercised over Roman women by male family members: *De Institutione Feminae Christianae* 3.20, 30.
194. Fischer 2002: 136-72, 262.
195. See Todd 1999: 70-3.
196. See Todd 1999: 74-5.
197. Cf. Todd 1999: 83.
198. Erickson 1993: 154, 203.

Notes to pages 71-74

199. Sharpe 1999: 229, 233.
200. Willen 1988: 561.
201. Fletcher 1995: 403; Sharpe 1999: 234-5, 239.
202. See Lovell 2006: 197-8, 327.
203. Erickson 1993: 192; Fletcher 1995: 25, 72; Sharpe 1999: 228.
204. Deal 1998.
205. Botelho 2002a: 234-6.
206. Wiltenburg 1992: 14.
207. Willen 1992.
208. Stretton 1998: 10-11, 49-50.
209. Amussen 1988: 93; Todd 1994: 430; Stretton 1998: 208-15.
210. Hanawalt 1992: 37; Mate 1998: 130-1.
211. Whittle 1998: 62.
212. Rosenthal 1984: 39-40; Todd 1985: 77-9; Wiesner 2000: 91.
213. Erickson 1993: 196-7; Rosenthal 1993: 37; Wood 1994: 59; Foyster 1999: 112; on the poor cf. Boulton 1990; Todd 1994 and below.
214. Todd 1985: 79; Todd 1994: 427-9; Whittle 1998: 63; see Oris and Ochiai 2002: 72-3.
215. Shepard 2003.
216. Carlton 1978: 122-3; Brodsky 1986: 122-3; Bennett 1992b: 71; Goldberg 1992b: 273; Hanawalt 1993: 160; Todd 1994: 440; Mate 1998: 34-5; Foyster 1999: 108; Pelling 1999: 51-4; Shepard 2003: 239. This is the usual pattern, certainly in western European cultures: Oris and Ochiai 2002: 66-9. For an exception from Elizabethan London, where widows and widowers evidently remarried with equal alacrity, see Brodsky 1986: 134.
217. Panek 2004: 15.
218. Laurence 1994: 46.
219. Macfarlane 1986: 235; Hanawalt 1993: 148; Brundage 1995: 44; Hanawalt 1996: 208. For a change in the early modern period, see below.
220. Brodsky 1986: 132; Franklin 1986: 199. Widows, however, seem generally to have respected the rule of the London Court of Orphans requiring them to defer remarriage until an inventory of the husband's estate was completed, a process that took over a year on average: Carlton 1978: 123.
221. Rawcliffe 1994: 88.
222. Levy 2003a: 147-52.
223. Rosenthal 1993: 36-7; a study of the widows of peers who died in war from 1450-1500 yields similar results: Rosenthal 1992: 135, as does a study of elite widows between 1450 and 1550: Harris 2002: 162; cf. Mate 1998: 125 on aristocratic widows in Sussex.
224. Rosenthal 1991: 236; Wiltenburg 1992: 142-44; Hanawalt 1993: 160; Rosenthal 1993: 38-9; cf. Harris 2002: 164-6.
225. Brodsky 1986: 125-7; Boulton 1990: 336; Foyster 1999: 112-13.
226. Archer 1984: 27; Loengard 1993: 61, 69-70; Walker 1993b: 83; Hanawalt 1993: 144-5; McCarthy 2004: 146.
227. Harris 2002: 160-1.
228. Rosenthal 1991: 213-15.
229. Hanawalt 1993: 143; Walker 1993b: 97-8.
230. Bennett 1992b: 100; Hanawalt 1993: 148-9; although cf. Gates 1995.
231. Brodsky 1986: 123.
232. Rappaport 1989: 370.
233. Boulton 1990.

Notes to pages 74-78

234. Keene 1994: 26; Hanawalt 1996: 209-10; Hanawalt 2005: 143.
235. Goldberg 1992b: 55.
236. Goldberg 1992b: 267-72, 278; see also Hanawalt 1996: 208, 212; McCarthy 2004: 149-50.
237. Hanawalt 1993: 147; see also Macfarlane 1986: 235-6; Erickson 1993: 198.
238. Brodsky 1986: 132; Boulton 1990: 335; Bennett 1992b: 75; Barron 1994: xvii; Keene 1994: 26; Mate 1998: 126.
239. Brodsky 1986: 130; see also Boulton 1990: 336-7; cf. Carlton 1978: 122 for a very different pattern in the Devonshire village of Colyton.
240. Remarriage might be a way to escape gossip, or worse: Leyser 1995: 181. While economic security no doubt played a role in the decision to remarry (or not), it receives less explicit emphasis in the sources: see Erickson 1993: 91.
241. Donahue 1993: 195-6.
242. Donahue 1993: 197-8.
243. Mate 1998: 131.
244. Brundage 1995: 46-7.
245. Laurence 1994: 65-6; Foyster 1999: 111.
246. There is some disagreement in the scholarship on this point: Rosenthal 1991: 191; Hanawalt 1992: 36; Laurence 1994: 50; Hufton 1995: 231; Leyser 1995: 172; Mate 1998: 97; Stretton 1998: 36, 197-201; Whittle 1998: 57-8; Botelho 2002b: 67-8.
247. Amussen 1988: 72-5.
248. Erickson 1993: 100-1, 144, 149; Harris 2002: 18-24: separate estates for wives are attested as early as the late fifteenth century; Foyster 1999: 118. By the same token, the unmarried state, even for those never married, was not necessarily an unhappy one: Erickson 1993: 83.
249. Donahue 1993: 198-202.
250. Brodsky 1986: 143.
251. Todd 1985: 54-5, 72-4; Erickson 1993: 166-7; Hanawalt 1996: 209. The ecclesiastical courts did not penalize widows for remarriage in succession on intestacy: Erickson 1993: 180.
252. See Cressy 1997: 439; Lovell 2006: 140.
253. Walker 2003: 143.
254. See Panek 2004: 8-9.
255. See Oakes 1990: 93-7, 110, citing a double literary tradition, one branch of which counselled against remarriage, the other of which advised widows in their choice of a new husband, a double tradition that intersected on the question of young widows, 276-98; Panek 2004: esp. 5-7, 27-8, 39-69, 79-92, 109-28, 136-41, 149-201.
256. Todd 1985: 80-2; Todd 1994: 430; Foyster 1999: 109-11; see above for evidence from the stage. Note the reinterpretation of *1 Timothy* by Edward Topsell in 1596 as imposing a duty on younger widows to remarry: Panek 2004: 33.
257. Carlton 1978: 127-8; Hufton 1995: 68, 109, 222-3; Pelling 2001; Levy 2003a: 155; Panek 2004: 54-69, 75-9, 104-5, 130-56, 167-86, 193-4, 200.
258. See Brodsky 1986: 143; Boulton 1990: 336-45; Erickson 1993: 198-200; Todd 1994: 431-43; Whittle 1998: 62; Sharpe 1999: 223.
259. Wiesner 1998: 85, 139-40; Wunder 1998: 188.
260. Koch 1991: 1, 8, 40; Strasser 2004: 48-9.
261. Wiesner 1998: 116-18.
262. Wiesner 1998: 117.
263. Opitz 1991: 26.

Notes to pages 78-82

264. Koch 1991: 43-55.
265. Wiesner 1986: 22. Widows could name guardians for their minor children in their wills: Koch 1991: 58. They seem to have preferred females as recipients of bequests: Johner 1987: 42.
266. Wiesner 1998: 86-7. In Bavaria, at any rate, a wife specifically had to reserve such a right for herself or it fell to her husband: Strasser 2004: 49, 191.
267. Koch 1991: 77.
268. Wiesner 1998: 88.
269. Opitz 1991: 29; Wunder 1998: 191; Ozment 2001: 25; Hurwich 2006: 156.
270. Strasser 2004: 47-9, 100-2.
271. Strauss 1986: 241; Koch 1991: 48-50; Harrington 1995: 28, 33, 123-6.
272. For Augsburg, where resort to one or the other type appears to have been conditioned by class, see Roper 1989: 41; for Nuremberg, Wiesner 1998: 86-7.
273. Roper 1989: 173, 176; Koch 1991: 48-50, 69; Harrington 1995: 194-5; Wiesner 2000: 37.
274. Wiesner 1998: 86.
275. This is a general statement, and local variations were many: Harrington 1995: 194.
276. Wiesner 1986: 27.
277. Koch 1991: 52-8. The marriage gift might have two components, the matching gift (*Widerlegung*) and morning gift (*Morgengabe*): Strasser 2004: 49; Hurwich 2006: 28, 41-51.
278. Wiedemann 2001: 36; see also Gerhards 1962: 170-1.
279. See Nov. 117.5 (a. 542), with Wesener 1979.
280. Wiesner 1998: 81; Hurwich 2006: 6-7, 30-40.
281. Spieß 1993: 10, 13, 131-98, 327-37.
282. Wiesner 1998: 140 compares her status to that of the *feme sole* in England.
283. Roper 1989: 148, 169-74, 188-9; Wiesner 1998: 87, 140; Wunder 1998: 186.
284. Opitz 1991: 38-40; Wiesner 1986: 31. Wunder 1998: 33 claims that the legal position of widows was weaker than that of wives, citing frequent accusations of witchcraft.
285. See Freist 1999: 169.
286. Opitz 1991: 47-8.
287. Wiesner 1986: 23-5 (when a husband and father died, his widow and children generally were given their own guardians); Johner 1987: 14-17 (an exception from late medieval Freiburg, where widows could without evident difficulty act as guardians to their minor children); Koch 1991: 56-8 (widows could act as guardians only if they renounced remarriage and certain legal protections, and if their husbands had not appointed someone else in his will); Freist 1999: 169 (widows might gain custody only alongside male guardians from a decedent husband's family).
288. Ozment 2001: 74.
289. Wiesner 1986: 23-5; Johner 1987: 14-17 (an exception from late medieval Freiburg, where guardians for women were regarded as an advantage, not a restriction, and functioned as a privilege enjoyed by the wealthy); Roper 1989: 170-1, 188-9, 193, 203-5; Koch 1991: 84-6; Opitz 1991: 29; Holthöfer 1997: 410-26; Wiesner 1998: 82, 86, 140; Wunder 1998: 187-8; Freist 1999: 169. On the older gender guardianship, become largely formal in nature by the late Middle Ages and employed at most for the protection of the widow, see Gerhards 1962: 169.
290. Wiesner 2000: 91. Not all widows were marginal of course. See, for example, the essays on noble widows in Schattkowsky 2003.

Notes to pages 82-86

291. Wiesner 1998: 8-11.
292. Wunder 1998: 42.
293. Harrington 1995: 217-24; Miller 1998: 27-8; Wunder 1998: 45.
294. Roper 1989: 225.
295. Wiesner 1998: 138; Strasser 2004: 64.
296. On the emergence of the ideology of *patria potestas* since the Renaissance, see Herlihy 1985: 115-17. For its reception in Bavaria, see Strasser 2004: 49, 100-2.
297. Koch 1991: 3-6, 12; Harrington 1995: 194; Wiesner 1998: 85-8, 92; Wiesner 2000: 38-9; Spieß 2003: 105; Streich 2003: 168-9.
298. Koch 1991: 182-6.
299. Koch 1991: 187-9; Wiesner 2000: 38-9.
300. Wiesner 1998: 87.
301. Roper 1989: 63; Wiesner 1998: 91-6, 116-18.
302. Strasser 2004: 8.
303. In Geneva, a new marital property law was enacted in 1568, four years after Calvin's death, that seriously compromised the rights of widows: Witte and Kingdon 2005: 395-6.
304. Roper 1989: 252-3.
305. Wunder 1998: 186.
306. Wiesner 2000: 130-1.
307. Roper 1989: 32; Hufton 1995: 95-6; Wiesner 2000: 128.
308. Wunder 1998: 137-8.
309. Hufton 1995: 238-9.
310. Opitz 1991: 33.
311. Johner 1987: 38-41; Opitz 1991: 33-4; Freist 1999: 167; Wiesner 2000: 113, 131-2.
312. Opitz 1991: 33-5; Freist 1999: 167.
313. Johner 1987: 18.
314. Spieß 1993: 149, 162-72, 175, 179-81, 189, 192-6; Wunder 1998: 32-3; Wiedemann 2001: 37.
315. Freist 1999: 169; Wiesner 2000: 132-3.
316. Wunder 1998: 89; Freist 1999: 167.
317. Wunder 2002: 22-3; Schattkowsky 2003: 32.
318. Wiesner 1986: 77.
319. Wiesner 1986: 5; Roper 1989: 48, 134; Koch 1991: 239-40; Wunder 1998: 33.
320. Wunder 1998: 62.
321. Roper 1989: 52; Wiesner 1998: 174; Freist 1999: 168; Strasser 2004: 65.
322. Wunder 1998: 142.
323. Roper 1989: 225.
324. Wiesner 1986: 93-5.
325. Roper 1989: 117.
326. Wiesner 1986: 172; Wunder 1998: 142; Ozment 2001: 23.
327. Freist 1999: 167.
328. Wiesner 1998: 165-6.
329. Herlihy 1990: 179; Koch 1991: 30, 77-8; Wunder 1998: 166; Wiesner 2000: 104-6.
330. Hufton 1995: 247-9.
331. Roper 1989: 49.
332. Roper 1989: 49.
333. Wiesner 1986: 92, 157-87; Herlihy 1990: 173, 179-80, 186.

Notes to pages 86-89

334. Roper 1989: 50-2.
335. Wiesner 1986: 3, 151, 157-63; Wiesner 1998: 143, 174, 179-80; Wunder 1998: 76; Freist 1999: 167. It is possible to locate the existence of restrictions on women in some crafts as early as the fourteenth century, but they seem to acquire a real momentum only in the early modern period: see Wiesner 1986: 174-8, 181-2.
336. Wiesner 1998: 173.
337. Koch 1991: 236.
338. Roper 1989: 49.
339. Wiesner 1986: 157.
340. Wiesner 1986: 46.
341. Strasser 2004: 156.
342. Wiesner 1998: 8, 148, 161.
343. Strasser 2004: 169.
344. Wiesner 1986: 40.
345. Wiesner 1998: 91.
346. Koch 1991: 69-76; Wiesner 1998: 121.
347. A controversial point: Roper 1989: 41, 44-5; Wiesner 1998: 132, 139; Wunder 1998: 66-75, 80-1.
348. Wunder 1998: 79-81; Wiedemann 2001: 37.
349. Wunder 1993: 29; Roper 1989: 41; Wiesner 1998: 161-2, 205; Wiesner 2000: 129.
350. Koch 1991: 240-4.
351. Wunder 1993; Strasser 2004: 9.
352. Wiesner 1986: 32.
353. Wiesner 1986: 33, 156, 165; Wiesner 1998: 144-5, 185.
354. Male offenders were ejected from the guild: Wiesner 1986: 153.
355. Wiesner 1998: 167-73, 180; Wiesner 2000: 127.
356. Wiesner 1986: 49-55, 190-2; Roper 1989: 46; Wunder 1998: 87; Freist 1999: 168; Wiesner 2000: 104.
357. Wunder 1998: 68, 72; Hurwich 2006: 41-4.
358. See Wunder 1998: 89-94.
359. Freist 1999: 166.
360. Strasser 2004: 65.
361. Gerhards 1962: 141-5, 150, 156-8; Jussen 2000: 321-7; Ingendahl 2003: 273.
362. Wiesner 1998: 11-12, 166.
363. Wiesner 1986: 31; Spieß 1993: 191. Squabbles frequently arose with family members over inheritances: Arnold 2003: 62-3.
364. Wiesner 1998: 12, 144.
365. Roper 1989: 52-3.
366. Koch 1991: 91, 244.
367. Koch 1991: 82-3; Wiesner 2001: 161.
368. Johner 1987; Wunder 1997: 51. The content of citizenship changed in the sixteenth century, as it became more gender-differentiated, to the disadvantage of women: see below.
369. Wiesner 1986: 75-9; Roper 1989: 9, 224; Koch 1991: 82; Wunder 1998: 166; Ozment 2001: 26. The goal of reducing the numbers of widows dependent on public alms motivated other aspects of policy as well: Strasser 2004: 214.
370. Roper 1989: 143.
371. Roper 1989: 249.
372. Strasser 2004: 67, 81.

Notes to pages 89-95

373. Wiesner 1986: 23-5.
374. Gerhards 1962: 119, 124-9; Wiesner 2000: 215-18.
375. Gerhards 1962: 134-40.
376. Johner 1987: 36; Roper 1989: 50-1; Wiesner 1998: 136-7; Wunder 1998: 132-4; Strasser 2004: 50-3.
377. Roper 1989: 143.
378. Roper 1989: 179.
379. Wunder 1998: 141.
380. Opitz 1991: 35-6.
381. Wunder 1998: 171-83.
382. Gerhards 1962: 94-8.
383. Koch 1991: 91, 127-8; Hurwich 2006: 188.
384. Koch 1991: 219-32.
385. Ingendahl 2003: 270, 278.
386. Roper 1989: 60; Wiltenburg 1992: 231.
387. Wiesner 1998: 175.
388. Wiesner 1986: 85, 114-18, 131-8, 158-9, 191-7; Wiesner 1998: 16.
389. Wiesner 1998: 144.
390. Ingendahl 2003: 278; Schattkowsky 2003: 27; Spieß 2003: 109-10; Streich 2003: 186.
391. See Taylor 1980: 97.
392. Roper 1989: 52-4; Wiltenburg 1992: 147; Wiedemann 2001: 38.
393. Roper 1994: 62.
394. Roper 1994: 192, 208.
395. Wiedemann 2001: 38; Fischer 2002: 162.
396. Wunder 1998: 61, 102; Wiedemann 2001: 40; Wiesner 2000: 273, 277.
397. Taylor 1980: 92-3; Wiedemann 2001: 37.
398. Gerhards 1962: 48, 53, 58, 83-5, 210-13, 225-8; Arden 1992; Runte 1998: 115-16; Ingendahl 2003: 275, 403; Feichtinger 2005: 198, 203.
399. Jussen 2000: 257-312.
400. Fischer 2002: 14, 31-2, 46.
401. Laurence 1997: 285.
402. The enclosure of religious women was ordained, if ambiguously, by Boniface VIII in 1298, and remained without strict enforcement for centuries: Wiesner 2000: 216; Strasser 2004: 73-5.
403. Gerhards 1962: 113, 129; cf. 224 on Johann Geiler von Kaisersberg; Fischer 2002: 54-72.
404. Fischer 2002: 73-135.
405. Matthew 22.30.
406. Fischer 2002: 173-94.
407. See Fischer 2002: 54-135.
408. Fischer 2002: 213-51, 268; Hurwich 2006: 181-9.
409. Wiltenburg 1992: 47.
410. Taylor 1980: 24-5, 107; Wiltenburg 1992: 77-8. Widow suicide, although a popular theme of German mythology, plays a very minor role in the literature and life of later periods: Gerhards 1962: 111; Taylor 1980:90.
411. Taylor 1980: 26-7; cf. Bawcutt 2005.
412. Cf. Jussen 2000 for a different understanding of these developments.
413. Strasser 2004: 82-3, 180.
414. Strasser 2004: 38.
415. Harrington 1995: 33-34; Witte 2002: 217-32.

416. Roper 1989: 211; Strasser 2004: 83.
417. Roper 1989: 52-3, 85, 108, 112, 130-1, 233; Freist 1999: 165. For late-medieval hostility to non-marital sex, anticipating Reform, see Strasser 2004: 175; Hurwich 2006: 173.
418. Wiesner 1998: 75, 77.
419. Strasser 2004: 23, 74, 84, 123-6, 139, 174-5.
420. Strasser 2004: 81.
421. Strasser 2004: 84.
422. Freist 1999: 176.
423. On the genre of the funeral sermon, which by 1600 had developed into an important vehicle for rendering personal virtues public, including those of widows, see Arnold 2003.
424. Taylor 1980: 27-8; Fischer 2002: 195-212.
425. Koch 1991: 203; Fischer 2002: 140; Witte 2002: 231; Ingendahl 2003: 274.
426. Harrington 1995: 79, 169; Wiesner 1998: 137-8; Strasser 2004: 83.
427. Strasser 2004: 64.
428. Strasser 2004: 176. For concerns about the sexual nature of wives, see Roper 1989: 201-2, 235.
429. Roper 1989: 53; Harrington 1995: 254-6, 271.
430. Wiesner 1998: 139.
431. Wiltenburg 1992: 17.
432. Roper 1994: 5.
433. Roper 1994: 192; Wiesner 2000: 268-73, 277.
434. Roper 1994: 207-12, 217; cf. 202-3.
435. Koch 1991: 151-7.
436. Wiesner 2000: 227.
437. Roper 1989: 54; Wiesner 1998: 37-46.
438. Bepler 2003: 305-13, 319; Streich 2003: 180.
439. Wunder 2002: 10-13, 24; Hufschmidt 2003: 350; Schattkowsky 2003: 18-22, 28.
440. See the essays by Günther, Koch, Marra, Puppel, Scholz, Streich and Wartenberg, in Schattkowsky 2003.
441. Wunder 2002: 25-6.
442. Ingendahl 2003: 271; Schattkowsky 2003: 31; Spieß 2003: 100-4; Streich 2003: 186-8.
443. Spieß 2003: 101.
444. Schleinert, Löwenstein and Scholz in Schattkowsky 2003.
445. Wiesner 2000: 232.
446. Wunder 1998: 181-3; Wiesner 2000: 223-4, 249, 295.
447. Wiesner 2000: 227-9; Wiesner-Hanks 2001: 161.
448. Strasser 2004: 39.
449. Wiesner 1998: 116-17, 125.
450. Wiesner 1998: 78, 100-1, 112.
451. Wiesner 1998: 52, 64, 77; Wunder 1998: 51.
452. Roper 1989: 252.
453. Roper 1989: 260; Wiesner 1998: 122.
454. Strasser 2004: 10-13, 47.
455. Strasser 2004: 85, 105, 111-19.
456. Roper 1989: 54-5; Wiesner 1998: 140; Wunder 1998: 81.
457. Roper 1989: 225.
458. Roper 1989: 132; Wunder 1998: 203.

Notes to pages 99-103

459. Strasser 2004: 10-13, 57, 65, 91, 111-17, 174-5.
460. Roper 1989: 180; Wunder 1998: 81, 84.
461. Roper 1989: 183-6; Hurwich 2006: 155.
462. Amussen 1988: 96-8, 112, 123-8, 159, 166-8; Roper 1994: 46-7, 109, 115; Fletcher 1995: 404; Miller 1998: 42-6.
463. Fletcher 1995: 19, 28.
464. Roper 1989: 188-91.
465. On the Germanic tradition of widow suicide, long superseded, see above in the notes.
466. Wunder 1998: 52-3.
467. Wunder 1998: 135-6.
468. Johner 1987: 35.
469. Freist 1999: 166.
470. Gerhards 1962: 217.
471. Spieß 1993: 135, 146-7, 158-61, 164, 181-9, 193-8.
472. Hurwich 2006: 106-9, 126-34.
473. See Wiesner 1998: 45.
474. Strasser 2004: 89-97.
475. Wiesner 1986: 7, 192; Wiedemann 2001: 35.
476. Ingendahl 2003: 274-77.
477. Koch 1991: 30-2.
478. Opitz 1991: 38; Wunder 1998: 136; Freist 1999: 166.
479. Hufton 1995: 222; Wunder 1998: 139.
480. Opitz 1991: 37.
481. Wunder 1998: 137.
482. Hurwich 2006: 133, 187.
483. Wunder 1998: 138.
484. One concern expressed was that a widow be young enough to bear children: Hurwich 2006: 123.
485. Wunder 1998: 138-9.
486. Hufton 1995: 223; Wunder 1998: 134; Freist 1999: 166.
487. Wunder 1998: 134, 139.
488. Wiesner 1986: 162; Harrington 1995: 241; Wunder 1998: 134; Freist 1999: 164. On Roman and canon law rules and their application, see Koch 1991: 28-9.
489. Gerhards 1962: 213-15; Opitz 1991: 41.
490. Wunder 1998: 139.
491. Spieß 1993: 421-4.
492. Wiesner 1986: 21; Harrington 1995: 191.
493. Roper 1989: 140.
494. Hurwich 2006: 9, 28, 86.
495. Wiesner 1986: 157, 162, 164; Roper 1989: 38.
496. Wiedemann 2001: 38; Hurwich 2006: 119-21.
497. Hurwich 2006: 158-9; cf. 161-5.
498. Wiedemann 2001: 35.
499. Koch 1991: 31-2, 54-5.
500. See Taylor 1980: 28; Roper 1989: 1; Laurence 1994: 272; Wiesner 1998: 202.
501. For older scholarship now deemed overly optimistic about gender equality in the Middle Ages, see Stretton 1998: 21.
502. Wunder 1998: 183; Ozment 2001: 28-42; Feichtinger 2005: 198, 203.

4. Modern England and the United States

1. In 1918 women over 30 with certain property or marital qualifications gained the franchise, which was extended to all women in 1928: Walby 1990: 161.
2. Hinde 2003: 201.
3. Klein 2004: 112, 116.
4. Hinde 2003: 216-17; Klein 2004: 108, 155. In 1921 about a quarter of women in their early thirties were unmarried: Abbott 2003: 44.
5. This despite a growing toll of deaths in industrial accidents, especially in the United States but also in England and elsewhere, which reached devastating proportions by the turn of the twentieth century, so much so that contemporaries did not hesitate to invoke the casualty rates of war, especially the Civil War, in comparison: Witt 2004: 2-3, 24-7, 41, 112. Such accidents had a disproportionate impact on men who were the sole support of wives and children: Witt 2004: 37.
6. This grew to 7.9 years by 1979: Goldman and Lord 1983: 178.
7. This was already six years in 1950-52: Anderson 1990: 16.
8. Wrigley and Schofield 1981: 437; Anderson 1990: 32-3; Lynch and Lee 1998: 105; Gordon and Nair 2003: 172. A study devoted to mid- to late nineteenth-century Glasgow shows that on average married men were seven years older than married women: Gordon and Nair 2003: 188.
9. Haines 2000: 319, who uses the term 'the white population'.
10. Wrigley and Schofield 1981: 437; Ruggles 1987: 106-11; Anderson 1990: 28; Curran 1993: 226; Gordon and Nair 2003: 172-3; Klein 2004: 126.
11. Hahn 2002: 35. An important development was the publication of information on marital status from the 1851 Census, which showed over one million never-married women who were more than 25 years of age in the British population: Green 2000: 201; Green and Owens 2003: 512.
12. See Taeuber and Taeuber 1971: 320; Anderson 1990: 31; Hareven and Uhlenberg 1995: 276.
13. Green 2000: 201-2; Green and Owens 2003: 513-17.
14. Klein 2004: 127-32.
15. Baldwin 1988: 228-9.
16. Riley 1988: 18, 86.
17. Mineau 1988: 140-1; Hareven and Uhlenberg 1995: 274-5.
18. Mineau 1988: 141, 149, 158.
19. Hareven and Uhlenberg 1995: 279.
20. Anderson 1990: 30.
21. Taeuber and Taeuber 1971: 285.
22. Perkin 1989: 2, 14-19; Staves 1990: 90, 145, 181; Davidoff et al 1999: 62, 144; Green 2000: 205-6.
23. Perkin 1989: 65-70; Staves 1990: 59-82, 98-9, 111-15, 131-61, 206.
24. Women of all marital statuses, and from all ranks of society, continued to be named as executors in wills or were called on to fulfil this function in case of intestacy: Gordon and Nair 2003: 196.
25. Perkin 1989: 16-17, 70-3; Staves 1990: 35, 49-50, 82, 127-33, 186.
26. Perkin 1989: 6, 51-2, 66; Staves 1990: 83-6, 115, 135, 151, 158-61, 194, 203; Finch 1994: 96-100; Davidoff et al 1999: 63.
27. Perkin 1989: 5-7, 71, 75, 115; Davidoff et al 1999: 63.
28. Staves 1990: 5, 27-49, 112-13. Personal property had a broader definition in the nineteenth century than in the early modern period: see Green 2000: 198.
29. Glendon 1989: 241.

30. Shanley 1989: 4, 33, 113.
31. Shanley 1989: 12-13, 19-20, 65-6, 99.
32. Shanley 1989: 129.
33. Writs of *habeas corpus* could no longer be used by a husband to regain custody of a wife from 1852, but only in 1891 did it become impossible to invoke one to secure custody of a wife already detained by her husband: Shanley 1989: 181-2.
34. Perkin 1989: 27-8, 293; Shanley 1989: 131-55; Behlmer 1998: 91; Davidoff et al 1999: 137-45. Until 1929, males could marry at 14 and females at 12 with parental consent, although for other purposes the age of majority was fixed at 21: Abbott 2003: 44.
35. Perkin 1989: 8, 296; Morris 1994: 174, 177-8, 190-1..
36. Perkin 1989: 25, 292-3, 301-3; Shanley 1989: 43-8.
37. Pateman 1988: 120; Perkin 1989: 304-5, 310; Shanley 1989: 14; Rose 1992: 51; Morris 1994: 172, 184-5, 190-1; Green and Owens 2003: 516.
38. Rose 1992: 63; Davidoff et al 1999: 44, 107, 143.
39. Lynch and Lee 1998: 120.
40. Shanley 1989: 70-4, 114, 125-30.
41. Combs 2004.
42. The numbers of divorces grew to 25,000 in 1961, 146,000 in 1981 and 153,000 in 1990: Behlmer 1998: 319.
43. Perkin 1989: 8, 116-17, 306-8; Shanley 1989: 174-6; Hammerton 1992: 57, 98, 118-33; Behlmer 1998: 177-225; Davidoff et al 1999: 145.
44. Witt 2004: 53.
45. Shanley 1989: 109-11.
46. For a list of nineteenth- and twentieth-century legislative acts affecting the family, see Davidoff et al 1999: 270-1.
47. Shanley 1989: 19-21, 113.
48. Perkin 1989: 98, 158, 246; Staves 1990: 204, 225-7; Davidoff et al 1999: 153.
49. Curran 1993: 223.
50. Shanley 1989: 10, 66.
51. Gordon and Nair 2003: 191-8. See also Green and Owens 2003: esp. 512, 516-19, 525, who show some single women, including widows, taking an active, and to all appearances successful, role in managing their investments; they are especially highly concentrated in the London area.
52. Green 2000: 217-22; Green and Owens 2003: 529-32.
53. The percentage of those living in towns doubled between 1801 and 1851, to about 50%. By 1850 only 5% of workers had jobs in factories and it was not until later in the century that the household-based workshop was virtually sundered from industrial production: Davidoff et al 1999: 26, 104.
54. Perkin 1989: 123-4, 181; Kertzer and Barbagli 2002: xxxvii.
55. Bradley 1989: 82-91.
56. Perkin 1989: 182-200.
57. Jordan 1999: 56-8.
58. Perkin 1989: 127-37, 156, 312; Rose 1992: 19; Miller 1998: 242.
59. Gillis 1985: 67, 184.
60. Rose 1994: 278-83.
61. Green 2000: 195.
62. Davidoff et al 1999: 192, 197-8; Witt 2004: 72-3, 95-6, 132, 181.
63. Winter 1983; Gillis 1985: 205, 239; Perkin 1989: 175-89; Rose 1992: 52, 77; Walkowitz 1992: 58; Rose 1994: 283-7; Laslett 1995: 48; Behlmer 1998: 276, 293;

Miller 1998: 176-8; Davidoff et al 1999: 107; Gente 2002; Wall 2002b: 11-12; Strange 2005: 196-200.
64. Pedersen 1993: 139-42, 152-9, 167-77.
65. See Abbott 2003: 52-3.
66. Perkin 1989: 296.
67. Hareven 1994: 133-4.
68. Perkin 1989: 158; Lynch and Lee 1998: 118-20.
69. Bradley 1989: 42-3; Perkin 1989: 164-5; Rose 1992: 82, 85; Skocpol 1992: 34, 249; Hareven 1994: 129; Behlmer 1998: 25; Strange 2005: 199.
70. Perkin 1989: 119, 130, 139, 162; Lynch and Lee 1998: 127.
71. Hufton 1995: 499.
72. Rose 1992: 15, 53, 84-6, 161, 185.
73. Rose 1992: 79, 88, 96-9. The 'male breadwinner family', as the object of a fair share of scholarly controversy, has been argued to be of recent vintage, caused by a variety of factors, uneven in its development, historically exceptional, linked to the early stages of the family life cycle, and complicated by great variation across cultures as well as by physical location and the sector of the economy within a society. See Janssens 1997 and the articles it introduces, especially that by Horrell and Humphries.
74. Rose 1992: 83-8, 166, 185.
75. Perkin 1989: 4, 158, 174-7.
76. Pateman 1988: 128-30; Perkin 1989: 235, 248-9; Lynch and Lee 1998: 109, 114, 128; Davidoff et al 1999: 152.
77. Davidoff et al 1999: 27-9.
78. Gillis 1985: 242; Perkin 1989: 127, 166; Rose 1992: 46, 80; Sharpe 1998: 10.
79. Behlmer 1998: 155; Gordon and Nair 2003: 180-3. The 'widening sphere' was in part a matter of perception, as women and their work became more visible to men: see Garrett 1995.
80. Gillis 1985: 246.
81. Sharpe 1998: 11.
82. Gillis 1985: 287-91.
83. Rose 1992: 72-80, 131-2; Hufton 1995: 509; Humphries 1995: 98-100; Lynch and Lee 1998: 110-11.
84. Bradley 1989: 204; Davidoff et al 1999: 106, 158-64, 178-80.
85. Gordon and Nair 2003: 184.
86. Curran 1993: 230.
87. Behlmer 1998: 283.
88. Rose 1992: 46, 76-7, 175, 188. Prominent among children admitted to the National Children's Home were the offspring of widows and abandoned wives: Gillis 1985: 246.
89. Curran 1993: 228-9.
90. See Laslett 1995: 50.
91. Walkowitz 1992: 105; Curran 1993: 235.
92. Bradley 1989: 47-9, 139, 151-2, 181, 210, 224; Davidoff et al 1999: 193.
93. See e.g. Curran 1993.
94. Gordon and Nair 2003: 190-8; Green and Owens 2003.
95. Perkin 1989: 64; Staves 1990: 158.
96. Perkin 1989: 84.
97. Perkin 1989: 54-5, 93-7, 99-101.
98. Gillis 1985: 187.
99. Perkin 1989: 39-40, 242.

Notes to pages 122-128

100. Perkin 1989: 56-7.
101. Gillis 1985: 220-3; Pateman 1988: 65-75, 117-20, 256; Perkin 1989: 39-40, 207-25, 241; Shanley 1989: 8, 60-1, 86, 156-7, 182; Hammerton 1992: 158-60.
102. Gillis 1985: 228.
103. Gillis 1985: 224-7; Bradley 1989: 40-1; Perkin 1989: 7, 133-4, 142, 213-19, 238-40, 265-6, 276; Hammerton 1992: 71; Miller 1998: 177, 188, 238-9, 263; Davidoff et al 1999: 27, 66-8, 101, 109-10, 125; Gordon and Nair 2003: 168.
104. Shanley 1989: 29; Davidoff et al 1999: 26.
105. Shanley 1989: 82; Behlmer 1998: 20, 24; Lynch and Lee 1998: 113-14; Wiesner-Hanks 2001: 165.
106. Perkin 1989: 148, 243, 268, 308; Vickery 1993: 383-401, 410-12; Behlmer 1998: 3, 24; Davidoff et al 1999: 68, 223; Gordon and Nair 2003: 179.
107. Gillis 1985: 252, 259; Perkin 1989: 223-31; Davidoff et al 1999: 129, 223.
108. Gillis 1985: 233-6, 288, 294, 299, 313; Perkin 1989: 54, 98, 232-40, 311, 315; Staves 1990: 279; Davidoff et al 1999: 79, 190, 246.
109. Gillis 1985: 252.
110. Gordon and Nair 2003: 167.
111. Shanley 1989: 5.
112. Gilbert and Gubar 2000: 10-11.
113. Strange 2005: 196.
114. Morley 1971: 70-5.
115. Thaden 1997: 92-109.
116. Kimball 1994.
117. Behlmer 1998: 18-19.
118. Perkin 1989: 313-14.
119. Perkin 1989: 250-72.
120. Shanley 1989: 8, 31, 50, 58, 62-3, 84, 188-9; Hammerton 1992: 2-7, 24, 31-3, 71-83, 107-11, 134-52, 167-9.
121. Gillis 1985: 237, 255, 263, 315-16; Davidoff et al 1999: 97, 208, 246.
122. Curran 1993: 227.
123. Rose 1994: 273-8.
124. Curran 1993: 218.
125. Green and Owens 2003.
126. Gordon and Nair 2003: 169-71, 177-8, 187-8.
127. Wall 2002b: esp. 150-4.
128. Wall 2002c.
129. Perkin 1989: 315; Behlmer 1998: 27.
130. See Gillis 1985: 4; Staves 1990: 159.
131. Gordon and Nair 2003: 198.
132. Anderson 1990: 29.
133. Curran 1993: 225-7. Anderson 1990: 31 breaks down the data by gender, with 9% of widows remarrying in the mid-nineteenth century, and the rate reaching 6.6% in the early 1900s. The rates for men are 14% and 8.9%, respectively.
134. Drake 1981: 289-93.
135. Hammerton 1992: 114.
136. Chinn 1988: 147, 156.
137. Perkin 1989: 60-1; Gordon and Nair 2003: 175 and above.
138. Gordon and Nair 2003: 174, 189-90.
139. Perkin 1989: 30, 52.
140. Perkin 1989: 30, 52, 182.

Notes to pages 128-133

141. Gillis 1985: 181, 236.
142. Basch 1982: 42, 180; Grossberg 1985: 14-15; Salmon 1986: xvi, 14, 41; Carter 1988: 279; Cott 2000: 12; Hartog 2000: 40-2, 77-8, 123-5, 146, 157-60, 169; Dubler 2003b: 1647.
143. Basch 1982: 23-6; Salmon 1986: 4-11, 22, 83-97, 101-17, 120-2, 148-9, 160-8, 183-8, 217.
144. Cott 2000: 6, 95; Hartog 2000: 39, 43, 53, 108-9, 118-20, 390.
145. Salmon 1986: 11, 93, 120, 160-4; Wilson 1992: 25-7.
146. Salmon 1986: 123, 141-6; Wilson 1992: 26; Hartog 2000: 144; Dubler 2003b: 1660-2, 1667-8. The inheritance right of widowers, known as curtesy, amounted to a life interest in the whole of decedent wife's real property: Salmon 1986: 144; Hartog 2000: 144; Dubler 2003b: 1661. States entering the Union after 1850 almost all favoured protection of the widow's 'homestead' to protection of dower. In fact, the majority of states eventually abolished dower and curtesy in favour of a statutory minimum share for the surviving spouse: Shammas et al 1987: 86. New York abolished dower in 1929: Dubler 2003b: 1649.
147. Scadron 1988b: 7; Wilson 1992: 29, 41-2. Some husbands sought to evade the protections afforded by dower, which seems to have lost efficacy over time: Dubler 2003b: 1662, 1670.
148. Wilson 1992: 31-40; Hartog 2000: 109, 120, 356, 359.
149. Hartog 2000: 170-4.
150. Wilson 1992: 44-54.
151. Wilson 1992: 137, 144.
152. Wilson 1992: 27-8; Hartog 2000: 118.
153. Basch 1982: 40, 227; Miller 1998: 127; Cott 2000: 7, 96, 257. An 1872 Supreme Court decision denying a married woman admission to a state legal bar characterized single women as 'exceptions to the general rule' and so dismissed them as irrelevant: Dubler 2003a: 798, 801.
154. Basch 1992: 108, 122.
155. Basch 1982: 148, 162-79; Grossberg 1985: 10; Hartog 2000: 18-19, 39, 43. The eighteenth-century legal authority William Blackstone, who discounted the role of equity in English law, was read as accurately reflecting that entire system by American reformers (and practically everyone else): Basch 1982: 43-57; Hartog 2000: 115-17, 121.
156. Hartog 2000: 24, 42, 117, 152, 167, 217, 282. Such arguments were eventually accepted by the courts, in some cases in the years after the Civil War, in South Carolina as late as 1938: Hartog 2000: 209, 300.
157. Basch 1982: 39, 131-2, 227.
158. Hartog 2000: 38, 55; Dubler 2003b: 1671-8.
159. Lebsock 1977; Basch 1982: 125, 137, 226; Grossberg 1985: 244; Wilson 1992: 27-8, 197; Shammas 1994: 24; Kahn 1996: 361-4; Hartog 2000: 39, 110, 176, 189-91; Geddes and Lueck 2002, arguing for the pursuit of a broader conception of male self-interest.
160. Worth noting is that the first law giving wives control over their earnings was passed by Massachusetts in 1855, the last by Georgia in 1943: Lebsock 1977: 209; Zeigler 1996: 70.
161. Basch 1982: 200-23; Siegel 1994b: 2150-4; Cott 2000: 54.
162. Chused 1994: 2222.
163. Shammas 1994.
164. Kahn 1996.
165. Siegel 1994a; Zeigler 1996.

Notes to pages 133-142

166. Basch 1982: 220.
167. See Basch 1982: 229-32.
168. Shammas et al 1987: 291-2; González 1988: 76; Schuele 1994; Kahn 1996: 380; Hartog 2000: 13-14, 321.
169. Shammas et al. 1987: 84.
170. Beecher et al 1988: 124-5.
171. Baldwin 1988: 234; Guy 1988: 197-200. Most states accepted 21 as the age of majority, a standard imported from the English tradition: DiMatteo 1994: 511.
172. Carter 1988: 271-5. There were some important differences in the rules between Arizona and New Mexico: see Carter 1988: 276.
173. Carter 1988: 278-9.
174. Grossberg 1985: 104; Riley 1988:21; Hartog 2000: 246-86.
175. Grossberg 1985: 73-80, 89, 97, 119; Cott 2000: 30-2, 38-9, 48.
176. Grossberg 1985: 234-50; Mason 1994: 60-1; Cott 2000: 15; Hartog 2000: 193-217.
177. Grossberg 1985: 242-7; Friedman et al 1996: 147, 152-3.
178. Hartog 2000: 144-6; Dubler 2003b: 1653, 1664-6.
179. Siegel 1994b: 2150-4; Hartog 2000: 360.
180. Hartog 2000: 144.
181. See Hartog 2000: 187.
182. Salmon 1986: 62, 76, 83, 93-7, 141, 167, 184, 215; Cott 2000: 11, 52-4; Hartog 2000: 53, 80, 101-2, 110-14, 136, 150-69; Dubler 2003b: 1678-89, 1691-4.
183. Dubler 2003b: 1649, 1655, 1694.
184. Witt 2004: 53-4.
185. Carter 1988: 289; Witt 2004: 11, 17, 190.
186. Witt 2004: 37-41, 126-33, 187, 190, 205-6.
187. Grossberg 1985: 117; Carter 1988: 279; Hartog 2000: 287-93; Dubler 2003b: 1652.
188. See Goldberg 1992b: 5-6; Miller 1998: 288.
189. Haber 1983: 31; Haber and Gratton 1994: 31-5, 69-70, 90-1; Klein 2004: 113.
190. Riley 1988: 118-19, 133-4.
191. Baldwin 1988: 230; Goodfriend 1988: 166; Shammas 1994: 26; Scadron 1988d: ix-xi; Scadron 1988b: 7; Hareven and Uhlenberg 1995: 273; Cott 2000: 166.
192. Kessler-Harris 1995; Witt 2004: 72-81, 114-17, 126-7, 200.
193. Miller 1998: 278.
194. Sommestad 1997: 154-63.
195. Wilson 1992: 29-30, 54-7, 111-12, 129.
196. Shammas et al 1987: 112-22.
197. Baldwin 1988: 234-5.
198. Shammas et al 1987: 195-206.
199. Wilson 1992: 2-5, 42.
200. Wilson 1992: 7.
201. Stanley 1998: 63.
202. In late nineteenth-century Arizona many widows found operating a farm without assistance from kin too great a challenge and sold the property. They tended to favour urban property as an investment: Baldwin 1988: 233.
203. Beecher et al 1988: 127, 133; Wilson 1992: 31, 58-60, 101-7, 120.
204. Baldwin 1988: 231-3, 239; Wilson 1992: 115-24, 131.
205. Wilson 1992: 59.
206. Wilson 1992: 124.

Notes to pages 142-147

207. Stanley 1998: 144-8.
208. Witt 2004: 35.
209. Cott 2000: 167.
210. Stanley 1998: 64.
211. Baldwin 1988: 265; Goodfriend 1988: 168, 174-7, 183-5, 191; Guy 1988: 202-10, 215-16; Scadron 1988a: 304-5; Wilson 1992: 5, 63-5; Hareven and Uhlenberg 1995: 282.
212. Lopata 1996; 47.
213. Sommestad 1997; 158-9.
214. Guy 1988; 210-12, 215. In late nineteenth-century Arizona, the relatively early average age at first marriage meant that few never-married women were hired compared to the United States as a whole: Guy 1988: 212.
215. Cott 2000: 167; see also Stanley 1998: 151-2.
216. Except among feminists, there was considerably less sensitivity over the work of freedwomen outside the home, suggesting that considerations of race and perhaps class played a role in the expression of this ideology: Stanley 1998: 188-90, 204.
217. Stanley 1998: 163-8, 172, 192.
218. Stanley 1998: 151-5, 215-16.
219. Cf. Scadron 1988b: 4, who suggests that before the demographic transition, there was a close link for many women between their widowhood and adulthood for their children.
220. Wilson 1992: 141, 149.
221. Goodfriend 1988: 178-80.
222. Haber and Gratton 1994: 31-4; Ruggles 2003; see also McGarry and Schoeni 2000: 221, 226, 233, who attribute the change in the twentieth century chiefly to the introduction of Social Security.
223. Riley 1988: 40, 47.
224. Wilson 1992: 157-62.
225. Goodfriend 1988: 170-3.
226. Guy 1988: 208; see also Baldwin 1988: 238.
227. Wilson 1992: 163-4.
228. Guy 1988: 209.
229. Baldwin 1988: 235; Beecher et al 1988: 130-1; Wilson 1992: 22, 69.
230. Goodfriend 1988: 180-2; Scadron 1988a: 304.
231. Grossberg 1985: 265-7; Wilson 1992: 71-99; Miller 1998: 176; Stanley 1998: 112-14, 131-136; see also Baldwin 1988: 236; Cott 2000: 276.
232. Goodfriend 1988: 182-3.
233. Guy 1988: 200.
234. See Hareven and Uhlenberg 1995: 273.
235. Beecher et al 1988: 123-33; Guy 1988: 207. At the peak of the phenomenon of polygynous marriage about 20% of the marriages in Utah fell into this category: Scadron 1988a: 302.
236. González 1988: 69-85.
237. Loustaunau 1988: 98-110.
238. Stanley 1998: 140, 194-216.
239. Kessler-Harris 1982: 81, 122; Baldwin 1988: 236; Carter 1988: 288; Goodfriend 1988: 170-2; Guy 1988: 208; Scadron 1988a: 306; Holmes 1990; Skocpol 1992: 65, 107, 139, 145; Wilson 1992: 73.
240. In 1893 pensions for disabled veterans, as well as for the widows and elderly parents of veterans, amounted to 40% of the federal budget: Cott 2000: 103.

Notes to pages 147-151

241. Baldwin 1988: 224-7.
242. Guy 1988: 196.
243. Dubler 2003b: 1653.
244. The cumulation of economic and moral criteria in evaluating eligibility is well illustrated by the distinction drawn in San Francisco between 'high type' and 'pauper type' widows, with the former judged more respectable and so eligible for greater benefits from the Widows' Pension Bureau: Skocpol 1992: 475.
245. Carter 1988: 287-9; Goodfriend 1988: 166-7, 184; Guy 1988: 201-5, 218-20; Scadron 1988a: 304; Skocpol 1992: 32-5, 95-6, 465-71; Gordon 1994: 19-20, 28-30, 45-51; Lopata 1996: 47; Cott 2000: 169-72; Dubler 2003b: 1700-7; Witt 2004: 203.
246. Carter 1988: 287.
247. Carter 1988: 289.
248. Carter 1988: 289-92; Guy 1988: 199, 205-6, 219; Skocpol 1992: 535-6; Cott 2000: 172-6, 179. On the changes to Social Security in 1939, see above.
249. Hartog 2000: 133-4.
250. Scadron 1988c: 261.
251. Grossberg 1985: 82, 251; Stanley 1998: 6-17; Cott 2000: 16-17, 25.
252. Salmon 1986: 61.
253. Grossberg 1985: 59; Stanley 1998: 181.
254. Stanley 1998: 23, 33, 240; Cott 2000: 61-3.
255. *Ephesians* 5.22-4, from a letter insecurely attributed to St Paul. See Stanley1998: 25-33, 44-50.
256. Grossberg 1985: 47-60, 146-50, 171, 183, 215, 227; Cott 2000: 159.
257. In fact, the negative equation of marriage and slavery dates as far back as Mary Astell in 1700: Grossberg 1985: 83, 90, 140-50, 175.
258. Stanley 1998: 176-86; Cott 2000: 63-7.
259. Grossberg 1985: 98, 121; Cott 2000: 68-74.
260. Grossberg 1985: 120; Cott 2000: 25-6, 72-3, 116.
261. Cott 2000: 124-31.
262. Cott 2000: 168, 181.
263. González 1988: 80-2.
264. Scadron 1988a: 308; Hartog 2000: 19-20, 37.
265. Wilson 1992: 87-9.
266. Reinhart et al 1998: 29-32.
267. Riley 1988: 74; Wilson 1992: 12.
268. Wilson 1992: 11, 21-2.
269. Wilson 1992: 134, 155, 165-6.
270. Scadron 1988c: 246; Wilson 1992: 15.
271. Scadron 1988c: 261; Wilson 1992: 11-12.
272. González 1988: 102.
273. Beecher et al 1988: 120-1.
274. Scadron 1988b: 13.
275. Scadron 1988c: 258.
276. Scadron 1988c: 264-5; Wilson 1992: 19.
277. González 1988: 101.
278. Beecher et al 1988: 119-20; cf. Scadron 1988c: 245.
279. Scadron 1988c: 262, 265.
280. Wilson 1992: 23, 31, 103-4.
281. Wilson 1992: 135-6.
282. Shammas et al 1987: 119-20.
283. Beecher et al 1988: 134.

Notes to pages 151-159

284. González 1988: 82; Wilson 1992: 170.
285. Riley 1988: 137-8.
286. Riley 1988: 156-63, 178-87.
287. Riley 1988: 198; Scadron 1988a: 305.
288. Goodfriend 1988: 184.
289. See Dubler 2003b: 1678.
290. Camfield 1997: 23, 36, 110-11.
291. See Morris 1992: 56-8.
292. Tracy 1995: 126-37.
293. Faust 1996: 110, 148-50; Revels 2004: 71, 139.
294. Revels 2004: 58-9.
295. Skocpol 1992: 145; Gordon 1994: 51.
296. Scadron 1988c: 264.
297. Hartog 2000: 11.
298. Guy 1988: 216.
299. Riley 1988: 2-4, 11, 54, 71-5, 102, 121, 195-201.
300. Riley 1988: 24, 163-5.
301. Reinhart et al 1998: esp. 39-41.
302. Grossberg 1985: 343.
303. Wilson 1992: 44, 55, 120, 137-43.
304. Mineau 1988: 150-3. On the difficulty in tracking remarriage in some sources because of such factors as name change, see Baldwin 1988: 229.
305. Hareven and Uhlenberg 1995: 276-84; see also Beecher et al 1988: 130.
306. Cott 2000: 78.
307. Loustaunau 1988: 96; Mineau 1988: 141.
308. Ruggles 2003: 155.
309. Hareven and Uhlenberg 1995: 281.
310. Scadron 1988: 4, 9; Hartog 2000: 90, 284.
311. Riley 1988: 22, 74, 80.
312. Hartog 2000: 20, 244-5, 284, 378.
313. See Dubler 2003a: 806-8, 814.
314. See Dubler 2003a: 808, 811; Dubler 2003b: 1648.

5. Conclusion: Widows in history

1. Davidoff et al 1999: 48.
2. See Scadron 1988a: 301.
3. Wiesner 2000: 3-7.
4. Dubler 2003b: 1644.
5. For example, the traditional link between citizenship and property holding has excluded most males in history from full civic standing: see Cott 2000: 27.
6. See Cott 2000: 44 for an important illustration.
7. Staves 1990: 85.
8. Salmon 1986: 39.
9. Staves 1990: 36, 111, 116, 120.
10. Pateman 1988: 48-54, 172-6, 231; Koch 1991: 197; Wunder 1998: 55; Wiesner-Hanks 2001: 163.
11. Bradley 1989: 47.
12. Staves 1990: 135, 142, 222.
13. Staves 1990: 35, 82, 86.
14. See Wunder 1998: 203-5; Wiesner-Hanks 2001: 162.

15. See Staves 1990: 83, 221.
16. Staves 1990: 203.
17. Salmon 1986: 13.
18. Staves 1990: 111, 129-30.
19. Bradley 1989: 41-2.
20. Staves 1990: 128.
21. Staves 1990: 161, 221.
22. Bradley 1989: 238.
23. Staves 1990: 7, 120-9.
24. See Staves 1990: 25.
25. Staves 1990: 169; Cott 2000: 13-15.
26. Cott 2000: 52.
27. Pateman 1988: 21, 85, 126-30; Staves 1990: 223.
28. Bradley 1989: 225.
29. Pateman 1988: 126, 135.
30. See Wiesner-Hanks 2001: 5-6.
31. Pateman 1988: 48-54, 172-6; Staves 1990: 224-6.
32. Staves 1990: 227-8.
33. Bradley 1989: 226.
34. See Frier and McGinn 2003: 8.
35. See Miller 1998: xvii.
36. Vickery 1993: 401-14.
37. See, for example, the different accounts of Pateman 1988: 19-22, 214; Miller 1998: 291-3.
38. Dubler 2003b: 1644.
39. Hahn 2002: 52-4.
40. Bradley 1989: 34; Miller 1998: 294.
41. Bennett 1997.

References and further reading

Abbott, M. (1993), *Family Ties: English Families 1540-1920* (London: Routledge).
Abbott, M. (2003), *Family Affairs: A History of the Family in 20th Century Britain* (London: Routledge).
Amtower, L. (2003), 'Chaucer's sely widows', in Amtower and Kehler (eds): 119-32.
Amtower, L. and Kehler, D. (eds) (2003), *The Single Woman in Medieval and Early Modern England: Her Life and Representation* (Tempe, AZ: Arizona Center for Medieval and Renaissance Studies).
Amussen, S.D. (1988), *An Ordered Society: Gender and Class in Early Modern England* (Oxford: Basil Blackwell).
Andersen, Ø. (1987) 'The widows, the city and Thucydides (II.45.2)', in *Symbolae Osloenses* 62: 33-49.
Anderson, M. (1990), 'The social implications of demographic change', in F.M.L. Thompson (ed.), *Cambridge Social History of Britain, 1750-1950*, 2 (Cambridge: Cambridge University Press): 1-70.
Archer, R.E. (1984), 'Rich old ladies: The problem of late medieval dowagers', in T. Pollard (ed.), *Property and Politics: Essays in Later Medieval English History* (Gloucester: Alan Sutton): 15-35.
Archer, R.E. (1992), '"How ladies ... who live on their manors ought to manage their households and estates": Women as landholders and administrators in the later Middle Ages', in Goldberg (1992a): 149-81.
Archer, R.E. and Ferme, B.E. (1989), 'Testamentary procedure with special reference to the executrix', in *Reading Medieval Studies* 15: 3-34.
Arden, H.M. (1992), 'Grief, widowhood, and women's sexuality in medieval French literature', in Mirrer: 305-19.
Arjava, A. (1996) *Women and Law in Late Antiquity* (Oxford: Oxford University Press).
Arnold, M. (2003), 'Mourning widows: Portraits of widows and widowhood in funeral sermons from Brunswick-Wolfenbuettel', in Levy (2003b): 55-74.
Astolfi, R. (1996), *La lex Iulia et Papia[4]* (Padua: Casa Editrice Dott. Antonio Milani).
Aubry, Y. (1989), 'Pour une étude du veuvage féminin à l'époque moderne', in *Histoire, Economie et Société* 8: 223-36.
Bagnall, R.S. and Frier, B.W. (1994), *The Demography of Roman Egypt* (Cambridge: Cambridge University Press).
Bailey, J. (2003), *Unquiet Lives: Marriage and Marriage Breakdown in England, 1660-1800* (Cambridge: Cambridge University Press).
Bailey, M. (1996), 'Demographic decline in late medieval England: Some thoughts on recent research', *Economic History Review* 49.1: 1-19.
Baker, P. (1984), 'The domestication of politics: Women and American political society, 1780-1920', *American Historical Review* 89.3: 620-47.
Baldwin, D.J. (1988), 'A successful search for security: Arizona Pioneer Society widows', in Scadron (1988d): 224-42.

References and further reading

Bardet, J.-P. and Dupâquier, J. (eds) (1998), *Histoire des populations de l'Europe*, vol. 2 (Paris: Librairie Arthème Fayard).
Barrett, C.J. (1977), 'Women in widowhood (1960s and 1970s)', in *Signs* 2: 856-68.
Barron, C.M. (1989), 'The "Golden Age" of women in medieval London', in *Reading Medieval Studies* 15: 35-58.
Barron, C.M. (1994), 'Introduction: The widows' world in later medieval London', in Barron and Sutton: xiii-xxxiv.
Barron, C.M. and Sutton, A.F. (eds) (1994), *Medieval London Widows, 1300-1500* (London: The Hambledon Press).
Basch, F. (1986), 'Women's rights and the wrongs of marriage in mid-nineteenth-century America', in *History Workshop* 22: 18-40.
Basch, N. (1982) *In the Eyes of the Law: Women, Marriage, and Property in Nineteenth-Century New York* (Ithaca, NY: Cornell University Press).
Bassler, J.M. (1996) *1 Timothy, 2 Timothy, Titus* (Nashville, TN: Abingdon Press).
Bawcutt, P. (2005), 'Women talking about marriage in William Dunbar and Hans Sachs', in S. Roush and C.L. Baskins (eds), *The Medieval Marriage Scene: Prudence, Passion, Policy* (Tempe, AZ: Arizona Center for Medieval and Renaissance Studies): 101-14.
Beecher, M.U. et al (1988), 'Widowhood among the Mormons: The personal accounts', in Scadron (1988d): 117-39.
Behlmer, G.K. (1998), *Friends of the Family: The English Home and its Guardians, 1850-1940* (Stanford, CA: Stanford University Press).
Bennett, H.V. (2002), *Injustice Made Legal: Deuteronomic Law and the Plight of Widows, Strangers and Orphans in Ancient Israel* (Grand Rapids, MI: Wm. B. Eerdmans Publishing Co.).
Bennett, J.M. (1989), 'Feminism and history', in *Gender & History* 1.3: 251-72.
Bennett, J.M. (1992a), 'Medieval women, modern women: Across the great divide', in D. Aers (ed.), *Culture and History 1300-1600: Essays on English Communities, Identities and Writing* (New York, NY: Harvester Wheatsheaf): 147-75.
Bennett, J.M. (1992b), 'Widows in the medieval English countryside', in Mirrer: 69-114.
Bennett, J.M. (1993), 'Women's history: A study in continuity and change', in *Women's History Review* 2.2: 173-84.
Bennett, J.M. (1996), *Ale, Beer, and Brewsters in England: Women's Work in a Changing World, 1300-1600* (New York, NY: Oxford University Press).
Bennett, J.M. (1997), 'Confronting continuity', in *Journal of Women's History* 9.3: 73-94.
Bennett, J.M. and Froide, A.M. (eds) (1999), *Single women in the European Past, 1250-1800* (Philadelphia, PA: University of Pennsylvania Press).
Bepler, J. (2003), '"Zu meinem und aller dehrer die sichs gebrauchen wollen, nutzen, trost, undt frommen": Lektüre, Schrift, und Gebet im Leben der fürstlichen Witwen in der Frühen Neuzeit', in Schattkowsky: 303-19.
Block, D.I. (2003), 'Marriage and family in Ancient Israel', in Campbell: 33-102.
Blom, I. (1991), 'The history of widowhood: A bibliographic overview', in *Journal of Family History* 16: 191-210.
Blundell, S. (1995), *Women in Ancient Greece* (Cambridge, MA: Harvard University Press).
Bonfield, L. et al (eds) (1986), *The World We Have Gained: Histories of Population and Social Structure* (Oxford: Basil Blackwell).
Botelho, L. (2002a), 'Images of old age in early modern cheap print: Women, witches, and the poisonous female body', in Ottaway et al: 225-46.

References and further reading

Botelho, L. (2002b), '"The old woman's wish". Widows by the family fire?: Widows' old-age provisions in rural England, 1500-1700', in *History of the Family* 7.1: 59-78.
Botelho, L. (2004), *Old Age and the English Poor Law, 1500-1700* (Woodbridge: The Boydell Press).
Botelho, L. and Thane, P. (eds) (2001), *Women and Ageing in British Society Since 1500* (Harlow: Longman).
Boulton, J. (1990), 'London widowhood revisited: The decline of female remarriage in the seventeenth and early eighteenth centuries', in *Continuity and Change* 5.3: 323-55.
Bowersock, G.W. (1978), *Julian the Apostate* (London: Duckworth).
Bradley, H. (1989), *Men's Work, Women's Work: A Sociological History of the Sexual Division of Labour in Employment* (Minneapolis, MS: University of Minnesota Press).
Bradley, K.R. (1991), *Discovering the Roman Family: Studies in Roman Social History* (Oxford: Oxford University Press).
Bratcher, R.G. (1983), *A Translator's Guide to Paul's Letters to Timothy and to Titus* (London: United Bible Societies).
Bremmer, J.N. (1987), 'The old women of Ancient Greece', in J. Blok and P. Mason (eds), *Sexual Asymmetry: Studies in Ancient Society* (Amsterdam: J.C. Gieben): 191-215.
Bremmer, J.N. (1995), 'Pauper or patroness: The widow in the early Christian Church', in Bremmer and van den Bosch: 31-57.
Bremmer, J.N, and van den Bosch, L. (eds) (1995), *Between Poverty and the Pyre: Moments in the History of Widowhood* (London: Routledge).
Brodsky, V. (1986), 'Widows in late Elizabethan London: Remarriage, economic opportunity and family orientations', in Bonfield et al: 122-54.
Brown, P. (1988) *The Body and Society: Men, Women and Sexual Renunciation in Early Christianity* (New York, NY: Columbia University Press).
Brown, P. (2002) *Poverty and Leadership in the Later Roman Empire* (Hanover, NH: The University Press of New England).
Brown, R.E. (1997), *An Introduction to the New Testament* (New York, NY: ABRL Doubleday).
Brundage, J.A. (1987), *Law, Sex, and Christian Society in Medieval Europe* (Chicago, IL: University of Chicago Press).
Brundage, J.A. (1992), 'Widows as disadvantaged persons in medieval canon law', in Mirrer: 193-206.
Brundage, J.A. (1993), 'Widows and remarriage: Moral conflicts and their resolution in classical canon law', in Walker (1993c): 17-31.
Brundage, J.A. (1995), 'The merry widow's serious sister: Remarriage in classical canon law', in R.R. Edwards and V. Ziegler (eds), *Matrons and Marginal Women in Medieval Society* (Woodbridge: The Boydell Press): 33-48.
Buitelaar, M. (1995), 'Widows' worlds: Representations and realities', in Bremmer and van den Bosch: 1-18.
Camfield, G. (1997), *Necessary Madness: The Humor of Domesticity in Nineteenth-Century American Literature* (New York, NY: Oxford University Press).
Campbell, K.M. (ed.) (2003), *Marriage and Family in the Biblical World* (Downers Grove, IL: InterVarsity Press).
Cantor, N.F. (2002), *In the Wake of the Plague: The Black Death and the World it Made* (New York, NY: Harper Perennial).
Cardman, F. (1999), 'Women, ministry, and church order in early Christianity', in

References and further reading

R.S. Kraemer and M.R. D'Angelo (eds), *Women and Christian Origins* (New York, NY: Oxford University Press): 300-29.

Carlson, C.L. and Weisl, A.J. (eds) (1999) *Constructions of Widowhood and Virginity in the Later Middle Ages* (New York, NY: St Martin's Press).

Carlton, C. (1978) 'The widow's tale: Male myths and female reality in 16th and 17th century England', in *Albion* 10.2: 118-29.

Carter, H.S. (1988), 'Legal aspects of widowhood and aging', in Scadron (1988d): 271-300.

Cavallo, S. and Warner, L. (eds) (1999), *Widowhood in Medieval and Early Modern Europe* (Harlow: Longman).

Chance A.M. (1992), 'Shakespeare's widow', in R. Eaden et al (eds), *Shakespeare and the World Elsewhere* (Adelaide, Australia. Proceedings of the Australian and New Zealand Shakespeare Association): 23-35.

Chen, M.A. (2000), *Perpetual Mourning: Widowhood in Rural India* (Oxford: Oxford University Press).

Chinn, C. (1988), *They Worked All Their Lives: Women of the Urban Poor in England, 1880-1939* (Manchester: Manchester University Press).

Chused, R.H. (1983), 'Married women's property law: 1800-1850', in *Georgetown Law Journal* 71: 1359-425.

Chused, R.H. (1985), 'Late nineteenth century married women's property law: Reception of the Early Married Women's Property Acts by courts and legislatures', in *American Journal of Legal History* 29.1: 3-35.

Chused, R.H. (1994), 'History's double edge: A comment on "Modernization of marital status law"', in *Georgetown Law Journal* 82: 2213-25.

Clark, E. (1990), 'City orphans and custody laws in medieval England', in *American Journal of Legal History* 34: 168-87.

Clark, E.A. (1989), 'Theory and practice in late ancient asceticism: Jerome, Chrysostom, and Augustine', in *Journal of Feminist Studies in Religion* 5.2: 25-46.

Clark, E.A. (2005), 'Dissuading from marriage: Jerome and the asceticization of satire', in Smith (2005a): 154-81.

Cohen, D. (1991), *Law, Sexuality and Society: The Enforcement of Morals in Classical Athens* (Cambridge: Cambridge University Press).

Cokayne, K. (2003), *Experiencing Old Age in Ancient Rome* (London: Routledge).

Combs, M.B. (2004), 'Wives and household wealth: The impact of the 1870 British Married Women's Property Act on wealth-holding and share of personal resources', in *Continuity and Change* 19.1: 141-63.

Cooper, K. (1996), *The Virgin and the Bride: Idealized Womanhood in Late Antiquity* (Cambridge, MA: Harvard University Press).

Corvisier, J.-N. (1999), 'Guerre et démographie en Grèce à la période classique', in *Pallas* 51: 57-79.

Cott, N.F. (2000), *Public Vows: A History of Marriage and the Nation* (Cambridge, MA: Harvard University Press).

Courtney, E. (2001), *A Companion to Petronius* (Oxford: Oxford University Press).

Cox, C.A. (1998), *Household Interests: Property, Marriage Strategies, and Family Interests in Ancient Athens* (Princeton, NJ: Princeton University Press).

Crawford, P. (1985), 'Women's published writings: 1600-1700', in Prior (1985a): 211-82.

Cressy, D. (1997), *Birth, Marriage, and Death: Ritual, Religion, and the Life Cycle in Tudor and Stuart England* (Oxford: Oxford University Press).

Crick, J. (1999), 'Men, women, and widows: Widowhood in pre-Conquest England', in Cavallo and Warner: 24-36.

References and further reading

Curran, C. (1993) 'Private women, public needs: Middle-class widows in Victorian England', in *Albion* 25.2: 217-36.

Davidoff, L. et al (1999), *The Family Story: Blood, Contract and Intimacy, 1830-1960* (London: Longman).

Davies, M. (1996), *The Pastoral Epistles* (Sheffield: Sheffield Academic Press).

Deal, L.K. (1998), 'Widows and reputation in the Diocese of Chester, England, 1560-1650', in *Journal of Family History* 23.4: 382-92.

Delarue, F. (2001), 'Le dossier du *De Matrimonio* de Sénèque', in *Revue des Études Latines* 79: 163-87.

Derosas, R. and Oris, M. (eds) (2002), *When Dad Died: Individuals and Families Coping with Family Stress in Past Societies* (Bern: Peter Lang).

de Vries, J. (1994), 'Population', in T.A. Brady Jr, H.A. Oberman and J.D. Tracy (eds), *Handbook of European History, 1400-1600: Late Middle Ages, Renaissance and Reformation* I (Leiden: E.J. Brill): 1-50.

Didion, J. (2006), *The Year of Magical Thinking* (New York, NY: Alfred A. Knopf).

Dietz, M.G. (1987), 'Context is all: Feminism and theories of citizenship', in *Daedalus* 116.4: 1-24.

DiGiulio, R.C. (1989), *Beyond Widowhood: From Bereavement to Emergence and Hope* (New York, NY: The Free Press).

Dillon, M. (2002), *Girls and Women in Classical Greek Religion* (London: Routledge).

DiMatteo, L.A. (1994), 'Deconstructing the myth of the "infancy law doctrine": From incapacity to accountability', in *Ohio Northern University Law Review* 21: 481-525.

Dixon, S. (1988), *The Roman Mother* (Norman, OK: University of Oklahoma Press).

Dixon, S. (2001), *Reading Roman Women: Sources, Genres and Real Life* (London: Duckworth).

Donahue, C. (1993), 'Female plaintiffs in marriage cases in the Court of York in the later Middle Ages: What can we learn from the numbers?', in Walker (1993c): 183-213.

Drake, M. (1981), 'The remarriage market in mid-nineteenth century Britain', in Dupâquier et al: 287-96.

Dubler, A.R. (2003a), '"Exceptions to the general rule": Unmarried women and the "constitution of the family"', in *Theoretical Inquiries in Law* 4: 797-816.

Dubler, A.R. (2003b), 'In the shadow of marriage: Single women and the legal construction of the family and state', in *Yale Law Journal* 112: 1641-715.

Dupâquier, J. et al (eds) (1981), *Marriage and Remarriage in Populations of the Past* (London: Academic Press).

Elm, S. (1994), *'Virgins of God': The Making of Asceticism in Late Antiquity* (Oxford: Oxford University Press).

Erickson, A.L. (1993), *Women and Property in Early Modern England* (London: Routledge).

Erickson, A.L. (1999), 'Property and widowhood in England, 1660-1840', in Cavallo and Warner: 145-63.

Erler, M.C. (1994), 'Three fifteenth-century vowesses', in Barron and Sutton: 165-83.

Evans Grubbs, J. (2001), 'Virgins and widows, show-girls and whores: Late Roman legislation on women and Christianity', in R.W. Mathisen (ed.), *Law, Society, and Authority in Late Antiquity* (Oxford: Oxford University Press): 220-41.

Evans Grubbs, J. (2002), *Women and the Law in the Roman Empire: A Sourcebook on Marriage, Divorce, and Widowhood* (London: Routledge).

References and further reading

Fantazzi, C. and Matheeussen, C. (eds) (1996), *Juan Luis Vives: De Institutione Feminae Christianae* (2 vols) (Leiden: E.J. Brill).

Faust, D.G. (1996) *Mothers of Invention: Women of the Slaveholding South in the American Civil War* (Chapel Hill, NC: University of North Carolina Press).

Fauve-Chamoux, A. and Sogner, S. (eds) (1994), *Socio-Economic Consequences of Sex-Ratios in Historical Perspective, 1500-1900* (Milan: Università Bocconi).

Fee, G.D. (1988), *1 and 2 Timothy, Titus* (Peabody, MA: Hendrickson Publishers).

Feichtinger, B. (1995), *Apostolae Apostolorum: Frauenaskese als Befreiung und Zwang bei Hieronymus* (Frankfurt am Main: Peter Lang).

Feichtinger, B. (2005), 'Change and continuity in pagan and Christian (invective) thought on women and marriage from antiquity to the Middle Ages', in Smith (2005a): 182-209.

Finch, J. (1994), 'Do families support each other more or less than in the past?', in M. Drake (ed.), *Time, Family and Community: Perspectives on Family and Community History* (Oxford: Blackwell): 91-105.

Finley, M.I. (1999), *The Ancient Economy^2* (rev. ed.) (Berkeley, CA: University of California Press).

Fischer, D. (2002), *Witwe als weiblicher Lebensentwurf in deutschen Texten des 13. bis 16. Jahrhunderts* (Frankfurt am Main: Peter Lang).

Fletcher, A. (1995), *Gender, Sex and Subordination in England, 1500-1800* (New Haven: Yale University Press).

Foyster, E. (1999), 'Marrying the experienced widow in early modern England: The male perspective', in Cavallo and Warner: 108-24.

Foxhall, L. (1989), 'Household, gender and property in Classical Athens', in *Classical Quarterly* 39.1: 22-44.

Foxhall, L. (1996), 'The law and the lady: Women and legal proceedings in Classical Athens', in L. Foxhall and A.D.E. Lewis (eds), *Greek Law in its Political Setting: Justifications not Justice* (Oxford: Oxford University Press): 133-52.

Franklin, P. (1986), 'Peasant widows' "liberation" and remarriage before the Black Death', in *Economic History Review^2* 39.2: 186-204.

Freist, D. (1999), 'Religious difference and the experience of widowhood in seventeenth- and eighteenth-century Germany', in Cavallo and Warner: 164-78.

French, S. (2003) 'A widow building in Elizabethan England: Bess of Hardwick at Hardwick Hall', in Levy (2003b) 161-6.

Friedman, L.M. et al (1996), 'Guardians: A research note', in *American Journal of Legal History* 40.2: 146-66.

Frier, B.W. (2000), 'Demography', in *Cambridge Ancient History^2* 11: 787-816.

Frier, B.W. and McGinn, T.A.J. (2003), *A Casebook on Roman Family Law* (New York, NY: Oxford University Press).

Froide, A.M. (2005), *Never Married: Single Women in Early Modern England* (Oxford: Oxford University Press).

Gagarin, M. (1998), 'Women in Athenian courts', in *Dike* 1: 39-51.

Gardner, J.F. (1986), *Women in Roman Law and Society* (Bloomington: Indiana University Press).

Gardner, J.F. (1993), *Being a Roman Citizen* (London: Routledge).

Garrett, E.M. (1995), 'The dawning of a new era? Women's work in England and Wales at the turn of the twentieth century', in *Histoire Sociale/Social History* 56: 421-64.

Gates, L.A. (1995), 'Widows, property, and remarriage: Lessons from Glastonbury's Deverill Manors', in *Albion* 27.4: 19-35.

References and further reading

Geddes, R. and Lueck, D. (2002), 'The gains from self-ownership and the expansion of women's rights', in *American Economic Review* 92.4: 1079-92.

Gente, M. (2002), 'Family ideology and the Charity Organization Society in Great Britain during the First World War', in *Journal of Family History* 27.3: 255-72.

Gerhard, U. (ed.) (1997), *Frauen in der Geschichte des Rechts: Von der Frühen Neuzeit bis zur Gegenwart* (Munich: Verlag C.H. Beck).

Gerhards, G. (1962), *Das Bild der Witwe in der deutschen Literatur des Mittelalters* (Diss. Bonn).

Gilbert, S.M. (2006), *Death's Door: Modern Dying and the Ways We Grieve* (New York, NY: W.W. Norton).

Gilbert, S.M. and Gubar, S. (2000), *The Madwoman in the Attic: The Woman Writer and the Nineteenth-Century Literary Imagination*[2] (New Haven: Yale University Press).

Gillis, J.R. (1985), *For Better, For Worse: British Marriages, 1600 to the Present* (Oxford: Oxford University Press).

Glendon, M.A. (1989), *The Transformation of Family Law: State, Law, and Family in the United States and Western Europe* (Chicago, IL: University of Chicago Press).

Goldberg, P.J.P. (ed.) (1992a), *Woman is a Worthy Wight: Women in English Society, c. 1200-1500* (Far Thrupp: Alan Sutton).

Goldberg, P.J.P. (1992b), *Women, Work, and Life Cycle in a Medieval Economy: York and Yorkshire c. 1300-1520* (Oxford: Oxford University Press).

Golden, M. (1981), 'Demography and the exposure of girls at Athens', in *Phoenix* 35: 316-31.

Goldman, N. and Lord, G. (1983), 'Sex differences in life cycle measures of widowhood', in *Demography* 20.2: 177-95.

González, D.J. (1988), 'The widowed women of Santa Fe: Assessments on the lives of an unmarried population, 1850-80', in Scadron (1988d): 65-90.

Goodfriend, J.D. (1988), 'The struggle for survival: Widows in Denver, 1880-1912', in Scadron (1988d): 166-94.

Gordon, E. and Nair, G. (2003), *Public Lives: Women, Family and Society in Victorian Britain* (New Haven: Yale University Press).

Gordon, L. (1994), *Pitied But Not Entitled: Single Mothers and the History of Welfare, 1890-1935* (New York, NY: The Free Press).

Gowing, L. (1996), *Domestic Dangers: Women, Words, and Sex in Early Modern London* (Oxford: Oxford University Press).

Graham, H. (1992), '"A woman's work ...": Labour and gender in the late medieval countryside', in Goldberg (1992a): 126-48.

Green, D.R. (2000), 'Independent women, wealth and wills in nineteenth-century London', in J. Stobart and A. Owens (eds), *Urban Fortunes: Property and Inheritance in the Town, 1700-1900* (Aldershot: Ashgate): 195-222.

Green, D.R. and Owens, A. (2003), 'Gentlewomanly capitalism?: Spinsters, widows, and wealth holding in England and Wales, c. 1800-1860', in *Economic History Review* 56.3: 510-36.

Grossberg, M. (1985), *Governing the Hearth: Law and the Family in Nineteenth-Century America* (Chapel Hill, NC: University of North Carolina Press).

Günther, L.-M. (1993), 'Witwen in der griechischen Antike: Zwischen Oikos und Polis', in *Historia* 42.3: 308-25.

Guy, D.J. (1988), 'The economics of widowhood in Arizona, 1880-1940', in Scadron (1988d): 195-223.

Haber, C. (1983), *Beyond Sixty-Five: The Dilemma of Old Age in America's Past* (Cambridge: Cambridge University Press).

References and further reading

Haber, C. and Gratton, B. (1994), *Old Age and the Search for Security: An American Social History* (Bloomington, IN: Indiana University Press).

Hahn, S. (2002), 'Women in older ages – "old" women?', in *History of the Family* 7.1: 33-58.

Haines, M.R. (2000), 'The white population of the United States, 1790-1920', in M.R. Haines and R.H. Steckel (eds), *A Population History of North America* (Cambridge: Cambridge University Press): 305-69.

Haines, M.R. and Goodman, A.C. (1995), 'A home of one's own: Aging and home ownership in the United States in the late nineteenth and early twentieth centuries', in Kertzer and Laslett: 203-26.

Hajnal, J. (1965), 'European marriage patterns in perspective', in D.V. Glass and D.E.C. Eversley (eds), *Population in History: Essays in Historical Demography* (Chicago, IL: Aldine Publishing Company): 101-43.

Hammerton, A.J. (1992), *Cruelty and Companionship: Conflict in Nineteenth-Century Married Life* (London: Routledge).

Hanawalt, B.A. (1992), 'The widow's mite: Provisions for medieval London widows', in Mirrer: 21-45.

Hanawalt, B.A. (1993), 'Remarriage as an option for urban and rural widows in medieval England', in Walker (1993c): 141-64.

Hanawalt, B.A. (1996), 'Patriarchal provisions for widows and orphans in medieval London', in M.J. Maynes et al (eds), *Gender, Kinship, Power: A Comparative and Interdisciplinary History* (London: Routledge): 201-13.

Hanawalt, B.A. (2005), 'The dilemma of the widow of property for late medieval London', in S. Roush and C.L. Baskins (eds), *The Medieval Marriage Scene: Prudence, Passion, Policy* (Tempe, AZ: Arizona Center for Medieval and Renaissance Studies): 135-46.

Hanson, A.E. (2000), 'Widows too young in their widowhood', in D.E.E. Kleiner and S.B. Matheson (eds), *I Claudia II: Women in Roman Art and Society* (Austin, TX: University of Texas Press): 149-65.

Hareven, T. (1994), 'The gendered division of labour in the transition from cottage industry to factory', in Fauve-Chamoux and Sogner: 125-37.

Hareven, T. and Uhlenberg, P. (1995), 'Transition to widowhood and family support systems in the twentieth century, Northeastern United States', in Kertzer and Laslett: 273-99.

Harrington, J.F. (1995), *Reordering Marriage and Society in Reformation Germany* (Cambridge: Cambridge University Press).

Harris, B. (2002), *English Aristocratic Women, 1450-1550: Marriage and Family, Property and Careers* (Oxford: Oxford University Press).

Hartog, H. (2000), *Man and Wife in America: A History* (Cambridge, MA: Harvard University Press).

Hatcher, R. (2003), 'Understanding the population history of England, 1450-1750', in *Past and Present* 180: 83-130.

Heid, S. (2000), *Celibacy in the Early Church: The Beginnings of a Discipline of Obligatory Continence for Clerics in East and West* (transl. M.J. Miller) (San Francisco, CA: Ignatius Press).

Helmholz, R.H. (1993), 'Married women's wills in later medieval England', in Walker (1993c): 165-82.

Hemelrijk, E.A. (1999), *Matrona Docta: Educated Women in the Roman Élite from Cornelia to Julia Domna* (London: Routledge).

Henderson, J. (1987), 'Older women in Attic old comedy', in *Transactions of the American Philological Association* 117: 105-29.

References and further reading

Herlihy, D. (1985), *Medieval Households* (Cambridge, MA: Harvard University Press).
Herlihy, D. (1990), *Opera Muliebria: Women and Work in Medieval Europe* (New York, NY: McGraw-Hill).
Hill, B. (1993), 'Women's history: A study in change, continuity or standing still?', in *Women's History Review* 2.1: 5-22.
Hinde, A. (2003), *England's Population: A History Since the Domesday Survey* (London: Hodder Arnold).
Holcombe, L. (1983), *Wives and Property: Reform of the Married Women's Property Law in Nineteenth-Century England* (Toronto: University of Toronto Press).
Holderness, B.A. (1984), 'Widows in pre-industrial society: An essay upon their economic functions', in R.M. Smith (ed.), *Land, Kinship and Life-Cycle* (Cambridge: Cambridge University Press): 423-42.
Holmes, A.E. (1990), '"Such is the price we pay": American widows and the Civil War pension system', in M.A. Vinovskis (ed.), *Toward a Social History of the Civil War: Exploratory Essays* (Cambridge: Cambridge University Press): 171-95.
Holthöfer, E. (1997), 'Die Geschlechtsvormundschaft: Ein Überblick von der Antike bis ins 19. Jahrhundert', in Gerhard: 390-451.
Honeyman, K. and Goodman, J. (1991), 'Women's work, gender conflict, and labour markets in Europe, 1500-1900', in *Economic History Review* 44.4: 608-28.
Huber, (1990), *Das Motiv der 'Witwe von Ephesus' in lateinischen Texten der Antike und des Mittelalters* (Tübingen: Gunter Narr Verlag).
Hudson, G.L. (1994), 'Negotiating for blood money: war widows and the courts in seventeenth-century England', in J. Kermode and G. Walker (eds), *Women, Crime and the Courts in Early Modern England* (Chapel Hill, NC: University of North Carolina Press): 146-69.
Hufschmidt, A. (2003), 'Starke Frauen an der Weser?: Rahmenbedingungen und Lebenspraxis verwitweter Frauen in den Familien des niederen Adels um 1600', in Schattkowsky: 345-57.
Hufton, O. (1995), *The Prospect Before Her: A History of Women in Western Europe I. 1500-1800* (New York, NY: Vintage Books).
Humphreys, S.C. (1993), *The Family, Women and Death: Comparative Studies*[2] (Ann Arbor, MI: University of Michigan Press).
Humphries, J. (1987), '"...The most free from objection": The sexual division of labor and women's work in nineteenth-century England', in *Journal of Economic History* 47.4: 929-49.
Humphries, J. (1995), 'Women and paid work', in Purvis: 85-105.
Hunter, D.G. (1987), 'Resistance to the virginal ideal in late-fourth-century Rome: The case of Jovinian', in *Theological Studies* 48: 45-64.
Hunter, D.G. (2007), *Marriage, Celibacy, and Heresy in Ancient Christianity: The Jovinianist Controversy* (Oxford: Oxford University Press).
Hunter, V.J. (1989a), 'The Athenian widow and her kin', in *Journal of Family History* 14.4: 291-311.
Hunter, V.J. (1989b), 'Women's authority in Classical Athens: The example of Kleobule and her son (Dem. 27-9)', in *Echos du Monde Classique/Classical Views* n.s. 8: 39-48.
Hunter, V.J. (1994), *Policing Athens: Social Control in the Attic Lawsuits, 420-320 BC* (Princeton, NJ: Princeton University Press).
Hurwich, J.J. (2006), *Noble Strategies: Marriage and Sexuality in the Zimmern Chronicle* (Kirksville, MO: Truman State University Press).

References and further reading

Ingendahl, G. (2003), 'Elend und Wollust: Witwenschaft in kulturellen Bildern der Frühen Neuzeit', in Schattkowsky: 265-79.
Janssens, A. (1997), 'The rise and decline of the male breadwinner family?: An overview of the debate', in *International Journal of Social History* 42 (Suppl.): 1-23.
John, A.V. (ed.) (1986), *Unequal Opportunities: Women's Employment in England 1800-1918* (Oxford: Basil Blackwell).
Johner, E. (1987), 'Witwen in Freiburg um die Mitte des 15. Jahrhunderts', in *Freiburger Geschichtsblatter* 65: 7-42.
Johnson, L.T. (1996), *Letters to Paul's Delegates: 1 Timothy, 2 Timothy, Titus* (Valley Forge, PA: Trinity Press International).
Jordan, E. (1989), 'The exclusion of women from industry in nineteenth-century England', in *Comparative Studies in Society and History* 31.2: 273-96.
Jordan, E. (1999), *The Women's Movement and Women's Employment in Nineteenth-Century Britain* (London: Routledge).
Jussen, B. (2000), *Der Name der Witwe: Erkundungen zur Semantik der mittelalterlichen Bußkultur* (Göttingen: Vandenhoeck & Ruprecht).
Just, R. (1989), *Women in Athenian Law and Life* (London: Routledge).
Kahn, B.Z. (1996), 'Married women's property laws and female commercial activity: Evidence from the United States patent records, 1790-1895', in *Journal of Economic History* 56.2: 356-88.
Keene, D. (1994), 'Tanners' widows, 1300-1350', in Barron and Sutton: 1-27.
Kertzer, D.I. and Barbagli, M. (eds) (2002), *Family Life in the Long Nineteenth Century, 1789-1913* (New Haven: Yale University Press).
Kertzer, D.I. and Laslett, P. (eds) (1995), *Aging in the Past: Demography, Society, and Old Age* (Berkeley, CA: University of California Press).
Kessler-Harris, A. (1982), *Out to Work: A History of Wage-Earning Women in the United States* (New York, NY: Oxford University Press).
Kessler-Harris, A. (1995), 'Designing women and old fools: The construction of the Social Security amendments in 1939', in L.K. Kerber et al (eds), *US History as Women's History: New Feminist Essays* (Chapel Hill, NC: University of North Carolina Press): 87-106, 369-71.
Kimball, J. (1994), 'An ambiguous faithlessness: Molly Bloom and the Widow of Ephesus', in *James Joyce Quarterly* 31.4: 455-72.
Klein, H.S. (2004), *A Population History of the United States* (Cambridge: Cambridge University Press).
Koch, E. (1991), *Maior dignitas est in sexu virili: Das weibliche Geschlecht im Normensystem des 16. Jahrhunderts* (Frankfurt am Main: Vittorio Klostermann).
Kowaleski, M. (1999), 'Single women in medieval and early modern Europe: The demographic perspective', in Bennett and Froide: 38-81.
Krause, J.-U. (1994a), 'Die gesellschaftliche Stellung von Witwen im römischen Reich', in *Saeculum* 45: 71-104.
Krause, J.-U. (1994b), *Witwen und Waisen im römischen Reich* 1 (Stuttgart: Habes).
Krause, J.-U. (1994c), *Witwen und Waisen im römischen Reich* 2 (Stuttgart: Habes).
Krause, J.-U. (1995a), *Witwen und Waisen im römischen Reich* 3 (Stuttgart: Habes).
Krause, J.-U. (1995b), *Witwen und Waisen im römischen Reich* 4 (Stuttgart: Habes).
La Penna, A. (1985), 'Didone', in *Enciclopedia Virgiliana* 2: 48-57.
Laslett, P. (1972), 'Mean household size in England since the sixteenth century', in P. Laslett and R. Wall (eds), *Household and Family in Past Time* (Cambridge: Cambridge University Press): 125-58.

References and further reading

Laslett, P. (1988), 'Family, kinship, and collectivity as systems of support in pre-industrial Europe: A Consideration of the "nuclear-hardship" hypothesis', in *Continuity and Change* 3.2: 153-75.

Laslett, P. (1995), 'Necessary knowledge: Age and aging in the societies of the past', in Kertzer and Laslett: 3-77.

Laurence, A. (1994), *Women in England, 1500-1760: A Social History* (New York, NY: St Martin's Press).

Laurence, P. (1997), *Jérôme et le nouveau modèle féminin: La conversion à la 'vie parfaite'* (Paris: Institut d'Études Augustiniennes).

Lebsock, S.D. (1977), 'Radical reconstruction and the property rights of southern women', in *Journal of Southern History* 43.2: 195-216.

Levy, A. (2003a), 'Good grief: Widow portraiture and masculine anxiety in early modern England', in Amtower and Kehler: 147-64.

Levy, A. (2003b), *Widowhood and Visual Culture in Early Modern Europe* (Aldershot: Ashgate Publishing).

Leyser, H. (1995), *Medieval Women: A Social History of Women in England, 450-1500* (London: Weidenfeld and Nicolson).

Loengard, J.S. (1993), '*Rationabilis Dos*: Magna Carta and widow's "fair share" in the earlier thirteenth century', in Walker (1993c): 59-80.

Lopata, H.Z. (1996), *Current Widowhood: Myths and Realities* (Thousand Oaks, CA: Sage Publications).

Loustaunau, M.O. (1988), 'Hispanic widows and their support systems in the Mesilla Valley of Southern New Mexico, 1910-1940', in Scadron (1988d): 91-116.

Lovell, M.S. (2006), *Bess of Hardwick: First Lady of Chatsworth* (pb. ed.) (London: Abacus).

Lynch, K.A. and Lee, W.R. (1998), 'Permanences et changements de la vie familiale', in Bardet and Dupâquier: 103-30.

MacDonald, M.Y. (1996), *Early Christian Women and Pagan Opinion: The Power of the Hysterical Woman* (Cambridge: Cambridge University Press).

Macfarlane, A. (1986), *Marriage and Love in England: Modes of Reproduction, 1300-1840* (Oxford: Blackwell).

MacKinnon, A. (1995), 'Were women present at the demographic transition? Questions from a feminist historian to historical demographers', in *Gender & History* 7.2: 222-40.

Magson, B. (1996), 'Life expectations of the widows and orphans of freemen in London, 1375-1399', in *Local Population Studies* 57: 18-29.

Mason, M.A. (1994), *From Father's Property to Children's Rights: The History of Child Custody in America* (New York, NY: Columbia University Press).

Mate, M.E. (1998), *Daughters, Wives, and Widows After the Black Death: Women in Sussex, 1350-1535* (Woodbridge: Boydell Press).

Matthews, V.H. (2003), 'Marriage and family in the ancient Near East', in Campbell: 1-32.

May, R. (2005), 'Chaste Artemis and lusty Aphrodite: The portrait of women and marriage in the Greek and Latin novels', in Smith (2005a): 129-53.

McCarthy, C. (2004), *Marriage in Medieval England: Law, Literature, and Practice* (Woodbridge: The Boydell Press).

McGarry, K. and Schoeni, R.F. (2000), 'Social Security, economic growth, and the rise in elderly widows' independence in the twentieth century', in *Demography* 37.2: 221-36.

McGinn, T.A.J. (1997), 'The legal definition of prostitute in late antiquity', in *Memoirs of the American Academy in Rome* 42: 73-116.

References and further reading

McGinn, T.A.J. (1998), *Prostitution, Sexuality, and the Law in Ancient Rome* (New York, NY: Oxford University Press).
McGinn, T.A.J. (1999), 'Widows, orphans, and social history', in *Journal of Roman Archaeology* 12.2: 617-32.
McGinn, T.A.J. (2004a), 'Missing females?: Augustus' encouragement of marriage between freeborn males and freedwomen', in *Historia: Zeitschrift für alte Geschichte* 53.2: 200-8.
McGinn, T.A.J. (2004b), *The Economy of Prostitution in the Roman World: A Study of Social History and the Brothel* (Ann Arbor, MI: University of Michigan Press).
McIntosh, M.K. (1998), 'Networks of care in Elizabethan English towns: The example of Hadleigh, Suffolk', in P. Horden and R. Smith (eds), *The Locus of Care: Families, Communities, Institutions, and the Provision of Welfare Since Antiquity* (London: Routledge): 71-89.
McIntosh, M.K. (2005), *Working Women in English Society: 1300-1620* (Cambridge: Cambridge University Press).
McMillan, A. (transl. and ed. 1987), *The Legend of Good Women by Geoffrey Chaucer* (Houston, TX: Rice University Press).
McNamara, J. (1984), 'Cornelia's daughters: Paula and Eustochium', in *Women's Studies* 11: 9-27.
Mendelson, S. and Crawford, P. (1998), *Women in Early Modern England, 1550-1720* (Oxford: Oxford University Press).
Mikesell, M.L. (1983), 'Catholic and Protestant Widows in *The Duchess of Malfi*', in *Renaissance and Reformation* n.s. 7.4: 265-79.
Miller, P. (1998), *Transformations of Patriarchy in the West, 1500-1900* (Bloomington, IN: Indiana University Press).
Mineau, G. (1988), 'Utah widowhood: A demographic profile', in Scadron (1988d): 140-65.
Mirrer, L. (ed.) (1992), *Upon My Husband's Death: Widows in the Literature and Histories of Medieval Europe* (Ann Arbor, MI: University of Michigan Press).
Mitchell, L.E. (1992), 'Noble widowhood in the thirteenth century: Three generations of Mortimer widows, 1246-1334', in Mirrer: 169-90.
Moore, J.G. (2003), '(Re)creation of a single woman: Discursive realms of the Wife of Bath', in Amtower and Kehler: 133-46.
Morgan, L.A. (1991), *After Marriage Ends: Economic Consequences for Midlife Women* (Newbury Park, CA: Sage Publications).
Morley, J. (1971), *Death, Heaven and the Victorians* (Pittsburgh, PA: University of Pittsburgh Press).
Morris, L.A. (1992), *Women's Humor in the Age of Gentility: The Life and Works of Frances Miriam Whitcher* (Syracuse, NY: Syracuse University Press).
Morris, R.J. (1994), 'Men, women, and property: The reform of the Married Women's Property Act, 1870', in F.M.L. Thompson (ed.), *Landowners, Capitalists, and Entrepreneurs: Essays for Sir John Habakkuk* (Oxford: Oxford University Press): 171-92.
Moscucci, O. (1990), *The Science of Woman: Gynaecology and Gender in England, 1800-1929* (Cambridge: Cambridge University Press).
Nelson, S.M. (1988), 'Widowhood and autonomy in the Native American Southwest', in Scadron (1988d): 22-41.
Nightingale, P. (2005), 'Some new evidence of crises and trends of mortality in late medieval England', in *Past and Present* 187: 33-68.
Norrback, A. (2001), *The Fatherless and the Widow in the Deuteronomic Covenant* (Åbo, Finland: Åbo Akademi University Press).

References and further reading

Oakes, E.T. (1990), *Heiress, Beggar, Saint, or Strumpet: The Widow in the Society and on the Stage in Early Modern England* (Diss. Vanderbilt).
Offen, K. (1997), 'A comparative European perspective: Comment on "confronting continuity"', in *Journal of Women's History* 9.3: 105-13.
Opitz, C. (1991), 'Emanzipiert oder Marginalisiert?: Witwen in der Gesellschaft des späten Mittelalters', in B. Lundt (ed.), *Auf der Suche nach der Frau im Mittelalter: Fragen, Quellen, Antworten* (Munich: Wilhelm Fink Verlag): 25-48.
Oris, M. and Ochiai, E. (2002), 'Family crisis in the context of different family systems: Framework and evidence on "when Dad died"', in Derosas and Oris: 17-79.
Osborne, R. (2004), 'Law, the democratic citizen, and the representation of women in Classical Athens', in R. Osborne (ed.), *Studies in Ancient Greek and Roman Society* (Cambridge: Cambridge University Press): 38-60.
Ottaway, S.R. et al (eds) (2002), *Power and Poverty: Old Age in the Pre-Industrial Past* (Westport, CT: Greenwood Press).
Owen, M. (1996), *A World of Widows* (London: Zed Books).
Ozment, S. (2001), *Ancestors: The Loving Family in Old Europe* (Cambridge, MA: Harvard University Press).
Palazzi, M. (1990), 'Female solitude and patrilineage: Unmarried women and widows during the eighteenth and nineteenth centuries', in *Journal of Family History* 15: 443-59.
Palmore, E. (1987), 'Cross-cultural perspectives on widowhood', in *Journal of Cross-Cultural Gerontology* 2: 93-105.
Panek, J. (2004), *Widows and Suitors in Early Modern English Comedy* (Cambridge: Cambridge University Press).
Parkin, T.G. (2003), *Old Age in the Roman World: A Cultural and Social History* (Baltimore: Johns Hopkins University Press).
Pateman, C. (1988), *The Sexual Contract* (Stanford, CA: Stanford University Press).
Patterson, C.B. (1987), '*Hai Attikai*: The other Athenians', in *Helios* 13.2: 49-67 (= M. Skinner [ed.], *Rescuing Creusa: New Methodological Approaches to Women in Antiquity* [Lubbock, TX: Texas Tech]).
Patterson, C.B. (1998), *The Family in Greek History* (Cambridge, MA: Harvard University Press).
Pedersen, S. (1993), *Family, Dependence, and the Origins of the Welfare State: Britain and France, 1914-1945* (Cambridge: Cambridge University Press).
Pelling, M. (1999), 'Finding widowers: Men without women in English towns before 1700', in Cavallo and Warner: 37-54.
Pelling, M. (2001), 'Who most needs to marry? Ageing and inequality among women and men in early modern Norwich', in Botelho and Thane: 31-42.
Pelling, M. and Smith, R.M. (eds) (1991), *Life, Death, and the Elderly: Historical Perspectives* (London: Routledge).
Perkin, J. (1989), *Women and Marriage in Nineteenth-Century England* (Chicago, IL: Lyceum Books).
Pfister, C. (1996), 'The population of late medieval and early modern Germany', in R. Scribner (ed.), *Germany: A New Social and Economic History* (London: Arnold): 33-62.
Pölönen, J. (2002), 'The division of wealth between men and women in Roman succession (ca. 50 BC-AD 250)', in R. Berg et al (eds), *Women, Wealth and Power in the Roman Empire* (Rome: Institutum Romanum Finlandiae): 147-79.
Pomeroy, S.B. (1997), *Families in Classical and Hellenistic Greece* (Oxford: Oxford University Press).

References and further reading

Prior, M. (ed.) (1985a), *Women in English Society: 1500-1800* (London: Methuen and Co).
Prior, M. (1985b), 'Women in the urban economy: Oxford, 1500-1800', in Prior (1985a): 93-117.
Purvis, J. (ed.) (1995), *Women's History: Britain, 1850-1945* (London: UCL Press).
Rappaport, S. (1989), *Worlds Within Worlds: Structures of Life in Sixteenth-Century London* (Cambridge: Cambridge University Press).
Rathbone, D. (2006), 'Poverty and population in Roman Egypt', in M. Atkins and R. Osborne (eds), *Poverty in the Roman World* (Cambridge: Cambridge University Press): 100-14.
Rawcliffe, C. (1994), 'Margaret Stodeye, Lady Philipot (d. 1431)', in Barron and Sutton: 85-98.
Reinhart, C.J. et al (1998), 'The sexual politics of widowhood: The virgin rebirth in the social construction of nineteenth- and early twentieth-century feminine reality', in *Journal of Family History* 23.1: 28-46.
Revels, T.J. (2004), *Grander in Her Daughters: Florida's Women During the Civil War* (Columbia, SC: University of South Carolina Press).
Riley, G. (1988), *The Female Frontier: A Comparative View of Women on the Prairie and the Plains* (Lawrence, KS: University Press of Kansas).
Roberts, A. (1999), 'Helpful widows, virgins in distress: Women's friendship in French romance of the thirteenth and fourteenth centuries', in Carlson and Weisl: 25-48.
Roper, L. (1989), *The Holy Household: Women and Morals in Reformation Augsburg* (Oxford: Oxford University Press).
Roper, L. (1994), *Oedipus and the Devil: Witchcraft, Sexuality and Religion in Early Modern Europe* (London: Routledge).
Roper, L. (2004), *Witch Craze: Terror and Fantasy in Baroque Germany* (New Haven: Yale University Press).
Rose, S.O. (1992), *Limited Livelihoods: Gender and Class in Nineteenth-Century England* (Berkeley, CA: University of California Press).
Rose, S.O. (1994), 'Widowhood and poverty in nineteenth-century Nottinghamshire', in J. Henderson and R. Wall (eds), *Poor Women and Children in the European Past* (London: Routledge): 269-91.
Rosenthal, J.T. (1984), 'Aristocratic widows in fifteenth-century England', in B.J. Harris and J.K. McNamara (eds), *Women and the Structure of Society: Selected Research from the Fifth Berkshire Conference on the History of Women* (Durham, NC: Duke University Press): 36-47, 259-60.
Rosenthal J.T. (1991), *Patriarchy and Families of Privilege in Fifteenth-Century England* (Philadelphia, PA: University of Pennsylvania Press).
Rosenthal, J.T. (1992), 'Other victims: Peeresses as war widows, 1450-1500', in Mirrer: 131-52 (= *History* 72 [1987]: 213-30).
Rosenthal, J.T. (1993), 'Fifteenth-century widows and widowhood: Bereavement, reintegration, and life choices', in Walker (1993c): 33-58.
Ruggles, S. (1987), *Prolonged Connections: The Rise of the Extended Family in Nineteenth-Century England and America* (Madison, WI: University of Wisconsin Press).
Ruggles, S. (2003), 'Multigenerational families in nineteenth-century America', in *Continuity and Change* 18.1: 139-65.
Runte, H.R. (1998), '*Translatio Viduae*: The Matron of Ephesus in four languages', in *Romance Languages Annual* 9: 114-19.

References and further reading

Ste. Croix, G.E.M. de (1970), 'Some observations on the property rights of Athenian women', in *Classical Review* n.s. 20.3: 273-8.
Sallares, R. (1991), *The Ecology of the Ancient Greek World* (Ithaca, NY: Cornell University Press).
Saller, R.P. (1994), *Patriarchy, Property and Death in the Roman Family* (Cambridge: Cambridge University Press).
Salmon, M. (1986), *Women and the Law of Property in Early America* (Chapel Hill, NC: University of North Carolina Press).
Salzman, M.R. (2002), *The Making of a Christian Aristocracy: Social and Religious Change in the Western Roman Empire* (Cambridge, MA: Harvard University Press).
Scadron, A. (1988a), 'Conclusion', in Scadron (1988d): 301-12.
Scadron, A. (1988b), 'Introduction', in Scadron (1988d): 1-21.
Scadron, A. (1988c), 'Letting go: Bereavement among selected Southwestern Anglo widows', in Scadron (1988d): 243-70.
Scadron, A. (ed.) (1988d), *On Their Own: Widows and Widowhood in the American Southwest, 1848-1939* (Urbana, IL: University of Illinois Press).
Schaps, D.M. (1979), *Economic Rights of Women in Ancient Greece* (Edinburgh: Edinburgh University Press).
Schaps, D.M. (1998), 'What was free about a free Athenian woman?', in *Transactions of the American Philological Association* 128: 161-88.
Schattkowsky M. (ed.) (2003), *Witwenschaft in der Frühen Neuzeit: Fürstliche und adlige Witwen zwischen Fremd- und Selbstbestimmung* (Leipzig: Leipziger Universitätsverlag).
Schen, C. (2001), 'Strategies of poor aged women and widows in sixteenth-century London', in Botelho and Thane: 13-30.
Schlegel, A. (1988), 'Hopi family structure and the experience of widowhood', in Scadron (1988d): 42-64.
Schofield, R. and Wrigley, E.A. (1981), 'Remarriage intervals and the effect of marriage order on fertility', in Dupâquier et al: 211-27.
Schroeder, J.A. (2004), 'John Chrysostom's critique of spousal violence', in *Journal of Early Christian Studies* 12.4: 413-42.
Schuele, D.C. (1994), 'Community property law and the politics of married women's rights in nineteenth-century California', in *Western Legal History* 7.2: 244-81.
Scott, J.W. (1999), *Gender and the Politics of History* (rev. ed.) (New York, NY: Columbia University Press).
Shammas, C. (1994), 'Re-assessing the Married Women's Property Acts', in *Journal of Women's History* 6.1: 9-30.
Shammas, C. et al (1987), *Inheritance in America from Colonial Times to the Present* (New Brunswick, NJ: Rutgers University Press).
Shanley, M.L. (1989), *Feminism, Marriage, and the Law in Victorian England* (Princeton, NJ: Princeton University Press).
Sharpe, P. (ed.) (1998), *Women's Work: The English Experience, 1650-1914* (London: Arnold).
Sharpe, P. (1999), 'Survival strategies and stories: Poor widows and widowers in early industrial England', in Cavallo and Warner: 220-39.
Shaw, B. (1997), 'Agrarian economy and the marriage cycle of Roman women', in *Journal of Roman Archaeology* 10: 57-76.
Shepard, A. (2003), *Meanings of Manhood in Early Modern England* (Oxford: Oxford University Press).

References and further reading

Siegel, R.B. (1994a), 'Home as work: The first women's rights claims concerning wives' household labor, 1850-1880', in *Yale Law Journal* 103: 1073-217.
Siegel, R.B. (1994b), 'The modernization of marital status law: Adjudicating wives' rights to earnings, 1860-1930', in *Georgetown Law Journal* 82: 2127-211.
Skocpol, T. (1992), *Protecting Soldiers and Mothers: The Political Origins of Social Policy in the United States* (Cambridge, MA: Harvard University Press).
Smith, J.E. (1984), 'Widowhood and ageing in traditional English society', in *Ageing and Society* 4.4: 429-49.
Smith, R.M. (1991a), 'Coping with uncertainty: Women's tenure of customary land in England, c. 1370-1430', in J. Kermode (ed.), *Enterprise and Individuals in Fifteenth-Century England* (Stroud: Alan Sutton): 43-67.
Smith, R.M. (1991b), 'The manorial court and the elderly tenant in late medieval England', in Pelling and Smith: 39-61.
Smith, W.S. (ed.) (2005a), *Satiric Advice on Women and Marriage from Plautus to Chaucer* (Ann Arbor, MI: University of Michigan Press).
Smith, W.S. (2005b), 'The Wife of Bath and Dorigen Debate Jerome', in Smith (2005a): 243-69 (= [with revisions] *Chaucer Review* 32 [1997] 129-45 and 26 [2002] 374-90).
Sogner, S. (1994), 'Introduction', in Fauve-Chamoux and Sogner: 9-16.
Sommerville, M.R. (1995), *Sex and Subjection: Attitudes to Women in Early Modern Society* (London: Arnold).
Sommestad, L. (1997), 'Welfare attitudes to the male breadwinning system: The United States and Sweden in comparative perspective', in *International Review of Social History* 42 (Suppl.): 153-74.
Spieß, K.-H. (1993), *Familie und Verwandtschaft im deutschen Hochadel des Spätmittelalters: 13. bis Anfang des 16. Jahrhunderts* (Stuttgart: Franz Steiner Verlag).
Spieß, K.-H. (2003), 'Witwenversorgung im Hochadel: Rechtlicher Rahmen und praktische Gestaltung im Spätmittelalter und zu Beginn der Frühen Neuzeit', in Schattkowsky: 87-114.
Spring, E. (1993), *Law, Land, and Family: Aristocratic Inheritance in England, 1300 to 1800* (Chapel Hill, NC: University of North Carolina Press).
Stanley, A.D. (1998), *From Bondage to Contract: Wage Labor, Marriage, and the Market in the Age of Slave Emancipation* (Cambridge: Cambridge University Press).
Staves, S. (1990), *Married Women's Separate Property in England, 1660-1833* (Cambridge: Cambridge University Press).
Steininger, C. (1997), *Die ideale christliche Frau (virgo-vidua-nupta): Eine Studie zum Bild der idealen christlichen Frau bei Hieronymus und Pelagius* (St Ottilien, Germany: EOS-Verlag).
Strange, J.-M. (2005), *Death, Grief and Poverty in Britain, 1870-1914* (Cambridge: Cambridge University Press).
Strasser, U. (2004), *State of Virginity: Gender, Religion, and Politics in an Early Modern Catholic State* (Ann Arbor, MI: University of Michigan Press).
Strauss, G. (1986), *Law, Resistance, and the State: The Opposition to Roman Law in Reformation Germany* (Princeton, NJ: Princeton University Press).
Streich, B. (2003), 'Anna von Nassau und ihre "Schwestern": Politische Gestaltungsmöglichkeiten fürstlicher Witwen in der Frühen Neuzeit', in Schattkowsky: 163-89.
Stretton, T. (1998), *Women Waging Law in Elizabethan England* (Cambridge: Cambridge University Press).

References and further reading

Stretton, T. (1999), 'Widows at law in Tudor and Stuart England', in Cavallo and Warner: 193-208.
Sutton, A.F. (1994), 'Alice Claver, Silkwoman (d. 1489)', in Barron and Sutton: 129-42.
Taeuber, I.B. and Taeuber, C. (1971), *People of the United States in the 20th Century* (Washington, DC: US Government Printing Office).
Taylor, I.C. (1980), *Das Bild der Witwe in der deutschen Literatur* (Darmstadt: Gesellschaft Hessischer Literaturfreunde).
Thaden, B.Z. (1997), *The Maternal Voice in Victorian Fiction: Rewriting the Patriarchal Family* (New York, NY: Garland Publishing).
Thurston, B.B. (1989), *The Widows: A Women's Ministry in the Early Church* (Minneapolis: Fortress Press).
Todd, B.J. (1985), 'The remarrying widow: A stereotype reconsidered', in Prior (1985a): 54-92.
Todd, B.J. (1990), 'Freebench and free enterprise: Widows and their property in two Berkshire villages', in J. Chartres and D. Hey (eds), *English Rural Society, 1500-1800* (Cambridge: Cambridge University Press): 175-200.
Todd, B.J. (1994), 'Demographic determinism and female agency: The remarrying widow reconsidered.... again', in *Continuity and Change* 9.3: 421-50.
Todd, B.J. (1999), 'The virtuous widow in Protestant England', in Cavallo and Warner: 66-83.
Tracy, S.J. (1995), *In the Master's Eye: Representations of Women, Blacks, and Poor Whites in Antebellum Southern Literature* (Amherst, MA: University of Massachusetts Press).
Treggiari, S. (1979), 'Lower class women in the Roman economy', in *Florilegium* 1: 65-86.
Treggiari, S. (1985), 'Iam Proterva Fronte: Matrimonial advances by Roman women', in J.W. Eadie and J. Ober (eds), *The Craft of the Ancient Historian: Essays in Honor of Chester G. Starr* (Lanham, MD: University Press of America): 331-52.
Treggiari, S. (1991), *Roman Marriage: Iusti Coniuges from the Time of Cicero to the Time of Ulpian* (Oxford: Oxford University Press).
Treggiari, S. (2003), 'Marriage and family in Roman society', in Campbell: 132-82.
van der Toorn, K. (1995), 'The public image of the widow in ancient India', in Bremmer and van den Bosch: 19-30.
Vickery, A. (1993), 'Golden age to separate spheres? A review of the categories and chronology of English women's history', in *Historical Journal* 36.2: 383-414.
Vuolanto, V. (2002), 'Women and the property of fatherless children in the Roman Empire', in R. Berg et al (eds), *Women, Wealth and Power in the Roman Empire* (Rome: Institutum Romanum Finlandiae): 203-43.
Wagener, U. (1994), *Die Ordnung des 'Hauses Gottes': Der Ort von Frauen in der Ekklesiologie und Ethik der Pastoralbriefe* (Tübingen: J.C.B. Mohr).
Walby, S. (1990), *Theorizing Patriarchy* (Oxford: Basil Blackwell).
Walby, S. (1997), *Gender Transformations* (London: Routledge).
Walcot, P. (1991), 'On widows and their reputation in antiquity', in *Symbolae Osloenses* 66: 5-26.
Walker, G. (2003), *Crime, Gender and Social Order in Early Modern England* (Cambridge: Cambridge University Press).
Walker, S.S. (1993a), 'Introduction', in Walker (1993c): 1-16.
Walker, S.S. (1993b), 'Litigation as personal quest: Suing for dower in the Royal Courts, circa 1272-1350', in Walker (1993c): 81-108.

References and further reading

Walker, S.S. (ed.) (1993c), *Wife and Widow in Medieval England* (Ann Arbor, MI: University of Michigan Press).

Walkowitz, J.R. (1992), *City of Dreadful Delight: Narratives of Sexual Danger in Late-Victorian London* (Chicago, IL: University of Chicago Press).

Wall, R. (1995), 'Elderly persons and members of their households in England and Wales from pre-industrial times to the present', in Kertzer and Laslett: 81-106.

Wall, R. (2002a), 'Elderly widows and widowers and their coresidents in late 19th- and 20th-century England and Wales', in *History of the Family* 7.1: 139-55.

Wall, R. (2002b), 'Introduction. Widows: Perceptions, demography, residence patterns and standard of living', in *History of the Family* 7.1: 3-12.

Wall, R. (2002c), 'The impact on the household of the death of the father in simple and stem family societies', in Derosas and Oris: 141-72.

Ward, J.C. (1994), 'Elizabeth de Burgh, Lady of Clare (d. 1360)', in Barron and Sutton: 29-45.

Watson, P.A. (1995), *Ancient Stepmothers: Myth, Misogyny and Reality* (Leiden: E.J. Brill).

Weiler, I. (1980), 'Zum Schicksal der Witwen und Waisen bei den Völkern der Alten Welt: Materialen für eine vergleichende Geschichtswissenschaft', in *Saeculum* 31: 157-93.

Weiler, I. (1988), 'Witwen und Waisen im griechischen Altertum: Bemerkungen zu antiken Randgruppen', in H. Kloft (ed.), *Sozialmassnahme und Fürsorge: Zur Eigenart antiker Sozialpolitik* (Graz: F. Berger u. Söhne): 15-33 (= *Grazer Beiträge* Suppl. 3).

Wesener, G. (1979), 'Pflichtteilsrecht und Unterhaltsanspruch des überlebenden Ehegatten in historischer Sicht', in B. Sutter (ed.), *Reformen des Rechts* (Graz: Leykam): 95-120.

Whatley, G. (1984), 'The uses of hagiography: The legend of Pope Gregory and the Emperor Trajan in the Middle Ages', in *Viator* 15: 25-63.

Whittle, J. (1998), 'Inheritance, marriage, widowhood and remarriage: A comparative perspective on women and landholding in North-East Norfolk, 1440-1580', in *Continuity and Change* 13.1: 33-72.

Wiedemann, I. (2001), *Die Schriften für Witwen in der Frühen Neuzeit* (Berlin: Verlag für Wissenschaft und Forschung).

Wiesner, M.E. (1986), *Working Women in Renaissance Germany* (New Brunswick, NJ: Rutgers University Press).

Wiesner, M.E. (1998), *Gender, Church and State in Early Modern Germany* (London: Longman).

Wiesner, M.E. (2000), *Women and Gender in Early Modern Europe*^{2} (Cambridge: Cambridge University Press).

Wiesner-Hanks, M.E. (2001), *Gender in History* (Oxford: Blackwell Publishers).

Willen, D. (1988), 'Women in the urban sphere in early modern England: The case of the urban working poor', in *Sixteenth Century Journal* 19.4: 559-75.

Willen, D. (1992), 'Godly women in early modern England: Puritanism and gender', in *Journal of Ecclesiastical History* 43.4: 561-80.

Wilson, L. (1992), *Life After Death: Widows in Pennsylvania, 1750-1850* (Philadelphia: Temple University Press).

Wiltenburg, J. (1992), *Disorderly Women and Female Power in the Street Literature of Early Modern England and Germany* (Charlottesville, VA: University Press of Virginia).

Winter, B.W. (2003), *Roman Wives, Roman Widows: The Appearance of New*

References and further reading

Women and the Pauline Communities (Grand Rapids, MI: Wm. B. Eerdmans Publishing Co.).

Winter, J. (1983), 'Widowed mothers and mutual aid in early Victorian Britain', in *Journal of Social History* 17.1: 115-25.

Witt, J.F. (2004), *The Accidental Republic: Crippled Workingmen, Destitute Widows, and the Remaking of American Law* (Cambridge, MA: Harvard University Press).

Witte, J. (2002), *Law and Protestantism: The Legal Teachings of the Lutheran Reformation* (Cambridge: Cambridge University Press).

Witte, J. and Kingdon, R.M. (2005), *Sex, Marriage, and Family in John Calvin's Geneva I: Courtship, Engagement, and Marriage* (Grand Rapids, MI: Wm. B. Eerdmans Publishing Co.).

Wood, R.A. (1994), 'Poor widows, c. 1393-1415', in Barron and Sutton: 54-69.

Wrigley, E.A. and Schofield, R.S. (1981), *The Population History of England, 1541-1871: A Reconstruction* (Cambridge, MA: Harvard University Press).

Wrigley, E.A. et al (1997), *English Population History from Family Reconstitution, 1580-1837* (Cambridge: Cambridge University Press).

Wunder, H. (1993), '"Jeder Arbeit ist ihres Lohnes Wert": Zur geschlechtsspezifischen Teilung und Bewertung von Arbeit in der Frühen Neuzeit', in K. Hausen (ed.), *Geschlechterhierarchie und Arbeitsteilung: Zur Geschichte ungleicher Erwerbschancen von Männern und Frauen* (Göttingen: Vandenhoeck and Ruprecht): 19-39.

Wunder, H. (1997), 'Herrschaft und öffentliches Handeln von Frauen in der Gesellschaft der Frühen Neuzeit', in Gerhard: 27-54.

Wunder, H. (1998), *He is the Sun, She is the Moon: Women in Early Modern Germany* (transl. T. Dunlap) (Cambridge, MA: Harvard University Press).

Wunder, H. (2002), 'Einleitung: Dynastie und Herrschaftssicherung: Geschlechter und Geschlecht', in H. Wunder (ed.), *Dynastie und Herrschaftssicherung in der Frühen Neuzeit: Geschlechter und Geschlecht* (Berlin: Duncker & Humblot): 9-27 (= *Zeitschrift für historische Forschung* Beiheft 28).

Zeigler, S.L. (1996), 'Wifely duties: Marriage, labor and the common law in nineteenth-century America', in *Social Science History* 20.1: 63-96.

Index

Acts of the Apostles, 38, 46
Aemilia Pudentilla, 30, 31, 34, 36, 173, 174
Agrippina the Younger, 33
Albert (Prince), 121, 122
Albertinus, Aegidius, 95
Alison, *see* Wife of Bath
Ambrose, 41, 43
Antonia the Younger, 36
Apuleius, 30, 31, 36, 173, 174
Archippe, 23, 26
Aristophanes, 24-6
Aristotle, 22, 111
Arizona, 134, 141, 144, 145, 147, 148, 152, 200
Astell, Mary, 201
Athens, 18-26, 30, 123, 165
Augsburg, 51, 80, 82, 86, 99, 102, 179, 188
Augustan legislation, 27, 28, 32, 35
Augustine, 40, 43, 46-7, 176, 177
Augustus, 28, 29, 32, 35, 36, 44

Bacharach, 96
Barry, John, 135
Basil of Caesarea, 177
Battle, Sussex, 63
Bavaria, 87, 95, 179, 188, 189
Beheim, Michael, 94
Bennett, Judith, 161
bereavement, *see* mourning
Bess of Hardwick, 1, 10, 61, 184
Bible, 36-8, 39, 44, 57, 66, 90, 149, 176
   see also Acts of the Apostles, Deuteronomy, Exodus, *First Corinthians*, *First Timothy*
Birmingham, 126
Black Death, 49-51, 53, 59-60, 63, 65, 74, 85, 108
Blackstone, William, 198
Braunschweig-Lüneberg, Elisabeth von, 97

Brigstock, Northamptonshire, 60
Bruno, Christoph, 96
Bucks County, PA, 141

California, 106, 133, 134, 136
capitalism, 2, 14, 105, 141, 159-61
Caroline (Queen), 122
Carthage, 177
Cartwright, William, 73
Catherine of Aragon (Queen), 70
Catholics, Catholicism, 17, 49-50, 66, 76, 82, 89, 95-6, 98-9, 146, 151, 179
Cato the Elder, 172-3
Chapman, George, 70
Charleton, Walter, 185
charity, 13, 30, 37, 39, 64, 71, 83, 85, 89, 90, 116, 117, 140, 144-6, 148, 153
chastity, 10, 14, 46, 66, 68-9, 93, 94
Chaucer, Geoffrey, 68-9, 185
Chester County, PA, 141
children
   exposure of, 19, 20
   of widows, *see* orphans
Christian, Christianity, 16, 36-47, 66, 71, 83, 90-104, 119, 123, 130-1, 143, 149-50
Chrysilla, 26
Cicero, 31
citizen, citizenship, 1, 2, 8, 17, 18, 21, 23, 26, 29, 74, 78, 82, 89, 96, 98-9, 102, 105-6, 114, 124, 140, 154, 157-8, 163, 190, 202
Civil War (England), 50, 51, 66, 184
Civil War (U.S.), 107, 147, 149, 152, 159, 194, 198
Clark, Alice, 2
Clark, Elizabeth, 177
class differences, 2-4, 10, 14, 18-20, 23-6, 30, 33-5, 36, 41, 43, 44, 52, 53, 59-61, 69, 72-4, 81, 85, 93,

Index

97-8, 100, 101, 107, 113, 114-15, 118-19, 121, 123, 125-6, 128, 142-3, 156, 162, 165, 169, 170, 171, 172, 177
Clement of Alexandria, 175, 177
Cleobule, 23, 26
Clifford, Lady Anne, 61
Clodia Metelli, 31
Colorado, 134, 135, 148
Colyton, Devonshire, 187
concubinage, 8, 82, 167
Congreve, William, 69
Connecticut, 129, 130
Constantine, 47
Consultationes Zacchaei et Apollonii, 46
Contagious Diseases Acts, 123
Cornelia, 34, 42, 185
Cornelius (Pope), 46
Cornelius Nepos, 30
Council of Trent, 93, 95
coverture, 55-8, 65, 74-81, 102, 105, 109-14, 128-30, 135-9, 148-50, 155
Criseyde, 68
custody, 12, 83, 100, 105, 111, 129, 131, 135-6, 139, 188, 195
Cyprian, 177

Dante Alighieri, 67
De Bono Viduitatis, 40
demography, 7, 12, 18-21, 39, 47-8, 51-5, 63, 99, 106-8, 140, 157, 168
Demosthenes, 23
Denver, 144, 145
Des Teufels Netz, 94
Deuteronomy, 37-8
De Viduis, 41
Dickens, Charles, 124
Didion, Joan, 169
Dido, 44, 68, 70, 173
District of Columbia, 106, 136
division of labour by gender, 4, 13-14, 23, 38, 62-3, 87, 110, 118, 120, 123, 125, 140, 142, 153-4, 158-62
divorce, divorcées, 8, 12, 19-20, 28-9, 34-5, 41, 53-4, 91, 97, 105, 108, 111-13, 124, 131-2, 135, 140, 145, 149-50, 154, 157, 167, 169, 174, 195
dower, 56-7, 59-60, 66, 74, 79, 109-10, 129-31, 134-7, 139, 147, 159, 181, 198

dowry, 21-2, 27-9, 34, 56, 64, 79-80, 82, 102, 130, 180, 181
Dunbar, William, 185

economic privilege, 8, 13-14, 22-3, 29-30, 59-65, 84-8, 103, 114-21, 139-48, 159-63
education of women, 15, 42-4, 70, 88, 106, 123, 152, 161
Egenolff, Margarethe, 88
Egypt, 18, 29, 33, 34, 36, 37, 170, 174, 174
Elizabeth I (Queen), 1, 61, 184
Enlightenment, 98, 150, 158, 161
Erickson, Amy, 59
Essex, 126
Euripides, 25
Evangelical Christianity, 116, 119, 120, 122, 125-6, 131-2, 143, 149
Exodus, 37
Eyb, Albrecht von, 94

family
  nuclear structure of, 21, 55, 64-5, 124, 127, 138, 157
  values, 42-43, 82-4, 161-2
  see also orphans
family wage ideal, 116, 118, 120, 138, 140, 142, 155
feminism, feminists, 1-4, 7-8, 14, 68, 74, 103, 110, 112, 113, 114, 117, 122-3, 125-7, 132-3, 136, 138, 146, 149, 152, 162, 165, 200
Finley, Moses, 1, 7-8
First Corinthians (1 Corinthians), 39, 42, 83, 93
First Timothy (1 Timothy), 38-40, 42, 43, 45, 46, 48, 70, 71, 77, 93, 94, 96, 97, 187
Frankfurt, 88
freedom of movement, 8, 14-15, 23-5, 30-4, 88-99, 103-4, 121-8, 148-53, 160-3
Freiburg, 84, 100, 188
French Revolution, 158
Froide, Amy, 53
Fulvia, 35

Galen, 94
Geminianus Monachensis, 95
Geneva, 189

226

Index

George IV (King), 122
Georgia, 198
Glasgow, 127, 194
Gortyn, 21-2
Gregory (Pope), 67
Groß, Erhart, 9, 93-4
guardians, guardianship, 12, 21-2, 27, 29, 31, 57, 60, 65, 78, 81-3, 97-8, 99, 111, 129, 131, 134, 136, 188
guilds, 62, 74, 84-7, 89-90, 101-2, 118, 183

Hajnal, John, 52
Helvidius, 45, 177
Henry VIII (King), 181
Hippocratics, 94
Homer, 25, 171
homework, 117, 142
Hopkins, Gerard Manley, 124
household, significance of, 13, 21-2
Hunter, Virginia, 23
hypergamy, female, 80
hypogamy, female, 10, 15, 36, 73, 74, 77, 80, 91, 92, 100, 102, 124

Idaho, 134
Indiana, 135
industrialism, industrialization, 2, 105, 141
insurance, 116-17, 121, 140, 145, 147, 148
Isis, 174
Iulia Procilla, 29

Jerome, 9, 16, 37, 40-8, 67-9, 92-5, 176, 177, 178, 185
Jesus Christ, 94
John Chrysostom, 46, 177
John of Salisbury, 33, 69
jointure, 57, 64, 74, 109, 110, 114, 130, 181
Jovinian, 45-6, 177, 178
Joyce, James, 125
Judaism, 16, 36-8
Judith, 94, 176
Julian, 47
Jussen, Bernhard, 9, 91
Justinian, 79
Juvenal, 31

Kempe, Margery, 65

Krause, Jens-Uwe, 6

Lancashire, 115, 126
Langland, William, 67
Laslett, Peter, 53
law, *see* private law
Livia Iulia, 35
London, 57, 58, 59, 62, 73, 74, 77, 108, 112, 115, 116, 179, 180, 181, 186, 195
Los Angeles, 141
Louisiana, 134
Luther, Martin, 95, 96
Lutheran, Lutheranism, 50, 95-7
 see also Protestant, Protestantism; Reformation

Magna Carta, 74
Mair, Appollonia, 86
male breadwinner ideal, 116, 117, 118, 119, 138, 140, 146, 196
Marcella, 34
marriage, 5, 9-13, 20, 26-8, 34, 39, 42-5, 55, 59, 63-4, 68-71, 74-80, 82, 84, 87-9, 92-104, 106, 110-15, 118-32, 135, 137, 140, 143, 145-50, 155, 157-8, 160-1, 163
 age at first, 12, 18-20, 26, 52-4, 107, 157, 179-80
 ideals of, 8, 26, 35, 75, 88, 95, 112-13, 118-27, 130-1, 137, 148-50, 153, 155, 160-1
 with or without *manus*, 26-8, 157-8
'marriage bar', 119-20
married women, 2, 6-9, 11-12, 17-19, 25-31, 37, 41, 44-7, 49, 52, 54, 56, 59, 61-2, 66, 70-2, 75-6, 77-83, 85-6, 88, 90-9, 100-3, 105, 109-23, 125-43, 145-9, 154-5, 157, 159-61, 163-4, 167, 173, 177, 180, 187, 188, 192, 194, 195, 196
Married Women's Property Acts (MWPA), 112-13, 132-9, 141, 146, 151
Martial, 30, 31, 34
Martineau, Harriet, 111
Maryland, 129
Mary Tudor (Queen), 70
Massachusetts, 129, 130, 198
mater familias / matrona, 29-30, 41
Maximilian I, 95

227

Index

Menander, 171
Methodist, Methodism, 123
microhistory, 4, 6
Middleton, Thomas, 70, 185
Mississippi, 132, 133
Mormons, 8, 122, 145, 151
mos maiorum, 41, 44
mourning, 11, 15-16, 32, 35, 73, 76, 101, 124, 150-1, 153
Munich, 88, 89, 95, 101
MWPA, *see* Married Women's Property Acts

Naevoleia Tyche, 34, 182
Nero, 32
Nevada, 134, 135
never-married women, 2, 6-9, 12, 15, 20, 29, 36-7, 41-2, 44-7, 53-4, 59, 62, 64, 66-8, 70, 78, 82-3, 92-5, 101, 107, 114, 124, 127-8, 155, 158-9, 164, 167, 174, 177, 194, 200
New Mexico, 134, 146, 151
New York, 106, 132, 133, 135, 136, 138
Nottinghamshire, 120, 127
Nuremberg, 51, 78, 83, 101, 188

Oliphant, Margaret, 125
'order of widows', 40, 178
Oregon Trail, 154
Origen, 45
orphanages, 46, 86, 143
orphans, 5- 6, 8, 11, 21-4, 26, 28, 29, 34, 36, 37, 40, 42, 45, 46, 56, 57, 60, 64, 65, 76, 79, 81, 83-5, 108, 109, 110, 115-17, 120, 126, 127, 129, 131, 134, 136, 138, 140, 142-8, 150, 153, 155, 170, 175, 176, 180, 181, 185, 186, 196, 200
Ovid, 68, 69, 173

Page, William, 71
patria potestas, 26-7, 34, 83, 126, 189
patriarchy, *passim*
 definition of, 7
 forms of, 4, 15, 158, 161-4
 historiography of, 3-4, 14
Paul, St, 38, 39, 42, 43, 71, 83, 93, 149, 201
Pelagius, 45-6
Peloponnesian War, 19-20, 169
Penelope, 25

Pennsylvania, 129, 130, 131, 141, 142, 143, 144, 145, 153
pension(s), 79, 100, 109, 117, 127, 140, 146-7, 152, 181, 184, 200, 201
Pericles, 19
periodization, 4-5, 49-50, 156-7, 162-4, 165
Petronius, 32-3, 69, 92
Phaedrus, 32-3, 69, 92
Philadelphia, 141, 144
Philemon, 171
Pizan, Christine de, 67
plague, *see* Black Death
Pliny the Younger, 31
polygyny, 134, 150, 153, 154, 167, 169, 200
Poor Law, *see* Poor Relief
Poor Relief, 61, 64, 71, 72, 109, 115, 116, 120, 137, 144, 145
poverty, 5, 8, 10, 23, 26, 30, 39, 42, 43, 47, 55, 57, 61, 63, 64, 67, 71-2, 73, 74, 79, 84-5, 88, 89, 90, 93, 103, 110, 115-16, 120, 127, 128, 132, 133, 137, 141, 142, 144-5, 146-8, 155, 156, 157, 167, 175, 186
private law, 12-13, 21-2, 26-9, 55-9, 60, 63-4, 77-84, 103, 105-6, 109-14, 128-39, 141, 140-2, 143, 144, 145, 146, 147, 149, 151, 153, 154-5, 158-9, 163, 180-1, 187, 189, 198
 of contracts, 78, 80-1, 112, 129, 131, 133, 136, 137, 143, 144, 146, 149
 of property, 12, 21-2, 27-8, 55-6, 58-60, 63-4, 78-84, 109-13, 128-39, 141, 145, 146, 147, 151, 159, 180-1, 189, 198
 of succession, 12, 21-2, 27-8, 55-60, 64, 78-81, 83, 84, 109-12, 115, 130-2, 134-5, 140-2, 145, 151, 153, 170, 180-1, 187
 of torts, 113-14, 129, 138
prostitutes, 54, 82, 90, 120, 123
prostitution, 3, 42-3, 63, 82, 85, 95, 99, 117, 122, 128, 131, 142
Protestant, Protestantism, 49-50, 71, 75-6, 82, 88, 95-101, 130, 149, 179
 see also Evangelical Christianity; Lutheran, Lutheranism; Methodist, Methodism; Puritan, Puritanism; Quaker, Quakerism

228

Index

Puritan, Puritanism, 49, 72, 77, 129, 149

Quaker, Quakerism, 123, 129
Querelle des Dames, 67, 90

Ralph Roister-Doister, 69
Reformation, 17, 49-50, 53-4, 61, 66, 73, 75-6, 83, 89, 92, 95-99, 102-4, 105, 160, 179, 192
Regensburg, Berthold von, 92-3
remarriage, 8, 10, 11-13, 15-16, 19-21, 24-6, 28-9, 31, 33-6, 38-44, 47, 52-4, 56-8, 60-1, 63-6, 69-71, 72-7, 79-80, 82-4, 86, 90, 92-4, 96-7, 99-102, 103-4, 108, 128, 129, 130, 153-4, 132, 135, 136, 148, 150, 151, 152, 155, 157, 158, 171, 175, 183, 186, 187, 197, 202
Riley, Glenda, 153
Rome, 16, 18-21, 26-36, 45, 46, 47, 157, 158
Romulus, 33, 69

Sachs, Hans, 94
Salvian, 179
Santa Fe, 145-6, 150
Sassia, 31
Scadron, Arlene, 6
Scotland, 105, 127
second Punic War, 20
Shakespeare, William, 70, 185
social constructionism, 5, 7, 8, 13, 90, 174
socialist, socialism, 122-3, 150
Sophocles, 25
Smith, Barbara Leigh, 109
Social Security, 140, 148, 200
South Carolina, 129, 135, 198
Spangenberg, Johannnes, 96
Sparta, 22, 170
Speyer, 102
spinsters, *see* never-married women
stepmothers, 24, 33, 36
Stanton, Elizabeth Cady, 152
Stoicism, Stoics, 42
Stow, Marietta, 132
Stowe, Harriet Beecher, 106, 125
Strasbourg, 51, 89, 102
strict settlement, 109, 110, 111, 112, 121, 131, 181

Suffolk, 126
suffrage, 1, 3, 114, 123, 134, 139, 154

Tacitus, 29, 185
Teichner, Heinrich der, 94
Tertullian, 40, 42, 43, 44, 175, 177
Texas, 134
Thirty Years' War, 51, 88, 98, 100, 179, 180
Thucydides, 19
Topsell, Edward, 187
Trajan, 67
trust, 27, 28, 57, 74, 109, 110, 111, 112, 121, 128, 130, 131
Twain, Mark, 152

Ummidia Quadratilla, 31
univira, 34-6, 44
Utah, 134, 135, 153, 200

Verania, 31
Vergil, 44, 68, 173
Veturia, 185
Victoria (Queen), 109, 121, 122, 139
Virginia, 129
virginity, 9, 67, 95, 99
virgins, *see* never-married women
Vives, Juan Luis, 70-1, 72, 76, 92, 96, 151, 185

Wales, 105, 127
Walpole, Horace, 1, 10
Washington, 134
Webster, John, 76-7
Wharton, Edith, 106
Whitcher, Frances Miriam, 152
widowers, 11, 15, 27, 34, 36, 41, 53-4, 71, 73, 101-2, 108, 127-8, 138, 143, 153-4, 157, 168, 172, 175, 180, 186, 198
Widow of Ephesus, 32-33, 36, 68, 69, 70, 91-2, 125, 185
Widow of Sarepta, 94
widows, *passim*
  children of, *see* orphans
  definition of, 8
  employment of, *see* economic privilege
  litigation by, 12, 15, 31, 49, 56, 65, 75, 81-2, 85, 88-9, 101, 138, 151
  marginalization of, 8, 9, 14, 15, 23,

Index

24, 26, 31, 33, 42, 45, 61, 71, 85, 97, 115, 118, 120, 124, 150, 154, 160, 188
  residence of, 15, 24, 26, 34, 61-2, 64-6, 71, 80, 89-90, 97, 99, 100, 126-7, 143-4, 139-40, 150, 171, 183, 195
  typology of, 9-11, 21, 25, 29, 41-2, 67-72, 90-7, 103-4, 124-5, 152, 156, 185, 201
  violence toward, 15, 33, 66, 90
  see also economic privilege, freedom of movement, private law, remarriage
Wife of Bath, 68, 185
wife, wives, *see* married women
witches, witchcraft, 10, 33, 66, 71-2, 91, 96-97, 188
Wollstonecraft, Mary, 122
workmen's compensation, 116, 138
World War I, 107, 113, 116, 117, 120
World War II, 117
Württemburg-Mömpelgard, Barbara Gräfin von, 98
Wycherley, William, 69
Wyclif, John, 67

Xenophon, 26

York, 50, 52, 75